ADVANCE PRAISE FOR

THE BUDDHIST ANALYSIS OF MATTER

"A dazzling textual exposition of the analysis of matter in Theravāda Abhidhamma, connecting Buddhist philosophy, psychology, and ethics."
—G. A. Somaratne, assistant professor, Centre of Buddhist Studies, The University of Hong Kong

"This is a rebirth of a classic in modern Buddhist studies. Written in the 1960s, a good enough time for any academic work to be replaced by more modern works in the relevant field of study, Professor Karunadasa's treatise still stands tall. Although a scholar is not expected to write the last word on a subject, if it has happened we have to be humble enough to acknowledge it. *The Buddhist Analysis of Matter* belongs to that rare class of works, the members of which are not too many."
—Asanga Tilakaratne, School of Buddhist Studies, Philosophy and Comparative Religion, Nalanda University, Rajgir, Bihar

"This is groundbreaking research in the Buddhist philosophical analysis of matter, with many new ideas. Professor Karunadasa skillfully presents his ideas in such a way that readers easily follow his logical arguments."
—Guang Xing, associate professor and director, Centre of Buddhist Studies, The University of Hong Kong

THE BUDDHIST ANALYSIS OF MATTER

Y. KARUNADASA

Wisdom

Wisdom Publications
199 Elm Street
Somerville, MA 02144 USA
wisdomexperience.org

First Published: Department of Cultural Affairs of the Government of Sri Lanka, Sri Lanka, 1967. Second Print: Buddhist Society of Singapore, Singapore, 1989. Second Edition: Centre of Buddhist Studies of the University of Hong Kong, Hong Kong, 2015. Published in Hong Kong by the Centre of Buddhist Studies of the University of Hong Kong, 2015

LIBRARY OF CONGRESS CATALOGING-IN-PUBLICATION DATA

Names: Karunadasa, Y., author.
Title: The Buddhist analysis of matter / Y. Karunadasa.
Description: Somerville, MA, USA: Wisdom Publications, 2020. | Previously published: Hong Kong: Centre of Buddhist Studies of the University of Hong Kong, 2015. | Includes bibliographical references and index.
Identifiers: LCCN 2019044570 (print) | LCCN 2019044571 (ebook) | ISBN 9781614294511 (hardcover) | ISBN 9781614294672 (ebook)
Subjects: LCSH: Matter—Religious aspects—Buddhism.
Classification: LCC BQ4570.M37 K37 2020 (print) | LCC BQ4570.M37 (ebook) | DDC 294.3/4—dc23
LC record available at https://lccn.loc.gov/2019044570
LC ebook record available at https://lccn.loc.gov/2019044571

ISBN 978-1-61429-451-1 ebook ISBN 978-1-61429-467-2

24 23 22 21 20 5 4 3 2 1

Cover photo: Buddha head from the early Ayutthaya Period, Photo © Luca Tettoni / Bridgeman Images. Cover design by Graciela Galup. Interior design by James D. Skatges.

Printed on acid-free paper that meets the guidelines for permanence and durability of the Production Guidelines for Book Longevity of the Council on Library Resources.

Printed in the United States of America.

PUBLISHER'S ACKNOWLEDGMENT

The publisher gratefully acknowledges the generous help of the Hershey Foundation in sponsoring the production of this book.

CONTENTS

FOREWORD

THIS ADMIRABLE BOOK began life more than half a century ago as a doctoral thesis for the School of Oriental Studies at the University of London, and when in due course it was published (by the government of Sri Lanka), Edward Conze, the most eminent Buddhologist of the day, wrote that it was "likely to be the last word on the subject for some time to come." There can be little doubt that the same judgment could be repeated today. Although in the interim the serious study of Pāli and its early literature so far declined that, if one excludes a few monastics in Theravāda monasteries in Asia (who are not likely to read scholarly work in English), the number of those equipped to appreciate it almost dwindled away, there is now a keen interest all over the world in the study of Pāli, both in lay Buddhist circles and in institutes of higher learning, and since there is so little corresponding to this book available, it meets a need.

Clearly, the great majority of those who are likely to want to read a book about early Buddhism are attracted to the subject out of a concern for its religious side. In his final chapter, "The Ethico-Philosophical Basis of the Buddhist Analysis of Matter," Professor Karunadasa faces this issue directly. In the chapter's opening paragraph he writes: "The Buddha himself says that as a religious teacher he teaches only two things: suffering and its cessation. Buddhism's analysis of the world of experience is undertaken not for its own sake but for evolving a rationale for its doctrine and discipline. Attention is not concentrated on the empirical world in and for itself. The Buddhist inquiry into the nature and constitution of matter and its relevance for Buddhism cannot be properly understood if the subject is divorced from its religious context."

He then goes straight on to write: "The close connection between the Buddhist analysis of matter and Buddhist ethics is indicated by the oft-recurring statement . . . [that] matter is something that is favorable to, or productive of . . . the fetters that bind the living being to *saṃsāric* existence." He continues: "The analysis of matter is thus necessitated by an ethical need . . . In the earlier texts where *rūpa* [matter] is explained in simple and general terms the ethical approach to the subject is much more pronounced. That *rūpa* is impermanent and that therefore it cannot be made the basis of true happiness is the main theme that runs throughout all such discussions."

The difficulty that the author cannot quite circumvent is that this straightforward explanation of the marginal position that matter holds in early Buddhist soteriology, while it is important, is hardly enough to fill a thesis or a book. Theoretical statements and arguments about matter are to be found in texts for more than a millennium after the time of the Buddha, and before long their connection to Buddhist ethics becomes increasingly tenuous. It is customary to call this theorizing "Buddhist philosophy," but it no longer underpins the Buddha's religious teachings and it is hard to see any interaction between these theories and Buddhism's core, the soteriological doctrines, which continue unaffected.

On the other hand, a historian can trace influence and interaction between the Pāli tradition and other ancient Indian cosmological teachings, both Buddhist and non-Buddhist, and here Prof. Karunadasa undoubtedly breaks new ground.

Prof. Karunadasa counts among his assets an exemplary clarity of thought and its natural concomitant, a gift for lucid exposition, and he conscientiously translates all Pāli terms and quotations. Nevertheless I think it has to be admitted that the very nature of his subject matter makes it inevitable that readers who do not know any Pāli will find it a challenge fully to understand even chapter 1, let alone what follows. However, the author has provided a one-page summary of the content of the book, containing no Pāli words, which is printed in the front of the book. I would recommend that newcomers to the subject first read this summary and then the final chapter, after which they will be better equipped to tackle the rest of the book.

Richard Gombrich
Emeritus Boden Professor of Sanskrit, University of Oxford

PREFACE

This work is an attempt to interpret the Buddhist view of matter as presented in Theravāda Buddhism, and is mainly based on the Abhidhamma, both of the earlier period containing the seven manuals of the Abhidhamma Piṭaka and of the later period containing Abhidhammic commentaries (*aṭṭhakathā*), subcommentaries (*ṭīkā*), and such compendiums as the Abhidhammatthasaṅgaha of Ācariya Anuruddha.

General observations on the Buddhist theory of matter are met with in almost all books dealing with Indian philosophy or with Buddhism in particular. These books, covering a wide period of oriental research, are too numerous to be mentioned here. Studies on some special aspects of the subject, undertaken mainly with a view to determining the nature of the earliest form of Buddhism—still a matter of controversy for some scholars—have appeared from time to time in the form of articles and monographs. Professor Stanislaw Schayer's article "Pre-canonical Buddhism" (1935), and Maryla Falk's monograph *Nāmarūpa and Dharmarūpa* (1943), for example, represent this category. Translations of four of the original texts—namely, the Dhammasaṅganī and its commentary, the Atthasālinī, the Visuddhimagga of Ācariya Buddhaghosa, and the Abhidhammatthasaṅgaha of Ācariya Anuruddha, wherein the subject under consideration is dealt with in greater detail—have also been made available. Mrs. Rhys Davids's translation of the Dhammasaṅganī, *A Buddhist Manual of Psychological Ethics* (1923), and Dr. S. Z. Aung's translation of the Abhidhammatthasaṅgaha, *Compendium of Philosophy* (1910), both with introductory essays, copious notes, and critical observations, deserve special mention.

The works indicated above have brought into relief some important aspects of the Buddhist view of matter as expressed in the sources of Theravāda Buddhism. However, so far no clear picture of the subject has emerged. Attention has tended to be largely concentrated on the broad philosophical implications arising from the Buddhist theory of matter. Consequently, the Buddhist analysis of matter as such remains less exhaustively dealt with. Hence it is that a critical and detailed examination of the Theravādins' list of *rūpa-dhammas*—these are the ultimate irreducible factors into which the material existence is analyzed—has become all the more necessary.

Furthermore, the extant writings have tended to be based more on the earlier sources, such as the Pāli canonical texts, and less on the later sources, such as the post-canonical commentaries and the kindred literature. In the comparatively late works of the Theravādins—for example, the Pāli *ṭīkās* and the Siṃhala *sannēs*, the Abhidhammic compendiums of the twelfth century and later—one meets with valuable data relating to the subject. That they have so far failed to attract much attention is shown by the absence of detailed accounts on the comparatively late developments of Theravāda Buddhism, such as (the Theravāda version of) the atomic theory, the theory of momentary being, and the denial of motion. Herein an attempt has been made to sift the material embodied in the works referred to, with a view to presenting a comprehensive account of the subject.

What has so far been observed about the Theravāda is less true about the other schools of Buddhism. For Professor Theodore Stcherbatsky's works, notably the *Central Conception of Buddhism*; Professor O. K. J. Rosenberg's *Die Probleme der buddhistischen Philosophie* (1924); and Dr. Mc Govern's *A Manual of Buddhist Philosophy*, vol. 1 (1924) have gone a long way to elucidating the Buddhist theories of matter as expressed in Sanskrit, Tibetan, and Chinese sources. Along with these should be mentioned Professor Louis de la Vallée Poussin's monumental translation of the Hiuan Tsang version of the Abhidharmakośa, under the title *L'Abhidharmakośa de Vasubandhu*, vols. 1–6 (1923–31). With its voluminous notes and critical observations, this translation has become an indispensable source book for a study of the doctrines and theories of Sanskrit Buddhism.

Although the present study is concerned with the Buddhist analysis of matter as expressed mainly in the sources of Theravāda Buddhism, an attempt has been made to take into consideration the parallel data found in the sources of non-Theravāda schools of Buddhism as well. This has been done with a view to bringing the subject into a wider perspective and to presenting it with a greater measure of precision. In this connection, the emphasis has fallen more on the Vaibhāṣika and Sautrāntika schools of Buddhism. These were two of the leading non-Mahāyāna schools with whom the Theravādins had much in common. Both schools subscribed to a realistic view of existence; the former had a tendency to extreme realism and the latter a predilection for—but certainly not a commitment to—subjectivism. Although less emphatic, these two trends are observable within the Theravāda commentarial exegesis. In the later works of the Theravādins, for instance, there is a marked tendency to declare as nominal what in the earlier are recognized as real.

In view of these circumstances, it was deemed proper that in elaborating the Theravāda analysis of matter, special attention should be paid to the doctrines and theories of the Vaibhāṣikas and the Sautrāntikas.

The Vijñānavādins' denial of matter does not come within the purview of this study. However, some passing comments on their attitude to the subject under consideration have been made wherever it was felt necessary.

* * *

The Buddhist Analysis of Matter was first published by the Department of Cultural Affairs of the Government of Sri Lanka in 1967. It was reprinted by the Buddhist Society of Singapore in 1989, with financial assistance from Nam Fatt Lam Buddhist Temple. I express my grateful thanks to Nam Fatt Lam Buddhist Temple for its generous act.

I express my thanks here to Professor Guang Xing, the director of the Centre of Buddhist Studies of the University of Hong Kong, for the keen interest he has evinced in this work when it was in preparation for the Hong Kong edition and Ms. Aosi Mak, teaching assistant at the Centre of Buddhist Studies, for generating the index and for formatting the manuscript.

The present edition is sponsored by Wisdom Publications, a non-profit organization, as its American edition. It will certainly ensure a wider circulation for the book.

I express here my deep sense of gratitude to Professor Richard Gombrich, the Emeritus Boden Professor of Sanskrit at the University of Oxford, for writing the foreword to this book.

In preparing this American edition, Dr. Mary Petrusewicz of Wisdom Publications went through the whole manuscript with meticulous care and made many valuable suggestions to enhance the overall quality of the book. I benefited much from her critical mind and sound sense. To her I express my grateful thanks.

Y. Karunadasa
Colombo, Sri Lanka
August 5, 2019

I

INTRODUCTION

ON THE BASIS of its occurrence in the philosophical terminology of the Pāli canon, at least four meanings of *rūpa* can be distinguished: Frequently it occurs in the (generic) sense of what is material, and with almost equal frequency in the more specific sense of what is visible—to be more precise, "the sphere of visibility." Rarely it is seen to figure as a simple substitute for the more specific compound *rūpa-dhātu* (*-loka*), which signifies the second of the three planes of existence recognized in Buddhist cosmology—what Mrs. Rhys Davids calls "the realm of attenuated matter"—and with almost equal rarity, as referring to four stages of ecstatic experience, technically and more specifically known as *rūpajjhāna*. These four may be represented as the generic, the specific, the cosmological, and the "psychological" meanings of the term.

Ācariya Buddhaghosa and Ācariya Dhammapāla, the two illustrious commentators of Theravāda Buddhism, collate as many as nine meanings (*attha*) in which the term in question is said to occur in the canonical works:

1. rūpakkhandha—the material aggregate
2. sarīra—the physical body of a living being
3. vaṇṇa—color
4. saṇṭhāna—form, figure, configuration
5. kasiṇa-nimitta—the "meditation-object"
6. paccaya—condition, cause
7. sabhāva—nature

The eighth and ninth are what we have introduced as the cosmological and "psychological" meanings. That the number is not exhaustive is recognized by the addition of the word *ādi*, "etc."[1]

Some of these items could, however, be brought under *rūpa* in the generic sense of matter. *Rūpakkhandha* (no. 1) is the first of the five components into which Buddhism analyzes the empiric individuality, the other four being *vedanā* (feelings), *saññā* (perceptions), *saṅkhāra* (synergies, formations), and *viññāṇa* (consciousness). Sometimes it is used in a wider sense to mean the totality of matter (*sabbaṃ rūpaṃ*).[2]

It may also be noted that in the Nikāyas sometimes it is used in a subjective sense, too, a usage that does not seem to have been retained in the post-Nikāyan works.[3] For the moment, we may overlook this latter usage. *Sarīra* (no. 2) can be considered as referring to the matter that enters into the composition of a living being.

That *rūpa* sometimes occurs in the sense of *vaṇṇa*, color (no. 3), is said to be supported by the oft-recurrent canonical statement *cakkhuñ ca paṭicca rūpe ca uppajjati cakkhuviññāṇaṃ*,[4] "depending on eye and the visible arises visual consciousness." According to the commentarial exegesis, the visible in this context means color.[5] But according to the Dhammasaṅgaṇī of the Abhidhamma Piṭaka, color as well as shape, form, or figure constitute the sphere of visibility (*rūpāyatana*).[6] The commentators,[7] however, ousted the latter from its traditional domain on the ground that in an absolute sense it was not visible and, as the Sautrāntika school of Buddhism did, explained it as a mental construction "superimposed on the difference of coloration."[8] It is in light of this subsequent development that we need to understand why the term "visible" in the quoted sentence is sought to be interpreted as color.

The mention of *saṇṭhāna*, form, figure (no. 4), is perhaps in order to recognize one of the general meanings of *rūpa*. But its mention separate from color (no. 3) is also a logical necessity arising from the abovementioned development.

For the moment let us confine ourselves to the Abhidhamma Piṭaka and take both items (nos. 3 and 4) as being represented by *rūpa* in its specific sense of what is visible. This, as interpreted in Buddhism, constitutes one of the subdivisions of *rūpa* in the sense of matter.[9]

Why *rūpa* is sometimes used to refer to *kasiṇa-nimitta*, the "meditation-object" (no. 5), is of course not far to seek. This is a name given to an object that could be profitably used for the practice of concentration that has the attainment of *jhāna* (absorption, ecstasy) as its end. According to the classical account given in the Visuddhimagga, at the initial stage of concentration the selected object is called *parikamma-nimitta*, the preparatory image. As the process of concentration gathers more and more intensity there comes a time when the original sensuous object is replaced by its corresponding mental image called *uggaha-nimitta*, the acquired image. With further progress in concentration, there emerges what is called *paṭibhāga-nimitta*, the counterimage, which is subtler than the immediately preceding one.[10]

Image, figure, sign, appearance—these are some of the general meanings of *rūpa*. And if the object of concentration is sometimes referred to by *rūpa*, then it is one of these general meanings that comes to our mind.

That *rūpa* is at times used in the sense of *paccaya*, condition (no. 6), does not seem to be supported by the example cited, a quotation from the Aṅguttaranikāya, which runs as follows: "*Sarūpā bhikkhave uppajjanti pāpakā akusalā dhammā no arūpā.*"[11] The commentary notes that *rūpa* in "*sarūpā*" and its negative "*arūpā*" should be understood as synonymous with *paccaya*.[12]

When the original passage where the sentence occurs is taken into consideration, considerable doubt arises on the validity of this explanation. Therein we find nine similar sentences, each differing only in respect of the first and the last words. Five of them come before the above sentence; they begin with (a) *sanimittā*, (b) *sanidānā*, (c) *sahetukā*, (d) *sasaṅkhārā*, and (e) *sappaccayā*, and end with the respective negatives. Four of them come after it; they begin with (f) *savedanā*, (g) *sasaññā*, (h) *saviññāṇā*, and (i) *saṅkhatārammaṇā*, and end with the respective negatives.[13]

Commenting on them, the commentator observes that *nidāna*, *hetu*, *saṅkhāra*, *paccaya*, *rūpa* in (b), (c), (d), (e), and *sarūpā* are all synonymous with *kāraṇa*, reason.[14] That *nidāna*, *hetu*, and *paccaya* as used in the Pāli texts carry more or less the same sense is, of course, understandable. But one fails to understand why *saṅkhāra* and *rūpa* too should be treated similarly. For one cannot fail to notice here the names of the five *khandhas* in *sarūpā*, *savedanā* (f), *sasaññā* (g), *sasaṅkhārā* (d), and *saviññāṇā* (h). However, it should be noted that in the passage in question the names of the five *khandhas* do not occur in the same order as they are usually enumerated. For the sentence beginning with *sasaṅkhārā* does not come between the two beginning with *sasaññā* and *saviññāṇā*.

It is to be noted that in respect of *savedanā*, *sasaññā*, and *saviññāṇā*, the same treatment is not given. It is specifically stated that *savedanā* means "*vedanāya sati*"—that is, when there is or because of *vedanā*. And it is also stated that the other two terms (and *saṅkhatārammaṇā*), too, should be understood in the same manner.[15]

This explanation fits in well with the context. And it seems to us that *sarūpā* and *sasaṅkhārā*, too, should be approached in the same way. That is to say, *sarūpā* = when there is or because of *rūpa*, and *sasaṅkhārā* = when there is or because of *saṅkhāra*. Viewed in this way, the two terms cannot be understood as synonymous with cause or condition. On the contrary, it shows that the two aggregates, *rūpa* and *saṅkhāra*, are causes or conditions in relation to something—that is, the arising of evil and unwholesome states of mind (*pāpakā akusalā dhammā*).

It is of much significance that in the list of meanings given by Ācariya Dhammapāla, *rūpa* in the sense of *paccaya* does not occur. Along with this may be mentioned that in one of the manuscripts collated by the PTS editor of the Aṅguttaranikāya Aṭṭhakathā II, the statement that *rūpa* and *saṅkhāra* are synonymous with *nidāna*, *hetu*, and *paccaya* is missing.[16]

Coming to no. 7, the example cited to show that *rūpa* sometimes means *sabhāva*, nature, appearance, is: "*Piyarūpe sātarūpe rajjati*,"[17] "One delights in what is of pleasant nature, in what is of delightful nature." This is reminiscent of a passage in the Yamaka of the Abhidhamma Piṭaka where, in the form of questions and answers, an attempt is made to unfold and delimit the implications of the term *rūpa*:

QUESTION: *Rūpaṃ rūpakkhandhoti*? (Is *rūpa rūpakkhandha*?)

ANSWER: *Piyarūpaṃ sātarūpaṃ rūpaṃ, na rūpakkhandho; rūpakkhandho rūpañ c'eva rūpakkhandho ca.* (*Piyarūpa* and *sātarūpa* are *rūpa* but not *rūpakkhandha*; *rūpakkhandha* is *rūpa* and is also *rūpakkhandha*).

QUESTION: *Na rūpakkhandho na rūpanti*? (What is not *rūpakkhandha* is not *rūpa*?)

ANSWER: *Piyarūpaṃ sātarūpaṃ na rūpakkhandho, rūpaṃ. Rūpañ ca rūpakkhandhañ ca ṭhapetvā avasesā na c'eva rūpaṃ na ca rūpakkhandho.* (*Piyarūpa* and *sātarūpa* are not *rūpakkhandha*, but *rūpa*. Apart from *rūpa* and *rūpakkhandha*, the rest are neither *rūpa* nor *rūpakkhandha*).[18]

This catechism is rather enigmatic. At first sight it seems to suggest that the Yamaka has recognized certain kinds of matter (*rūpa*) that it excludes from the aggregate of matter (*rūpakkhandha*).

Shwe Zan Aung, while agreeing that *rūpa* is often used in the sense of matter, refers to this catechism to show that sometimes the term is used to express states of mind. He translates and understands it as follows:

> Does [everything that is called] *rūpa* [belong to] the material group? [The eighty-one worldly classes of consciousness and their concomitants called] *rūpa* that is "attractive" and "pleasant" are called *rūpa*, but they do not belong to the material group. The twenty-eight material qualities . . . that

> go to make up the material group are designated *rūpa* and they belong also to the material group.
>
> [Again,] is anything that does not belong to the material group ever called *rūpa*? [such is the question.] Things attractive and desirable are called *rūpa* though they do not belong to the material group. Those things and that group apart, the remainder [namely, the eight classes of transcendental, i.e., lokuttara, consciousness and their concomitants; and nibbāna] are neither called *rūpa* nor do they go to make up the material group.[19]

It will be seen that this translation, with our bracketed clarification, explains satisfactorily the whole catechism. It will also be seen that the whole translation has become coherent and meaningful because of the two underlined and bracketed interpretations. To repeat:

1. "Piyarūpaṃ sātarūpaṃ" is interpreted to mean the eighty-one worldly classes of consciousness and their concomitants.
2. "*na c'eva rūpaṃ na ca rūpakkhandho*" = "*avasesā*" (neither *rūpa* nor *rūpakkhandha* = the rest) is interpreted to mean the eight classes of transcendental consciousness, their concomitants, and nibbāna.

It is implied that the items in (1) can be described as *piyarūpa* and *sātarūpa*, and that the items in (2) cannot be so described.

On the basis of this interpretative translation one could certainly say that in this particular passage of the Yamaka, *rūpa* is used not only to refer to the material aggregate but also to express states of mind. This same explanation appears in Mrs. Rhys Davids's Introduction to the Yamaka.[20] And Surendra Dasgupta, too, seems to have understood the passage in the same way when he refers to Yamaka I, 16, as an instance where *rūpa* is sometimes used in a subjective sense.[21]

There are, however, certain difficulties that militate against such a conclusion. At the very outset it should be stated that neither in the Yamaka nor in the commentary is it explicitly said that "*Piyarūpaṃ sātarūpaṃ*" and "*avasesā*" are to be understood in the same way as they are interpreted above. Could it, then, be taken as implied in the catechism and demanded by the context?

This, too, does not seem to be possible because of more positive difficulties. It may be noted here that in the Nikāyas a wide variety of things, mental as well as material, are described as *piyarūpa* and *sātarūpa*[22]—a fact pointing to the generality of their usage. Coming closer to the Yamaka: the same situation obtains even in the Abhidhamma Piṭaka. In the Vibhaṅga, for instance, we find sixty items enumerated as an answer to the question: What is *piyarūpa* and *sātarūpa*? Among them, ten are the first five sense-organs and the corresponding objective fields.[23] These ten items, it may be noted here, are included in the *rūpakkhandha*. It may then be asked that if some items included in the *rūpakkhandha* are describable as *piyarūpa* and *sātarūpa*, why is it that in the Yamaka what is *piyarūpa* and *sātarūpa* is completely excluded from the *rūpakkhandha*?

The question does not arise if the catechism is understood in light of certain exegetical methods pursued in the Yamaka. In unfolding the implications of terms, sometimes it lays emphasis on what appears to be obvious and seems to make more complex what is manifestly clear. The nature of the work is summarized by Nyānātiloka Thera when he observes: "To me it looks, as if this book was composed for examination purposes, or to get versed in answering sophistical and ambiguous or captious questions, on all the manifold doctrines and technical terms of Buddhist philosophy. The questions of identity, subordination, and coordination of concepts are playing a prominent part in our work, which tries to give a logical clearing up and delimitation of all the doctrinal concepts as to their range and contents."[24]

Following is an example of how it attempts to unfold the import of the term *gandha*.

QUESTION: Is *gandha* the *gandhāyatana*, the sphere of smell?

ANSWER: *Sīlagandha* (fragrance of virtue), *samādhigandha* (fragrance of concentration), and *paññāgandha* (fragrance of wisdom) are *gandha* but not *gandhāyatana*.[25]

The purpose is to show that *gandha* in its figurative usage (e.g., *paññāgandha*) should not be confused with *gandha* when it stands for smell, the objective field corresponding to the olfactory organ.

To take another example:

QUESTION: Is *sota* the *sotāyatana* (the organ of hearing)?
ANSWER: (Yes, but not always, e.g.,) *taṇhāsota* (the stream of craving) is (also) *sota* but not *sotāyatana*.[26]

Here, both *sotāyatana*, the organ of hearing, and *taṇhāsota*, the stream of craving, are called *sota* because it occurs in both words—although of course *sota* in *sotāyatana* is different in meaning from *sota* in *taṇhāsota*. In the former it means "ear" and in the latter "stream." And it is precisely in order to point out this difference that the whole catechism is set forth.

The catechism in question, too, should be understood in a similar way. In this particular context, *Piyarūpaṃ sātarūpaṃ* should be translated not as "things pleasant and desirable" (= Aung) but as "of pleasing and delightful 'nature'" (= Nyānātiloka).[27] Usually (but not always) when Pāli works refer to things pleasant and desirable they use the words *yam piyarūpaṃ sātarūpaṃ*[28] (= that which is pleasant and desirable). But that is not the main argument here. The moment we understand it as "things," we are at a loss to understand why they are completely excluded from the *rūpakkhandha*. For, as observed above, in the Vibhaṅga what is included in the *rūpakkhandha* is also described as *piyarūpa* and *sātarūpa*. And it is very unlikely that the Yamaka has deviated from this tradition.

Taking all these facts into consideration, we may then explain the four points of the catechism as follows:

1. *Piyarūpaṃ sātarūpaṃ* (of pleasing and delightful nature or appearance) is called *rūpa* in the same way as *taṇhāsota* is also called *sota*.
2. *Rūpa* (= *Piyarūpaṃ sātarūpaṃ*) is excluded from *rūpakkhandha* (material aggregate) in the same way as *sota* (=*taṇhāsota*) is excluded from *sotāyatana*. The exclusion of *piyarūpa* and *sātarūpa* from *rūpakkhandha* is tantamount to saying that the meaning of *rūpa* in the first two words is different from the meaning of *rūpa* in the compound *rūpakkhandha*. In the former it means (of pleasant and delightful) nature or appearance; in the latter, (aggregate of) matter.
3. *Rūpakkhandha* is called *rūpa* as well as *rūpakkhandha* in the same way as *sotāyatana* is called *sota* as well as *sotāyatana*. Here only one meaning of the term is taken into consideration.
4. The last statement: "Apart from *rūpa* (= *Piyarūpaṃ sātarūpaṃ*) and *rūpakkhandha*, the rest (*avasesā*) are neither *rūpa* nor *rūpakkhandha*" could be understood in the same way as: "Apart from chairs and tables, the rest are neither chairs nor tables." The words "the rest" (*avasesā*), according to this explanation, cannot be interpreted as referring only to the eight classes of transcendental consciousness, their concomitants, and nibbāna. They too are certainly included. But "the rest" means much more—that is, all except *rūpa* (*Piyarūpaṃ sātarupaṃ*) and *rūpakkhandha*.

The explanation we have given here may look strange. But when one considers how the Yamaka seeks to unfold the implications of *gandha* and *sota*, strangeness ceases to be a disqualification. Be it also repeated here that neither in the Yamaka nor in its commentary is it stated that "*Piyarūpaṃ sātarūpaṃ*" and "*avasesā*" (the rest) should be understood in the same way as they are interpreted in the quoted translation (underlined and given within brackets). Moreover, the present explanation does not contradict but falls in line with the situation that obtains in the Vibhaṅga. The whole purpose of the catechism is to clarify the implications of the term *rūpa* in the compound *rūpakkhandha* and to avoid its being confused with *rūpa* as it occurs in *piyarūpa* and *sātarūpa*. In fact, the commentary rightly observes that the questions in this catechism are asked for the sole purpose of clarifying the implications of terms—*vacana-sodhanatthaṃ*.[29]

We may then conclude that as far as this particular Yamaka catechism is concerned it is not correct to say that *rūpa* is used to express states of mind.

2

DEFINITION OF MATTER AND THE BASIC MATERIAL FACTORS

COMMENTARIAL EXEGESIS DEFINES *rūpa* in the sense of matter as that which has the characteristic of *ruppana*. *Ruppana* refers to mutability of matter, its susceptibility to being "deformed, disturbed, knocked about, oppressed, and broken." The use of the term in this sense is traceable to a sutta passage where the Buddha says: "And why, monks, do you say material form (*rūpa*)? It is deformed (*ruppati*), therefore it is called material form. Deformed by what? Deformed by cold, by heat, by hunger, by thirst, by flies, mosquitoes, wind, sunburn, and creeping things."[30]

The characteristic of *ruppana* is often paraphrased as *vikāra*. *Vikāra* is the alteration matter undergoes owing to such physical conditions as cold and heat. *Vikāra* in the sense of alteration is again paraphrased as *visaduppatti*—that is, "genesis of dissimilarity."[31] What this means should become clear in the context of the theory of moments, according to which all basic material and mental factors are of momentary duration. They disappear as soon as they appear without having time to undergo change. Therefore change came to be interpreted not as the alteration between two stages in the same material factor (*rūpadhamma*), but as the disappearance of one material factor and the immediate emergence in its place of another. Understood in this manner, what is called *visaduppatti* (genesis of dissimilarity) is not the dissimilarity between two stages of the same material factor, but the dissimilarity brought about by the disappearance of one material factor and the emergence in its place of another. The reference is to the appearance of a series of momentary material dhammas, where the succeeding dhamma is dissimilar to the immediately preceding one.[32] This phenomenon of "becoming dissimilar" is due to the impact of such adverse physical conditions as heat and cold (*sitādi-virodha-paccaya-sannidhāne visaduppatti yeva*).[33] Obviously the reference here is not to the empirically observable change in material things, what the commentary calls "evident decay" (*pākaṭa-jarā*). Rather, it refers to the never-stopping, infinitely graduated "incessant decay" (*avici-jarā*).[34]

In the Sarvāstivāda Abhidharma we find a somewhat different definition. Matter is that which has the characteristic of *pratighāta*. *Pratighāta* is resistance or impenetrability. This characteristic of matter is due to its extension in space (*yaddeśaṃ āvṛṇoti*): "Where there is an object with the characteristic of resistance (impenetrability), there cannot be at the same time another object that has the characteristic of resistance (impenetrability)": *Yatraikaṃ sapratighaṃ vastu tatra dvitīyasyotpattir na bhavati.*[35] This definition thus highlights the characteristic of spatial extension (*āvaraṇa-laksaṇa*), which makes matter resistant and impenetrable.

What is interesting to note here is that the Theravāda too recognizes this definition in an indirect way. This will become clear if we examine here the definitions given in the Theravāda to the four great elements of matter (*mahābhūta*)—namely, earth (*paṭhavī*), water (*āpo*), fire (*tejo*), and air (*vāyo*). The first represents solidity (*kakkhaḷatta*) and spatial extension (*pattharaṇa*), the second fluidity (*davatā*) and cohesion (*bandhanatta*), the third temperature of cold and heat (*sita*, *uṇha*), and the fourth distension (*chambhitatta*) and mobility (*samudīraṇa*). These four material elements are necessarily coexistent (*niyata-sahajāta*) and positionally inseparable, one from another (*padesato avinibhoga*).[36] They are therefore present in all instances of matter, beginning from the smallest material unit (*rūpa-kalāpa*) to anything bigger than that. Now the fact that the earth-element that represents solidity and spatial extension is said to be present in every instance of matter is another way of saying that every instance of matter is characterized by solidity (whatever be the degree) and by extension (whatever be the extant). This is another way of saying that every instance of matter has the characteristic of resistance/impenetrability (*pratighāta*).

Basic Material Factors

Rūpa-dhammas are the basic irreducible material factors. They are the basic constituents into which the whole of material existence is resolved. Their aggregation and interaction explains the variety and diversity of the physical phenomena of our world of experience. Apart from these material dhammas, no other matter is recognized. What is called "material substance" is explained away as a product of our own imagination. Any given instance of matter is therefore resolvable into these material dhammas without leaving any residue to be interpreted in a substantial sense. The dichotomy of substance and quality has no role to play in the Buddhist analysis of matter (or of mind). No material dhamma is either a substance or a quality of any other material dhamma.

A material dhamma is normally postulated as if it were a discrete entity. However, this does not mean that it has an independent and isolated existence. It is entirely for the convenience of definition and description that it is so postulated. For it always exists in inseparable association with a set of other material dhammas. Even when the analysis of matter "ended" in atomism (theory of *rūpa-kalāpa*), this principle of positional inseparability was not abandoned. For, as we shall see, even the so-called atom (*paramāṇu*) is, in the final analysis, a cluster of material dhammas (*rūpa-kalāpa*) one physically inseparable from another, all forming a "heterogeneous" unity.

In the course of this chapter we shall notice that some of the material dhammas represent certain phases, modalities, and characteristics of what really amounts to *rūpa* in the sense of matter. Strictly speaking, to introduce them as material dhammas is in a way to misrepresent their true nature. However, there is this justification for our doing so. The

Pāli commentators themselves observe that they are not true material dhammas, but nominal entities. Yet as a matter of convention (*rūḷhiyā*), they themselves refer to them by the same term. Hence if we, too, keep on introducing them as material dhammas, this, be it noted, is done as a matter of convention (*rūḷhi*).[37]

Although the Dhammasaṅganī of the Abhidhamma Piṭaka refers in all to twenty-seven material dhammas, the Pāli commentaries have increased the number to twenty-eight by adding heart-basis as the physical seat of mental activity. The final list is as follows.

a. Four great material elements: (1) earth (*paṭhavī*), (2) water (*āpo*), (3) fire (*tejo*), and (4) air (*vāyo*);
b. five sense-organs: (5) organ of sight (*cakkhu*), (6) organ of hearing (*sota*), (7) organ of smell (*ghāna*), (8) organ of taste (*jivhā*), and (9) organ of touch (*kāya*);
c. the objective sense-fields, with the exception of the tangible: (10) the visible (*rūpa*), (11) sound (*sadda*), (12) smell (*gandha*), and (13) taste (*rasa*);
d. three faculties: (14) faculty of femininity (*itthindriya*), (15) faculty of masculinity (*purisindriya*), and (16) material faculty of vitality (*rūpa-jīvitindriya*);
e. (17) heart-basis (*hadaya-vatthu*), (18) nutriment (*āhāra-rūpa*), and (19) space-element (*ākāsa-dhātu*);
f. two modes of self-expression: (20) bodily intimation (*kāya-viññatti*), and (21) vocal intimation (*vacī-viññatti*);
g. three characteristics of matter: (22) lightness of matter (*rūpassa lahutā*), (23) malleability of matter (*rūpassa mudutā*), and (24) wieldiness of matter (*rūpassa kammaññatā*);
h. four phases of matter: (25) production of matter (*rūpassa upacaya*), (26) continuity of matter (*rūpassa santati*), (27) decay of matter (*rūpassa jaratā*), and (28) impermanence of matter (*rūpassa aniccatā*).

Material Dhammas Included among the Objects of Mind (Dhammāyatana-rūpa)

The twenty-eight material dhammas are represented in the list of twelve *āyatanas* as follows. The first five sense-organs constitute the first five internal *āyatanas* (the sixth internal *āyatana*, i.e., *mana-āyatana*, is mental), and the four objective sense-fields constitute the first four external *āyatanas*. The four great material elements, with the exception of the water-element, constitute the fifth external *āyatana*. All the remaining material dhammas constitute a part of *dhamma-āyatana*—that is, the sixth external *āyatana* representing objects of mind.

It will be seen that altogether sixteen material dhammas are included in the *dhammāyatana*. They are cognized not through any of the physical sense-organs, but by mind, through a process of inference. The five physical sense-organs are also of this nature. For they refer not to the visible gross sense-organs, but to their subtle counterparts. They are known only as objects of mind-cognition. Hence, strictly speaking, they can also be included in the *dhammāyatana*. However, since they are already represented by five separate *āyatanas*, they are not designated as *dhammāyatana-rūpa*. We shall be using the term *dhammāyatana-rūpa*(*s*) to mean only those sixteen items that in the Abhidhamma are so designated.

There is general agreement among Buddhist schools that the first five material faculties and the corresponding five external sense-fields are *rūpa* in the sense of matter. From the point of view of early Buddhism, too, this is so. It is in regard to the category of *dhamma-āyatana-rūpa* that Buddhist schools differ. As we have seen, for the Theravāda it consists of sixteen items. For the Sarvāstivāda, on the other hand, there is only one *dharmāyatana-rūpa*, called *avijñapti-rūpa*. However, seven of the items in the Theravāda list have their counterparts in the Sarvāstivāda as well, but not as part of *dharma-āyatana-rūpa*. They are water-element, the two faculties of sex, nutriment, space-element, and the two modes of self-expression. These seven items, with the exception of nutriment, appear as subdivisions of other sense-fields. On the other hand, nutrition appears as a combination of three sense-fields. Such a difference as to the relative position of these seven items and the sense-fields presupposes a difference as to their interpretation. But this need not concern us here.

The Theravādins do not recognize under any guise the *avijñapti-rūpa*, which, for the Sarvāstivādins, is the one and only *dharmāyatana-rūpa*. The Dārsṭāntikas and the Sautrāntikas strongly criticize the very notion of *avijñapti-rūpa*, and oppose its elevation to the status of a dharma. For these two schools, it is only a mental construction with no corresponding objective counterpart. There is no evidence to suggest that the Sautrāntikas recognized any *dharmāyatana-rūpa*. For them, all that is material can be subsumed under the first five internal sense-organs and the corresponding five external sense-fields.

Two things emerge from the foregoing observations. One is that some Buddhist schools did not recognize *dhammāyatana-rūpa*. The other is that two leading schools that recognized it did not agree on what it should consist of. Both seem to suggest that the inclusion of some material dhammas in *dhammāyatana* is an innovation on the part of the Abhidharma/Abhidhamma.

However, the Theravāda Abhidhamma seeks to establish a link between *dhammāyatana-rūpa* and early Buddhist teachings. This it does on the basis of a sutta passage where we find material form (*rūpa*) defined in its totality: "*yaṃ kiñci rūpaṃ atītānāgata-paccuppanaṃ ajjhattaṃ vā bahiddhā vā oḷārikaṃ vā sukhumaṃ vā hīnaṃ vā paṇītaṃ vā dūre vā santike vā, sabbaṃ rūpaṃ*" (whatever material form past, present, or future, internal or external, gross or subtle, inferior or superior, far or near, all that material form . . .).[38]

It will be seen that this passage uses some pairs of words to embrace components of corporeality in their entirety. Two of them are (1) gross or subtle (*oḷārika* and *sukhuma*) and (2) far or near (*dūre* and *santike*). These two pairs, according to the Abhidhamma, are meant to distinguish *dhammāyatana-rūpa* from the rest. The five physical sense-organs and the five physical sense-objects are called "gross" (*oḷārika*) because their presence is easily apprehended through sensory impingement.

The other material dhammas included in *dhammāyatana* are called "subtle" (*sukhuma*) because they are not easily apprehended (*duppariññeyya*). They have to be known only as objects of mind-cognition through a process of inference. The distinction between gross and subtle is thus not based on the relative size of the object but on how their presence can be observed.[39] Likewise the other pair, far and near (*dūre* and *santike*), in this particular context does not signify spatial distance or proximity. The five physical sense-organs and the five physical sense-objects are called "proximate" because their contact (*ghaṭṭana*), resulting in visual consciousness, etc., witnesses to their very presence. Because of their being thus easily grasped (*gahaṇassa sukarattā*), they are called "proximate" (*santike*). "Far" signifies the *dhammāyatana-rūpas* because in contrast to the rest they are not easily apprehended (*duviññeyya*).[40]

We find the two terms "gross" (*audārika*) and "subtle" (*sūkṣma*) used in a similar sense in the Sarvāstivāda as well. Here "subtle" refers to *avijñapti*, the *dharmāyatana-rūpa*, and "gross" to all other material dharmas. An alternative explanation is that the pair does not indicate an absolute dichotomization, but are of relative application (*āpekṣikam*). What is subtle in relation to something could be gross in relation to something else. However, the Sarvāstivādins interpret near (*antika*) and far (*dūra*) in a different context to justify their theory of tri-temporality according to which the essence of the dharmas exists in all three temporal divisions. The material dharmas that exist now are "near" (*antika*). The material dharmas belonging to the future and past are "far" (*dūra*).[41]

It is very unlikely that the sutta passage has used the two pairs of words in such a technical sense. We can understand them in a direct and literal sense. What it seeks to lay stress on is the totality of material phenomena (*sabbaṃ rūpaṃ*), first with reference to time (past, present, or future), second with reference to a given individual (internal or external), third with reference to the nature of material form (gross or subtle), fourth with reference to its quality (inferior or superior), and finally with reference to its location (far or near). We find the same formula, with the necessary changes, applied to the other four aggregates as well, quite obviously to stress the idea of "all."

The original sutta meaning of the two terms is, in fact, retained in the Vibhaṅga of the Abhidhamma Piṭaka: "whatever other material form there is that is not proximate (*anāsanne*), that is not in the vicinity (*anupakkaṭṭhe*), that is far (*dūre*), and not near (*asantike*)—this is called material form that is 'far.' Whatever material form there is in proximity (*āsanne*), in near vicinity (*upakkaṭṭhe*), not far (*avidūre*), but near (*santike*)—this is called material form that is 'near.'"[42]

Equally significant is the explanation given by Bhadanta Śrīlāta, a celebrity of the Sautrāntika School: material dharmas that exist in a visible locality (*dṛṣya-deśa*) are near (*antika*); those that exist in an invisible locality (*adṛṣya-desa*) are far (*dūra*). The criterion is not whether the material dharmas are visible or not, for such a criterion would bring the sphere of visibility (*rūpāyatana*) under one heading and the remaining material dharmas under the other.

Another link the Abhidhamma establishes between *dhammāyatana-rūpa* and early Buddhist teachings is the *Saṅgīti Sutta* of the Dīgha-nikāya. This sutta says that all materiality is of three kinds: (a) visible and impinging (*sanidassana-sappaṭigha*), (b) non-visible and impinging (*anidassana-sappaṭigha*), and (c) non-visible and non-impinging (*anidassana-appaṭigha*). The sutta does not identify what and what material form is to be subsumed under each heading.

"Visible" (*sanidassana*), as the Abhidhamma says, is an exclusive adjective reserved for *rūpāyatana*, because of the obvious reason that it signifies "the visible," the sense-field of the organ of sight. "Impinging or with impact" (*sappaṭigha*) describes the five physical sense-organs and their sense-objects. For their contact is necessarily associated with some impact and is therefore grosser than that between mind and mind-objects. The other material dhammas (= *dhammāyatana-rūpa*) that are objects of mind-consciousness are, therefore, non-visible (*anidassana*) and non-impinging (*appaṭigha*).

Accordingly the twenty-eight material dhammas can be subsumed under the three headings, as follows:

1. Visible and impinging = the visible, i.e., the sense-field of the organ of sight (no. 10).
2. Non-visible and impinging = the five physical sense-organs and their sense-fields, except the visible (nos. 1, 3, 4 = the tangible, 5–9, 11–13).
3. Non-visible and non-impinging = material dhammas included in *dhammāyatana* (nos. 2, 14–28).

Among the sixteen *material* dhammas that come under *dhamma-āyatana*, only five can be traced to the Pāli suttas. These are the water-element (*āpo-dhātu*), faculty of femininity (*itthindriya*), faculty of masculinity (*purisindriya*), edible food (*kabaḷiṅkāra-āhāra*), and space-element (*ākāsa-dhātu*). Among these five items the water-element and edible food can certainly be included in *rūpa* in the sense of matter. However, it is very unlikely that the Pāli suttas understood them in such a way as to justify their inclusion in the *dhammāyatana*—that is, as two items of materiality that can be cognized only by the mind (*mano*). As to the two faculties of sex, what is important to remember here is that the suttas do not present them as two material dhammas cognizable only by the mind. This leaves us only with one item—namely, space-element. This, it seems to us, is the only item that we can subsume under the heading "non-visible and non-impinging." As we shall see in the sequel, when the Abhidhamma includes space-element among material dhammas, it means void region, the space bound by matter. This is the meaning it seems to assume in the Pāli suttas as well. We find the term "space-element" (*ākāsa-dhātu*) used in the suttas when they analyze the living being into six components: the four great material elements, space-element, and consciousness-element.

One question that arises here is why the Sarvāstivādins and the Sautrāntikas do not recognize space-element as a *dharmāyatana-rūpa*. As we shall see, for the Sarvāstivādins, too, it means void region (space delimited by matter), but for them it is something visible (*sanidarśana*). Hence they include it in the sense-field of the visible, not in *dharmāyatana*. The Sautrāntikas take an entirely different position:

space-element is a mental construct with no objective counterpart (*prajñaptisat*).

If we go by the *Saṅgīti Sutta*'s division of material form into three groups, it is only space-element that qualifies as a *dhammāyatana-rūpa*. Where the Abhidhamma shows a development in this regard is when it adds fifteen more items to this category. When we go through these items we will not fail to notice that most of them are not on par with other material dhammas. They merely signify certain modes, characteristics, and phases of other material dhammas. Then the question that arises here is why they are presented as separate material dhammas.

There seem to be two main reasons for this situation. One is the felt need to make the catalogue of material dhammas as exhaustive as possible so as to represent all material phenomena in our world of experience. The second is that, in doing so, not to introduce any distinction between substance and quality into the catalogue of material dhammas. Hence the real material dhammas as well as some of their modalities and characteristics are all presented under the common designation of rūpa-dhamma, or material factors. When Buddhism analyzes a thing into its basic constituents, the basic constituents are always presented as coordinate parallel factors and not as exhibiting a hierarchy. Through this strategy it avoids the substance-and-quality distinction intruding into the list of factors. The factors are presented not as one above or below another, but as one beside another. The idea is to show that the factors into which a composite thing is resolved are not fractions of a whole but coordinate factors, all connected according to the principles of conditionality.

The Real and the Nominal Material Dhammas

It was noted above that some material dhammas represent certain characteristics or modalities of other material dhammas. The difference between the two groups of material dhammas became more apparent in light of two new developments found in the commentarial exegesis.

One is the definition of *rūpa* in the sense of matter as that which has the characteristic of mutability (*ruppana*).[43] The other is the definition of *dhamma* as that which has its own-nature (*sabhāva*).[44] These two defining characteristics of *rūpa* and *dhamma* could not be applied to all material dhammas because of the obvious reason that some of them are merely indicative of certain properties of other material dhammas. Hence in order to make this distinction explicit, the commentaries make a division of all material dhammas into two groups, as *nipphanna* and *anipphanna*.

The positive term *nipphanna* with the intensive prefix *pari* (= *parinipphanna*) occurs in three of the Kathāvatthu controversies in a more or less technical sense. If a given thing is *parinipphanna*, it should have the following characteristics: it is conditioned (*saṅkhata*), dependently arisen (*paṭicca-samuppanna*), subject to decay (*khaya-dhamma*), subject to waning away (*vaya-dhamma*), in the nature of producing dispassion (*virāga-dhamma*), subject to cessation (*nirodha-dhamma*), and subject to change (*vipariṇāma-dhamma*). From this it follows that the term *parinipphanna* can be used to describe all conditioned dhammas, mental as well as material. The Pāli commentaries use the term, both in its ordinary and intensive forms, to carry the same implications.

Accordingly, the category of *nipphanna* (concretely produced) includes material dhammas produced by the four generative conditions of matter—namely, kamma, consciousness (*citta*), temperature (*utu*), and nutriment (*āhāra*).[45] This means that the opposite term *anipphanna* (non-concretely produced) refers to material dhammas that are not so produced. Nevertheless they are reckoned as material dhammas because they exist as modalities or attributes of other material dhammas, which have a real and concrete genesis due to the four generative conditions of matter. Only the latter have their own-natures (*attano sabhāvena siddha*), and therefore they alone can be apprehended through their own-natures (*sabhāvena pariggahetabba*). The rest are contrary thereto (*tabbiparīta*). Therefore another name for the *nipphanna* category is "matter having its own-nature" (*sabhāva-rūpa*). They are also called "matter having its own characteristic" (*salakkhaṇa-rūpa*) because they are marked by the three characteristics of impermanence, suffering, and non-self. Or else they alone have the three characteristics of the conditioned—namely, arising (*uppāda*), presence (*ṭhiti*), and dissolution (*bhaṅga*). A yet another name for the *nipphanna* category is "matter to be comprehended by insight" (*sammasana-rūpa*) because they can be made the objects of insight contemplation.[46]

The *nipphanna* category is also called "material matter" (*rūpa-rūpa*). The reason given for coining this reduplicated term is this: as a matter of convention, the term *rūpa* has also been used to denote things devoid of the nature of materiality and thus its meaning has become unduly stretched. Hence the need arises to reduplicate the term.[47] What this amounts to saying is that the opposite group, the *anipphanna* category, does not represent real material dhammas. Rather they represent certain modalities and attributes of matter. In this sense they are said to go together with the other group (*taggatika*). Strictly speaking, they have to be excluded from the list of twenty-eight material dhammas. This is why some subcommentaries fix the total number of conditioned dhammas at seventy-one and not at eighty-one. It is by excluding the ten items included in the *anipphanna* category.

Great Elements of Matter and Dependent Matter

Another well-known division of the twenty-eight material dhammas is the one into *mahābhūta,* the four great elements of matter, and *upādā-rūpa*, dependent matter. This division is often mentioned in the Pali suttas as well. As to the relative position of the two categories we have a clear statement in the Paṭṭhāna of the Abhidhamma Pitaka. As mentioned here, the four *mahābhūtas* are conditions by way of co-nascence (*sahajāta*), support (*nissaya*), presence (*atthi*), and no-disappearence (*avigata*) in relation to *upādā-rūpas*. The first means that the *mahābhūtas,* as they arise, serve as a condition for the arising, simultaneously with them, of the *upādā-rūpas.* Thus both groups arise at one and the same time. However, it is the *mahābhūtas* that function as the condition, while the *upādā-rūpas* become what is conditioned by them. Although the *upādā-rūpas* are co-nascent with the *mahābhūtas*, the *upādā-rūpas* are not a condition by way of co-nascence in relation to the *mahābhutas*. The next relationship between them is based on the condition by way of support (*nissaya*). This means that the *mahābhūtas* serve as a necessary support or foundation for the *upādā-rūpas* to depend on. The two conditions by way of presence (*atthi*) and non-disappearence (*avigata*) mean the same kind of condition. Here it means that the presence and non-disappearence of the *mahābhūtas* ensures the presence and the non-disappearence of the *upāda-rūpas*.

The above conditional relations show that the *upādā-rūpas* are dependent on the *mahābhūtas*. The *mahābhūtas* are also dependent, not, of course, on the *upādā-rūpas*, but on themselves. Each *mahābhūta* depends on the other three and therefore none of them can arise in isolation from the other three. This difference between the *mahābhūta* and the *upādā-rūpa* is summed up in a sub-commentary when it says: "that which clings to the *mahābhūtas* while being clung to by others, is not *upādā-rūpa*; that which clings to the *mahābhūtas* while being not clung to by another is *upādā-rūpa*."

In contemporary writings, *upādā-rūpa* has often been rendered as "derived materiality/matter." Such a rendering does not seem to represent the true position. *Upādā-rūpa* is not a variety of matter that is derived or evolved from the *mahābhūtas*. The notion of derivation or evolution is not consonant with Buddhist philosophy, because it presupposes the dichotomy between substance and quality. The moment we understand *upādā-rūpa* as a derivative from *mahābhūtas*, the former become qualities and the latter substances, a distinction categorically rejected by the Abhidhamma.

There is another important reason why we should not render *upādā-rūpa* as "derived matter/materiality." As we have already observed, dhammas are the basic constituents of mental and material existence. Therefore, none of them is further reducible to any other reality. If *upādā-rūpas* are derived from *mahābhūtas*, then the former are reducible to the latter; in such a situation, they forfeit their right to be designated as dhammas, for the simple reason that they are no more irreducible. If this is their true nature, then the list of material dhammas will get reduced to four—namely, the four *mahābhūtas*.

3

THE PRIMARY ELEMENTS

Most of the schools of Indian thought, notably the Sāṃkhya, the Vedānta, and the Medical Tradition as represented by Caraka and Suśruta, recognize five *mahābhūtas*, or elemental substances—namely, earth, water, fire, air, and ether/space (*ākāśa*).[48] That space is the fifth is admitted by the Nyāya-Vaiśesikas, too. But in many respects it differs from the other four: it is a non-corporeal (*amūrta*) substance devoid of tactility (*sparśa*) and characterized by ubiquity (*vibhū*), absolute continuity, and infinite magnitude. As such, unlike the other four substances, it is not, in the ultimate analysis, composed of atoms. Thus, although *ākāśa* is introduced as a *mahābhūta*, in view of its peculiar characteristics, it has to be distinguished from the other four and is, in a way, on a par with such intangible substances as *kāla*, time.[49] In Jainism, on the other hand, it is ranked with what is called *bhuda-catukka*, "the elemental tetrad," which consists of earth, water, fire, and air. Both space and the elemental tetrad are brought under the general heading *ajīva*, non-spirit; but only the latter is brought under the more specific *puggala*, matter.[50]

The Buddhist position in regard to this matter is similar to that of Jainism. That is to say, only earth, water, fire, and air are brought under the heading *mahābhūta*. It is of course true that, as pointed out by Mrs. Rhys Davids,[51] in the Nikāyas, sometimes space is enumerated immediately after, and apparently as coordinate with, the above four items.[52] But this does not mean that space is the fifth *mahābhūta*, just as much as *viññāna* (consciousness), which too is sometimes enumerated after the five items in question,[53] is not the sixth *mahābhūta*. When space and consciousness are mentioned along with earth, water, fire, and air, the general designation used in respect of all the six items is *dhātu*. On the other hand, the term *mahābhūta* is always used in a more specific sense—that is, as referring only to the last four items.

In the schools of Buddhist thought, too, the situation remains unchanged. True, on the nature of space, they advance more than one interpretation.[54] But on its non-recognition as a *mahābūta*, they all agree.

With this clarification as to the number of *mahābhūtas*, we may now proceed to consider how they are understood in Buddhism.

In the Nikāyas they are defined in simple and general terms and are illustrated mostly with reference to the constituents of the human body. Earth-element is that which is hard (*kakkhaḷa*) and rigid (*kharigata*)—for example, hair of the head or body, nails, teeth, skin, flesh, etc. Water-element is water (*āpo*), or that which is watery (*āpogataṃ*)—for example, bile, phlegm, pus, blood, sweat, tears, etc. Fire-element is fire or heat (*tejo*), or that which is fiery (*tejogataṃ*)—for example, the heat in the body that transmutes food and drink in digestion. Air-element is air (*vāyo*), or that which is airy (*vāyogataṃ*)—for example, "wind discharged upward or downward, wind in the abdomen or belly, vapors that traverse the several members, inhaling and exhaling of breath."[55]

These definitions seem to suggest that from its very beginning Buddhism did not make a radical departure from the popular conception of the *mahābhūtas*. There are, however, some Nikāya passages that clearly imply they were understood in a more abstract and technical sense[56]—that is, as we find them interpreted in the Abhidhamma.

It is really in the Abhidhamma that we are presented with a different conception of the *mahābhūtas*. Much of the earlier terminology is retained, but the earlier definitions are modified. The subject is presented in greater detail and with more precision. New theories have been evolved and new interpretations advanced, so as to bring the whole subject in line with the other subsequent developments of the doctrine.

For the Abhidhamma, too, *kakkhaḷa* and *khara*, which mean hard and rigid, respectively, bring out the essential nature of *paṭhavī-dhātu*, the earth-element.[57] The first is said to represent its characteristic (*lakkhana*) and the second its mode (*ākāra*).[58] The question is raised whether *kakkhaḷatta* (hardness) is itself not the earth-element. It is maintained that although this is the case, yet for the convenience of definition, the earth-element is said to possess the characteristic of *kakkhaḷatta*.[59]

It will be seen that according to the Nikāyan definition what is comparatively hard or rigid (*kakkhaḷa, kharigata*) is the earth-element, whereas according to the Abhidhammic definition the fact of hardness or rigidity (*kakkhaḷatta*) is itself the earth-element. The conception of earth-element in this way is not confined to the Theravāda alone. Parallel definitions are met with in other schools of Buddhist thought. In its chapter on the genesis of the world, the Mahāvastu says that when the living beings, who lived at a new evolution of the world, began to eat whole mouthfuls of the essence of this earth as food, their bodies came to possess the characteristics of heaviness (*gurutva*), roughness (*kharatva*), and solidity (*kakkhaṭatva*).[60] The implication is given that "heavy," "rough," and "solid" represent the essential nature of earth-element. The Abhidharmakośa and its Vyākhyā, too, use the latter two terms in defining the earth-element.[61] In the Abhidharmasamuccaya it is defined as *kaṭhinatā*,[62] a term that could be interpreted as meaning rigidity or solidity. As such this interpretation is almost the same as that given by the Theravādins. Thus there is general agreement among the Buddhist schools in maintaining that what is called earth-element stands for the phenomenon of hardness, rigidity, solidity, or compactness in matter.

The earth-element is also defined as that which extends or spreads out, *pattharatī ti paṭhavī*.[63] Extension is occupation in space. "Tridimensional extension gives rise to our idea of a solid body. As no two bodies can occupy the same space at the same time, Buddhists derive their idea of hardness (*kakkhaḷatta-lakkhana*) from *paṭhavī*."[64] Thus the interpretation of earth-element as the element of extension brings into relief a different method of approach.

In the commentaries we get futher discussions on the peculiar function of this element. Venerable Buddhaghosa observes that it acts as a foundation, a sort of fulcrum, and that it manifests itself as receiving (*sampaṭicchana-paccupaṭṭhānā*).[65] This has been further explained to mean that the other three primary elements are established on it (*paṭhavī-patiṭṭhitā*) and that therefore it serves as a support, a basis (*patiṭṭhānaṃ*) for them.[66] That this view is shared by the Vaibhāsikas, is shown by their contention that the "bearing up" or supporting (*saṃdhārana*) of ships by water (= ocean) is a sufficient ground for the inference that that the earth-element is present in water.[67] A Pali sub-commentary observes that what we conventionally call earth is the support of trees, mountains, etc., even so the earth-element is a support for the other material elements.[68]

Water-element represents the fact of viscidity (*sineha*) and cohesion or binding together in matter (*rūpassa bandhanattaṃ*).[69] *Bandhanatta* or cohesion refers more to its function. "For the water-element binds together iron, etc., in masses, makes them rigid. Because they are so bound, they are called rigid; similarly in the case of stones, mountains, palm-seeds, elephant-tusks, ox-horns, etc. All such things the water-element binds and makes rigid; they are rigid because of its binding."[70] *Paggharana,* flowing, and *nissanda-bhāva,* state of streaming, are also cited as two other characteristics of the water-element[71]—a view that suggests the popular and common-sense idea of water. However, this does not mean that water-element, as it came to be interpreted in the Abhidhamma, is identical with water. No primary element can exist independently of, or in isolation from, the other three. Hence the water-element is present not only in water but also in air, fire, etc.

In the schools of Sanskrit Buddhism, too, the water-element is defined in a similar manner. It stands for *dravatva*, liquidity, and *snehatva*, viscidity in material phenomena.[72] It may be noted here that the "*ap*" (water) substance of the Vaiśesikas, too, has the same two characteristics: *āpo dravah snigdhah.*[73] But, according to Vaiśesikas liquidity and viscidity are qualities inherent in the "*ap*" substance. No such dichotomy is recognized by the Buddhists. Not withstanding these metaphysical differences, the parallelism goes still further. The Vaiśesikas maintain that *saṃgraha*, cohesion or agglutination, is a distinct quality produced by fluidity and viscidity operating together.[74] The Buddhists maintain that water-element, which stands for the facts of liquidity and viscidity, performs the function of *saṃgraha*. Hence it is that according to the Vaibhāsikas, the phenomenon of cohering or non-broken continuity in a blazing fire is due to the presence therein of the water-element.[75] The same idea is recognized by the Theravādins too, when they say that the water-element manifests itself by its action of cohesion (*āpo-dhātu sangaha-paccupaṭṭhānā*).[76]

The fire-element signifies the phenomenon of heat, the term being used is *usmā* or *usumā*.[77] In the Sanskrit sources we get *usnatva*, and its corresponding Pali form, *unhatta*, is the standard term used in the Pali commentaries and sub-commentaries.

One significant feature of the Theravada conception of the fire-element concerns the question of *sīta*, cold. The Vaiśesikas, for instance, maintain that heat is the peculiar quality of the fire-substance (*tejasa usnatā*) and that cold is that of the water-substance (*apsu sītatā*).[78] Since the natural touch of water is cold, "other substances (bodies) are cold only in proportion to the extent to which water enters into their composition."[79] The Vaibhāsikas, too, associate cold with the water-element, as shown by their contention that the touch of cold in wind points to the presence therein of the water-element.[80] Bhadanta Srīlābha's view: "The fire-element exists in water, since it is more or less cold"[81] carries the implication that heat and cold are represented by the fire-element and the water-element, respectively.

The stance taken up by the Theravadins in regard to this question is quite different. In the works of the Abhidhamma Pitaka we do not get any explicit statement concerning the position of cold (*sīta*) in relation to the primary elements. Nevertheless there is no possibility of its being considered as represented by the water-element because this particular primary element, as maintained by the Theravadins, does not come within the sphere of the tangible (*phoṭṭhabbāyatana*). It is only in the commentarial exegesis that we are presented with a clear statement on this subject: "Although cold (*sītatā*) is known by the sense of touch, it is really the fire-element. The sensation of cold (*sīta-buddhi*) is obtained when the heat is less, for there is no distinct quality (*guna*) called cold. . . . Hence it is that during the summer season when people having first stayed in the sun enter the shade they experience the sensation of cold. And when they stay there for a long time they experience the sensation of heat."[82] Thus in the view of the Theravadins, cold is not the peculiar characteristic of the water-element as is believed by the Vaibhāsikas. Rather, it is the relative absence of heat. And heat is represented by the fire-element.

The characteristic function of fire-element is *paripācana*—that is, ripening or maturing. For this is the element that heats, matures, sharpens, and imparts heat to all other material elements.[83]

Vāyo-dhātu, the air-element, as defined in the Dhammasangani, signifies inflation or distension (*thambhitatta*), and fluctuation or mobility (*chambhitatta*).[84] While the other three primary elements stand for the facts of solidity, cohesion, and heat, this particular element represents the more restless and dynamic aspect of material phenomena.

The standard term used in the Pali commentarial works to describe the air-element is *samudīrana*, which means mobility or motion.[85] In the Sanskrit sources *samudīrana* occurs in combination with *laghu* or *laghutā* (light or lightness).[86] For the Theravadins, as we shall see in sequel, *lahutā* represents one of the secondary elements of matter. This seems to be the reason why they do not associate it with the air-element, which is one of the primary elements of matter. The Abhidharmakośa takes note of a similar problem, when it observes that according to a sūtra the air-element is lightness (*laghutva*) whereas according to the Prakaranas, *laghutva* is a secondary material element. It seeks to reconcile the two views by stating that "the dharma which has motion for its nature (*īranātmaka*) is the air-element. Its nature is manifested as lightness, and its function is manifested by its act of motion (*īrana-karman*)."[87] As the Theravadins conceive material lightness (*rū-*

passa lahutā) as a secondary element of matter, in their opinion it is not associated with one particular primary element but is dependent on all the four.[88] These are only minor differences. There is general agreement among the Buddhists that the air-element is representative of mobility or motion (*īrana, samudīrana*).

With the development of the theory of momentariness,[89] the above definition of the air-element could not be retained without modification. We shall discuss this theory in a later chapter. Suffice it to note here that according to it, all elements of existence, mental as well as material, are of momentary duration. They are characterized by instantaneous being in the sense that they arise and perish in continual succession projecting a picture of a relatively static existence. Closely connected with this theory is the denial of motion. As the Abhidharmakośa observes, "the conditioned perishes wherever it arises; it cannot go from one place to another."[90] If the air-element is representative of mobility or motion, how is this statement to be reconciled with the denial of motion?

In keeping with the theory of momentariness, motion is given a different interpretation: "by motion one understands a series of instantaneous states which arise in adjacent locations, just as when one speaks of the motion of a flame."[91] Accordingly, motion has to be understood, not as the movement of an element of matter from one locus in space to another (*deśāntara-gamana*), but as the appearance of different elements in adjacent locations (*deśāntarotpatti*).[92] For in the case of momentary elements, wherever appearance takes place there itself takes place disappearance: *yatraivotpattih tatraiva vinasah*.[93] The classic example given in this connection is the light of the lamp. The so-called light of the lamp, it is contended, is nothing but a common designation given to an uninterrupted production of a series of flashing points. When the production changes place one says that the light has changed. But in reality other flames have appeared in another place.[94]

It is interesting to notice that this new definition of motion has somehow or other found its way to Theravada Abhidhamma that flourished after the time of Venerable Buddhaghosa. In the earlier Pali commentaries air-element is understood as indicative of motion, but therein motion is not denied. In the later works, notably the ṭīkās, motion is denied; that is to say, it is interpreted as *desantaruppatti*, the appearance of momentary elements in adjacent locations, projecting a picture of relative duration.[95] This new development has necessitated a modification in the earlier definition of the air-element. Hence it is that the air-element is sought to be defined as the cause of "motion" (= *desantaruppatti*). It is that which causes or brings about the arising of momentary elements in adjacent locations (*desantaruppatti-hetu-bhāvena . . . gametī ti*).[96] The recognition, on the part of the Theravadins, of this new definition of motion is no matter for surprise for, as we shall see in a later chapter,[97] they, too, developed a theory of momentariness that, except for minor details, presents a close parallelism to that of the schools of Sanskrit Buddhism.

From the foregoing description of the four great elements it should appear that, as interpreted in the Abhidhamma, earth stands for solidity and extension, water for viscidity and cohesion, fire for the temperature of cold and heat, and air for motion or (according to the later interpretation) the cause of "motion." The four are not the qualities or attributes of what is called *bhūta-rūpa* (the primary matter); on the contrary, they are its constituents. In this respect, they are like the three *gunas* of Sāṃkhya, which form the constituents of prakrti, the ultimate causal nexus of the world of non-self.

The four great elements are coordinate and represent four distinct forces or phenomena in the realm of matter. The characteristics (*lakkhana*), functions (*rasa*), and manifestation (*paccupaṭṭhāna*) of one are different from those of another.[98] The non-alteration of their characteristics is constantly alluded to. However much one great element is influenced by the others, it never abandons its essential nature. In this connection the Atthasālinī refers to a sutta passage where it is stated that the four great elements might alter their characteristics sooner than it were possible for the Ariyan disciple, endowed with assured faith in the Buddha, to alter.[99] The clear implication is that both are impossibilities. What all this amounts to is that the four great elements, which stand for four distinct ultimate data of all material phenomena, are neither transmutable into one another nor reducible to a common ground.

There is, however, a way in which they group themselves into two pairs, each having one common characteristic: the earth-element and water-element are similar in heaviness (*garukattā sabhāgā*) and that fire-element and air-element are similar in lightness (*lahukattā sabhāgā*).[100] This theory seems to have been developed from the observation of some of the features of the *mahābhūtas* as understood in the popular or literal sense. It is also reminiscent of the contention of the Vaiśesikas—namely, that weight is possessed by only two elemental substances: earth and water.[101]

Another fundamental feature of the *mahābhūtas* as great elements of matter is that they always exist together (*sahajāta, sahabhū*). None of them can exist independently of the other three.[102] The nascence, subsistence, and evanescence of one do always synchronize with those of the others.[103] It is precisely for this reason that their relation is described as one of reciprocal co-nascence (*aññamañña-sahajāta*).[104] That is to say, since no great element can come into being independently of the others, in this sense, each great element is postulated as a condition by way of co-nascence (*aññamañña-sahajāta-paccaya*) in relation to the other three.[105]

The commentators seek to explan the mutual conditionality of the great elements under all possible combinations and permutations: Taking each one beginning with "earth" there are three others whose occurrence is due to that one, thus with three due to one, their occurrence takes place in four ways. Likewise each one beginning with "earth" occurs in dependence on the other three, thus with one due to three, their occurrence takes place in four ways. But with the last two dependent on the first two, with the second and fourth dependent on the first and third, with the first and third dependent on the second and fourth, with the first and forth dependent on the second and third, with the second and third dependent on the first and fourth, they occur in six ways with two elements due to two.[106] The fundamental principle involved in the relation by way of reciprocal co-nascence is that when one element arises, what is related to it, too, must arise simultaneously. With this as the basis, the commentators have shown how each of the great elements becomes, at one and the same time, the condition as well as the conditioned, in relation to the other three under different combinations and permutations.

Closely connected with this is the inseparability of the great elements. They exist in inseparable (*avinibhoga*) association: they are not positionally resolvable; one element cannot be separated from the rest.[107] Venerable Buddhaghosa explains this characteristic of inseparability in a rather mysterious way: "And just as, whomsoever the great creatures such as the spirits grasp hold of (possess), they have no standing place either inside him or outside him and yet they have no standing independently of him, so too these elements are not found to stand either inside or outside each other, yet they have no standing independently of one another."[108] What is attempted to show is that they have no thinkable standing place relative to each other.

This explanation as to the relative position of the great elements is sought to be justified on the following grounds: If they were to exist inside each other, then they would not perform their respective functions. If they were to exist otside each other, then they would be resolvable, and in such a case the theory of inseparability (*avinibbhuttavāda*) would have no validity. Therefore their standing place cannot be shown.[109]

Each great element assists the remaining three by performing its peculiar function: The earth-element, which is held together by water, maintained by fire, and distended by air, is a condition for the other three great primaries by acting as their foundation. The water-element, which is founded on earth, maintained by fire, and distended by air, is a condition for the other three primaries by acting as their cohesion. The fire-element, which is founded on earth, held together by water, and distended by air, is a condition for the other three primaries by acting as their maintaining. The air-element, which is founded on earth, held together by water, and maintained by fire, is a condition for the other three primaries by acting as their distension.[110] Thus each great element depends on, and is depended on by, the other three. Theirs is a case of mutual cooperation, a remarkable policy of give and take.

Since the four primaries exist always together, and since they are not separable one from another, the position taken up by the Buddhists in respect to the question of how they enter into the composition of different material aggregates is quite clear: in every instance of matter all the four great elements are necessarily present. On this view there is general agreement among the Buddhist schools. The Vaibhāsikas, for instance, maintain that the presence of water, fire, and air elements in an earthy substance is inferred from its cohesion, maturing, and expansion, respectively; the presence of earth, fire, and air in water is shown by its support of ships, its heat and motion; the presence of earth, water, and air in a blazing fire is shown by its solidity (*sthairya*), cohesion, or unbroken continuity and mobility; and the presence of earth, water, and fire in the air is shown by its action of holding up, its touch of cold, and its touch of heat.[111]

Accordingly, all material things or aggregates are necessarily "tetra-bhautic." This may be contrasted with the Vedantic view according to which there can be "mono-bhautic" substances as earthy, watery, etc. But this statement needs qualification.[112] For, in view of the Vedantins, there are five subtle elements (*sūksma-bhūtas*) corresponding to the five (gross) primaries. And according to the theory of *pañcīkarana*, quintuplication, "the five subtle elements are present as ingredients, though in different proportions, in each primary."[113] Hence from the standpoint of the *sūksma-bhūtas*, each and every material object turns out to be "penta-bhautic."

It is in fact the view of the Vaiśesikas that stands in clear contrast to the Buddhist theory. The differences between the Buddhists and the Vaiśesikas in regard to this question will be clear if we consider how the Buddhists explain the constitution of the human body. According to them, as mentioned earlier, it is composed of all the four primaries (*cātummahābhūmiko'yaṃ kāyo*). According to Vaiśesikas it is essentially earthy. The other substances do not enter it as its substantive or material causes.

The Vaiśesika theory is based on the following arguments: The conjunction of things perceptible and imperceptible is itself imperceptible. Hence, since space and air are imperceptible, to maintain that the human body is a conjunction of the five primaries is tantamount to saying that it is itself imperceptible.[114] Second, it is one of the theses of the Vaiśesikas that the quality in the effect is preceded by the corresponding quality in the cause.[115] It is also maintained that no effect can take place except through the combination of two component elements. Therefore, if earth unites with water to form a compound, the compound will be devoid of odor, for odor is present only in earth. Similarly a compound of earth and fire will have no odor and taste, for they are possessed only by earth. Likewise a compound of earth and air will be odorless, tasteless, and colorless, for odor, taste, and color belong to earth and not to air. Now all the foregoing qualities are present in the human body. Therefore it is to be concluded that it is not a combination of all the five elemental substances.[116]

The above argument of the Vaiśesikas is partly based on the contention that air possesses only touch; fire possesses color and touch, water possesses taste, color, and touch; and earth possesses smell and all the foregoing qualities. For the Buddhists smell, taste, color, etc., are not qualities of the great elements; they are a set of secondary elements dependent on the former. In fact, a theory similar to that of the Vaiśesikas is cited by Venerable Buddhaghosa only to be refuted as unsatisfactory. The main theme of his argument may be stated as follows: If smell were the special quality of earth, then the smell of cotton, which has an excess of earth in it, should be greater than that of fermented liquor, which has an excess of water in it. Again, if color were the special quality of fire, then the color of hot water, which has an excess of fire in it, should be brighter than that of cold water. Neither of these things is true. Therefore the theory in question should be abandoned.[117] It is also observed that of the four great elements that are not separable, one from another, one cannot say that this is a quality of that one or that is a quality of this one.[118]

The fact that Buddhism does not conceive the great elements as eternal and ever-perduring substances has also some relevance to its attitude toward the composition of material aggregates. A piece of ice, according to Buddhism, is composed of all the four primaries. Its solidity, cohesion, etc., point to their presence therein. For the Vaiśesikas, ice is essentially a watery (*ap*) substance. In their view all matter is ultimately reducible to the four kinds of eternally existing atoms—namely, the earthy, the watery, the fiery, and the airy. Since no substance is destroyable, decomposition of a compound means its reversal to the original position. Hence, when ice melts it becomes water, and water is ultimately composed of watery atoms.[119] From the Buddhist standpoint, whether ice remains as it is, or whether it becomes water when melted or vapor when excessively heated, in all these different states the four great elements are present.

Although all the four primaries are present in every instance of matter, yet there is no quantitative difference between them. In other words, they enter into the composition of material things in equal proportion.[120] There is as much water-element in a blazing fire as there is in wood or water. It is argued that if there were to be a quantitative difference between the primaries that enter into the composition of materal objects, then the thesis that they are inseparable would not be logical (*na yujjeyya*).[121] This theory is not confined to the Theravada alone. This is what the schools of Sanskrit Buddhism call "*tulya-bhūta-sad-bhāva*."[122]

If the great elements are present in equal proportion in each and every material thing, what explains the diversity of the latter? For it is a matter of common experience that in many respects a comparatively hard stone is different from water, and both from a blazing fire. Or to put it differently: Now the Theravadins say that the four primaries, with the exception of the water-element, are tangibles (*phoṭṭhabbāyatana*) while the schools of Sanskrit Buddhism say that all the four are tangibles.[123] Such being the case, what accounts for the diversity in tactile sensations? For it is a matter of common experience that one does not get the same sensation when one touches, say, a flower and a blazing fire.

The diversity, it is maintained, is not due to a difference in quantity (*pamāna*) but to a difference in capability (*sāmatthiya*) or extrusion (*ussada*).[124] That is to say, in a given material object one primary is more intense than the others. For instance, in a comparatively solid thing, say, in a stone, although all the primaries are present in equal proportion, yet the earth-element is more intense or more extruded than the others. So is water-element in water, fire-element in fire, and air-element in air.

In the Atthasālinī we get more details on this subject. It says that the four primaries (exept water-element) reach the avenue of the sense of touch simultaneously. Although they strike the sentient body simultaneously, yet bodily cognition of them does not arise at once. For the object of touch is determined by one of two alternative factors—namely, deliberate attention (*ābhuñjita-vasena*) and extrusion (*ussada-vasena*).[125]

The first alternative is illustrated as follows: When the bowl is filled with food and brought in, one who takes up a lump and examines whether it is hard or soft is considering only the element of extension, though there may be heat and mobility present. One who investigates by putting the hand in hot water is considering only the element of heat, though extension and mobility are present. One who lets the wind beat upon the body by opening the window in the hot season is considering, while the wind beats gently and softly, only the element of mobility, though extension and heat are present.[126]

The other alternative, where the element of deliberate attention is absent, is explained with reference to extrusiveness (*ussada*) of one element in relation to others. "But he who slips or knocks his head against a tree, or in eating bites on a stone, takes as his mental object only the element of extension on account of its extrusiveness, though where he slipped, etc., heat and mobility were present. One treading on fire makes only the element of heat his object owing to its extrusiveness, although extension and mobility are present therein. When a strong wind blows striking the ear as if to make one deaf, although extension and heat are present, the element of mobility alone is made the object owing to its extrusiveness."[127]

That intensity determines which element should become the object of touch is recognized by many of the schools of Sanskrit Buddhism, too. The Abhidharmakośa, too, poses the question as to why all the elements do not become the object of touch simultaneously. And the answer given is almost the same as that which we mentioned under the second alternative: "One perceives in a given aggregate such and such a thing (earth-element, etc.), which finds itself as the most intensive (*paṭutama, sphuṭatama*), and not the others."[128]

From the Abhidharmakośa one gathers that the scholiasts had advanced more than one explanation in respect of this subject. In the first place, there is the opinion of Bhadanta Śrīlābha, according to which the aggregates consist of the four great elements because, due to certain causes, the solid things become liquid, and so on. The fire-element exists in water because it is more or less cold. This view attempts to explain the differences in the objects of touch as being due to a quantitative difference of the primaries. Thus the degree of hotness of water is dependent on the quantity of fire-element with which it is mixed (*miśrībhāva, vyatibhāva*).[129] The Theravādins and the Vaibhāṣikas refuse to believe in a quantitative difference; such a difference, says the *ṭīkā* to the Visuddhimagga, does not accord well with the theory of the inseparability of the four primaries.[130] Śrīlābha's interpretation is criticized in the Abhidharmakośa itself. It says that the variability, say, of cold is due to the variability of the intensity of the water-element, and not due to the fact that it gets mixed with its opposite—that is, heat, which is represented by fire-element.[131]

Still more different is the explanation given by the Sautrāntikas: the great elements that are not perceived in a given aggregate exist *a l'etat de semence* (*bījatas, śaktitas, sāmarthyatas*), not in active capacity, not by way of own-nature (*svarūpatas*). This is why the Buddha was able to say: "In this piece of timber, there are many *dhātus* or mineral substances as potentialities and latencies."[132] This theory of the Sautrāntikas appears to be analogous to that of the Theravādins and the Vaibhāṣikas. There is, however, this fundamental difference to be noted: for the latter, excess (*adhikatā*) of one element means that it is characterized by more intensity or capability. They do not say that other elements are in an "*état de semence*." They say that in a given object of touch all the elements are present, and that those elements that are comparatively intense become the object of touch.

Closely connected with this principle of intensity (*ussada*) is another sense in which the names of the four primaries are used. According to the Abhidhammic interpretation, one cannot speak of material things as earthy, watery, fiery, and airy. For in each and every instance of matter all the primaries are present. Nevertheless, there is a sense in which the Ābhidhammikas speak of material aggregates named after the *mahābhūtas*. This has been established with reference to the above-mentioned principle of intensity. If in a given material aggregate the earth-element is characterized by a comparatively high degree of intensity (*ussada*) or capability (*sāmatthiya*), then (as a matter of convention) that material aggregate is also called "earthy." In such instances the term is sometimes followed by *adhika*, "excessive" (in intensity or capability)—for example, *paṭhavī-adhika*. Similarly are used the names of the other three primaries.[133]

This kind of description is, in a way, an attempt to accommodate the earlier conception of the primaries, according to which the hair, nails, teeth, etc., are earth; blood, mucus, etc., are water; and so on. However, as interpreted in the Abhidhamma, strictly speaking, no primary element is visible. The attribution of visibility, as the Abhidharmakośa says, is from the point of view of common usage: "In common parlance what one describes by the word 'earth' is but color and figure" (*pṛthivī varṇasaṃsthānaṃ ucyate lokasaṃjñaya*).[134]

According to the Kathāvatthu and its commentary, the Andhakas object to the recognition of primaries as not visible: "But do we not see earth, a stone, a mountain, water, fire blazing, trees waving in the wind . . . ?"[135] This objection, it needs barely any mention, has hardly any relevance to the Abhidhammic interpretation of the four primaries. It is only reminiscent of their earlier conception.

The inclusion of the four primaries in the sphere of touch (*phoṭṭhabbāyatana*) shows that although not visible, they are tangible. They can be known by the sense of touch. From the point of view of the Theravādins, this statement needs qualification. For as we have already indicated, in their opinion only three primaries—namely, earth, fire, and air—come under the sphere of touch. In contrast, the schools of Sanskrit Buddhism include all four in the sphere of the tangible.[136]

Why the Theravādins have excluded water-element from the sphere of the tangible is partly explained by what we have observed about the position of *sīta*, cold, in relation to the four primaries. Unlike, for instance, the Vaibhāṣikas, the Theravādins do not associate cold with the water-element. For the latter, cold is not a force distinct from, but is only the relative absence of, heat (= *tejo-dhātu*). As such, in the view of the Theravādins, both cold (*sīta*) and heat (*uṇha*), in other words, all degrees of temperature, are represented by, and therefore testify to the presence of, fire-element.[137]

Water-element, as stated above, is representative of *bandhanatta*, the fact of binding together or cohesion and *davatā,* fluidity. But this, according to Theravada Buddhism, is not felt by the sense of touch.[138] The point is illustrated by S. Z. Aung when he says: "When one puts his hand into cold water, the softness of water felt is not *āpo*, but *paṭhavī,* the cold felt is not *āpo*, but *tejo*; the pressure felt is not *āpo*, but *vāyo*."[139] Its cohesion and fluidity, whatever their degree of intensity or capability, are not felt by the sense of touch. Hence water-element is excluded from the sphere of the tangible and is included in the sphere of mental objects.[140] That is to say, it cannot be known by any of the senses other than the mind (*mano*). It is known by a process of inference.

The general position assigned to the *mahābhūtas* as great elements may now be considered. If one were to examine how they are interpreted in other systems of Indian thought one would notice that in Buddhism they were assigned a comparatively primary position. What the Sāṃkhya considers as *mahābhūtas* are not the ultimate irreducible constituents of matter, for they are evolved immediately from the *tanmātras* and ultimately from the *prakṛti*—that is, the uncaused first cause of the world of non-self.[141] According to the Vedāntins, the *mahābhūtas* are produced from the *sūkṣmabhūtas*. The former are a species of gross matter and the latter a species of subtle matter.[142] For the Jainas, the ultimate constituents of *puggala*, matter, are not the four elements (*dhādu-catukka*) but the homogeneous atoms (*paramāṇu*). The latter are recognized as the essential causes of the former.[143] The Nyāya-Vaiśeṣikas postulate four kinds of atoms corresponding to the four elemental substances—namely, earth, water, fire, and air.[144] This may be described as an attempt to reconcile the older theory of the *mahābhūtas* with the later atomic theory. Because of this fact, the four substances in question are not reduced to a secondary position.

In Buddhism, unlike in many other systems of Indian thought, the *mahābhūtas* are assigned a primary position in the sense that they are recognized as the ultimate irreducible data of matter. It is of course true that a given instance of matter consists of not only the four *mahābhūtas* but also of a set of *upādā-rūpas*, such as color, smell, etc. But these so-called *upādā-rūpas*, as conceived by the Buddhists, are always dependent on and therefore secondary to the *mahābhūtas*. Even the development of the theory of *rūpakalāpas*—that is, the Theravāda version of atomism—did not in any way reduce the *mahābhūtas* to a secondary position. For in every *rūpakalāpa*, the smallest unit of matter, all the four *mahābhūtas* are present.[145] Although they are postulated as the ultimate primary elements of matter, the *mahābhutas* are not to be understood as uncaused or as ever-perduring entities. They too come under the laws of "phenomenal" (*saṅkhata*) existence. As Venerable Buddhaghosa says, they are impermanent in the sense of liability to destruction (*khayaṭṭhena aniccā*), suffering in the sense of causing terror (*bhayaṭṭhena dukkhā*), and non-self in the sense of having no ever-perduring essence (*asāraṭṭhena anattā*).[146]

4

THE SECONDARY ELEMENTS: GROUP A

IT WAS OBSERVED earlier that only those material elements qualified by the positive term "concretely produced" (*nipphanna*) are real. They have the three characteristics of the conditioned—namely, coming into being, change-in-continuance, and complete cessation—and are brought about by the four generative conditions of matter—namely, consciousness, volitional act, temperature, and nutriment. They have not only their own-nature but also answer to the definition of matter. Among the twenty-four secondary material elements, fourteen are subsumed under the heading "concretely produced"—namely, the first five sense-organs, the first four objective fields, the faculty of femininity, the faculty of masculinity, the material faculty of life, material nutriment, and the physical base of mental activity. It is these items that we propose to examine in this chapter.

Sense-Organs

The first five sense-organs, conceived as five secondary material elements, are the organs of sight (*cakkhu*), hearing (*sota*), smell (*ghāna*), taste (*jivhā*), and touch (*kāya*).

On their nature as a species of matter, the Nikāyas are less informative. True, they figure oft and again in many a sutta. However, the purpose is not so much to explain their nature as a variety of matter.

Sometimes they occur in stock formulas where the causality of sense perception is explained;[147] oftener than not they occur in what may be described as hortative discourses where the Buddha is exhorting the disciples not to become victims to sensual pleasures lest they should fall short of the highest ideal.[148]

In the Abhidhamma Piṭaka they came to be described as *pasāda*.[149] Literally the term means clearness, brightness, serenity, or faith. But as a descriptive term of the sense-organs, it had not been used in the earlier Pāli texts. "Taken causatively," observes Mrs. Rhys Davids, "it may conceivably have meant either that which makes clear—a revealer as it were—or that which gratifies or satisfies, . . ."[150] It is in fact suggestive of both meanings, for the first indicates the receptive and reacting nature of the sense-organs, and the second brings into relief the part they play in the gratification of sensual pleasures.

In the Sanskrit sources, too, the sense-organs are described as *prasāda*. Considering the contexts in which it occurs,[151] it could also be said that in using this term the Buddhists are intent on showing that the sense-organs are of a very subtle and delicate matter. This is borne out by the fact that, according to the Dhammasaṅganī, they cannot be known by any of the senses other than the mind (*mano*).[152] The Vaibhāṣikas, too, conceive them in a similar way. They are suprasensible (*atīndriya*)[153] and translucent (*accha*). Because of this translucence, like the luminosity of a gem (*maṇiprabhāvāt*), they cannot be burnt or weighed.[154] Nor can they be cut into two. For example, when a part of the body is chopped off, thereby the body-sensibility (*kāya-prasāda*) does not multiply itself. For the part that is cut off is devoid of body-sensibility; this is inferred from the fact that, on the basis of the part that is separated, there does not arise tactile sensation.[155]

On this point Ācārya Yaśomitra makes this interesting observation: "How then could there be tactile sensation with reference to the tip of the nose when it is cut but not separated from the nose? Since it is connected with the nose the body-sensibility (*kāyendriya*) arises again. Hence there is no contradiction. But how is it that when the tails of house lizards, etc., are chopped off, they begin to vibrate if they are devoid of body-sensibility? This is due to the alteration or impact (*vikāra*) of the air-element."[156]

Since the sense-organs are conceived as a species of extremely subtle matter, it is explicitly stated that they should not be understood according to their popular conception. The Abhidharmakośa says that what in common parlance are known as eye, ear, etc. are the *adhiṣṭhāna*, the support, of the real sense-organs.[157] The same distinction is upheld in the Theravāda, too. The Atthasālinī remarks that the very purpose of using the term *pasāda* is to dismiss their popular conception. Each sense-organ (i.e., in a broad and general sense) consists of two parts: the compound or peripheral organ (*sasambhāra*) and the sentient organ (*pasāda*). The first is what we ordinarily mean by eye, ear, etc. The second is the real sense-organ, and has the first as its basis (*vatthu*).[158]

In pursuance of this distinction, the Visuddhimagga and the Atthasālinī give, in almost identical words, a long disquisition on the nature and constitution of the sense-organs: The *sasambhāra-cakkhu*, or the compound eye, is white from the abundance of phlegm, black from that of bile, red from that of blood, rigid from that of the element of extension, fluid from that of cohesion, hot from that of heat, and oscillating from that of mobility. The *pasāda-cakkhu*, or the sentient eye, is situated in the center of the compound eye. It permeates the ocular membranes as sprinkled oil permeates seven cotton wicks. It is served by the four elements doing the functions of sustaining, binding, maturing, and vibrating, just as a princely boy is tended by four nurses doing the functions of holding, bathing, dressing, and fanning him. It is not bigger in size than the head of a louse. The organ of hearing is situated in the interior of the compound organ, at a spot shaped like a finger ring and fringed by tender tawny hairs, and is tended by the four primary elements. The organ of smell is in the interior of the compound organ, at a spot shaped like a goat's hoof. The organ of taste is above the middle of the compound organ, at a spot shaped like the upper part of a torn lotus leaf. The organ of touch is to be found everywhere in this physical body like a liquid that soaks a layer of cotton.[159]

Although the organ of touch is said to be co-extensive with the whole body, yet the possibility of confusion (*saṅkara*) between the sense-organs as to their functions is repeatedly ruled out. The characteristic (*lakkhaṇa*), function (*rasa*), and manifestation (*paccupaṭṭhāna*) of one sense-organ are different from those of another. For instance, the organ of sight has the characteristic of being sensitive only to the sphere of visibility, but not to sounds, tastes, etc.; its function is to draw attention to its respective objective field only; and it manifests itself as the physical basis of visual consciousness, but not as the physical basis of auditory or any other kind of consciousness.[160]

Professor Stcherbatsky observes that the Buddhist conception of the sense-organs as composed of matter subtler than the things that become the corresponding objects is reminiscent of the Sāṃkhya view—namely, that matter developed along two different lines, the one with predominance of the translucent intelligence-stuff (*sattva*), the other with predominance of dead matter (*tamas*), resulting in sense-objects in their subtle (*tan-mātra*) and gross (*mahābhūta*) forms. But the fundamental difference, to which Professor Stcherbatsky himself draws attention, is that, unlike in the Sāṃkhya, in Buddhism the two groups are not conceived "as modifications or appurtenances of an eternal substance."[161]

Moreover, the force of this parallelism tends to fade away because of the circumstance that, in most of the systems of Indian thought, the sense-organs are conceived in a more or less similar manner. The Jainas speak of two kinds of sense-organs: *dravyendriya*, the physical sense-organ, and *bhāvendriya*, its psychical correlate. The former, in turn, consists of two parts: *nivṛtti*, the organ itself, and *upakaraṇa*, the supporting environment. According to Caraka, the sense-organs are distinct from their peripheral seats. The Mīmāṃsakas maintain that "the sense-organs consist in the faculty of potency (*śakti*) abiding in the sockets." The Sankarite Vedāntin is of the view that the organs of sight, hearing, smell, taste, and touch are composed of the sāttvic parts of light, ether, earth, water, and air, respectively.[162]

It is of course very likely that this somewhat common tradition is due to the influence of the Sāṃkhya on the other systems of Indian thought. It is also significant to notice that a similar view seems to have been held by Ajita Kesakambali, who, as we gather from the suttas, was contemporaneous with the Buddha. In the *Sāmaññaphala Sutta* he is recorded as having told King Ajātasattu that a human being is composed of four *mahābhūtas*—namely, earth, water, fire, and air—and that after his death, while the four *mahābhūtas* join with their respective groups (in the external world), his *indriyas* join the *ākāsa* (ether).[163] On the basis of its general usage, if *indriya* is understood as referring to the sense-organs, then the fact that they are said to join the *ākāsa* suggests that, in Ajita Kesakambali's view, they are a very delicate variety of matter.

The association of such characteristics as subtlety, transparence, and translucence with the sense-organs is understandable, for this is an attempt to explain the big problem as to why the sense-organs are sensitive to external phenomena.

Once the sense-organs were distinguished from the other *upādā-rūpas* by their being described as *pasāda-rūpa*, the next problem that required an explanation was why they were different, one from another.

There was the well-known theory of the Nyāya-Vaiśeṣikas: The difference is due to the circumstance that the organs of sight, hearing, smell, taste, and touch are composed of light, ether, earth, water, and air, respectively. Each organ is sensitive to the phenomenon that is the particular quality (*viśeṣa-guṇa*) of the substance that enters into its composition. Color, sound, smell, taste, and touch are the respective qualities of light, ether, earth, water, and air. As such they become the objects corresponding to the organs of sight, hearing, smell, taste, and touch, respectively. There is thus a community of interest between the sense-organ and the corresponding objective field.[164]

That this Nyāya-Vaiśeṣika theory, in a modified form, was accepted by certain Buddhists, is shown by some comments made by Ācariya Buddhaghosa on two similar theories. According to the first, among the primary elements that support the organ of sight, heat is in excess; likewise, in the case of the organs of hearing, smell, and taste, air, earth, and water are in excess. And, as for the organ of touch, there is no difference between the supporting primary elements. According to the second, the five sense-organs (in the order they are mentioned above) have, respectively, heat, ether (*vivara*), air, water, and earth in excess.[165]

The two views are cited only to be refuted. That they were advocated by certain Buddhists is clear from Ācariya Buddhaghosa's contention—namely, that those who put them forward should be pressed to quote a sutta in favor of their argument—an attempt, says Ācariya Buddhaghosa, in which they would be disappointed.[166] In the *ṭīkā* to the Visuddhimagga the first is attributed to certain Mahāsāṅghikas and is said to have been advocated by one Vasudhamma.[167] And in the Sinhalese *sannē* to the same work the second is attributed to the Abhayagirivāsins, the rival sect of the Mahāvihāra.[168]

Ācariya Buddhaghosa's argument is as follows: "But some give as their reason that it is because these (several sensitivities = sense-organs) are (respectively) aided by visible data, etc., as qualities of fire and so on. They should be asked, 'But who has said that visible data, etc., are qualities of fire and so on?' For it is not possible to say of primary elements which remain always inseparable, that 'This is a quality of this one, that is a quality of that one.' Then they may say, 'Just as you assume, from excess in such and such material things, the (respective) functions of upholding (*sandhāraṇa*) etc., for earth, etc., so from finding visibility, etc., (respectively) in a state of excess in material things that have fire in excess, one may assume that visible data, etc., are (respectively) qualities of these.' They should be told, 'We might assume it if there were more odour in cotton which has earth in excess than in fermented liquor which has water in excess, and if the colour of cold water were weaker than the colour of hot water which has heat in excess. But since neither of these is a fact you should therefore give up conjecturing the difference to be in the supporting primary elements.'"[169]

Ācariya Buddhaghosa's general refutation of the two theories is understandable. For, as represented by him, their underlying assumption is that color, smell, etc., are the qualities of the primary elements—a view to which Buddhism in general took strong exception. His own explanation, repeated by his successors, too, as to the difference between the sense-organs is based on an earlier tradition—namely, that they come into being through the action of kamma (*kammasamuṭṭhāna*).[170] The difference between the sense-organs, it is said with much emphasis, is due to the difference in the kamma of which they are the results.[171]

However, as pointed out by Dr. E. R. Sarathchandra, although the Buddhists rejected the Nyāya-Vaiśeṣika theory as regards the affinity between a given sense-organ and the corresponding sense-object, yet they seem to have been influenced by it in postulating the media in which the sensory stimuli traveled. The media for the organs of sight, hearing, smell, taste, and touch were, respectively, light (*āloka*), space or ether (*ākāsa*), air (*vāyo*), water (*āpo*), and earth (*paṭhavī*).[172]

Before we end this section we need examine why the sense-organs are called *indriya*. Buddhism interprets the term as expressive of power, dominance, or suzerainty (*ādhipacca, issariya*).[173] As the bases or supports (*vatthu, nissaya*) of the consciousness (*viññāṇa*), the sense-organs are said to weild a dominating influence on the former.[174] Since consciousness cannot arise without reference to a given sense-organ and the corresponding object, the question is raised as to why the former alone is called *indriya*. The answer is that the intensity of the consciousness is relative to the strength of the sense-organ. If the latter is "sharp," strong (*tikkha*), the former, too, becomes "sharp," strong; likewise if the latter is weak (*manda*), the former, too, becomes weak.[175]

Objective Fields

The Nikāyan descriptions of *rūpa* (the visible), *sadda* (sound), *gandha* (smell), *rasa* (taste), and *phoṭṭhabba* (the tangible) take a general form, determined mostly by ethical and practical considerations. They are not permanent (*anicca*) and have no abiding essence (*asāra*). Attachment to them cannot, therefore, be made the basis of true happiness. It only nourishes and prolongs "saṃsāric" existence. For the realization of the highest ideal, all sensual pleasures should be eschewed. But the visible, the audible, etc. are the five strands of sensual pleasures (*pañcakāma-guṇā*). Hence it is that they are sought to be described in such a way as to bring home the perils (*ādīnava*) that result from attachment to them and thereby to emphasize the need to eschew all kinds of craving in respect of them (*nissaraṇa*).[176]

This, in brief outline, is how the earlier texts approach the subject under consideration. In the post-Nikāyan works they have become the subject of a more detailed study. Certainly the ethical approach prevails, but the emphasis is not as pronounced as in the Nikāyas. Their treatment in the Abhidhamma Piṭaka is very laconic; the logical implications are not discussed. However, the commentaries and the sources of Sanskrit Buddhism help us to understand the descriptions in a wider perspective.

Let us take *rūpāyatana*, the sphere of the visible, first. In the Dhammasaṅganī under *rūpāyatana* are enumerated first some examples of color: blue, yellow, red, white, etc., and then some examples of figure: circular, oval, square, hexagonal, etc.[177] As far as the inclusion of both items under *rūpāyatana* is concerned, this explanation is fundamentally the same as that of the Vaibhāṣikas.

They, too, maintained that the visible consisted of color (*varṇa*) as well as figure (*saṃsthāna*). The visible can be color without being figure (*saṃsthāna-nirapekṣaṃ*)—for example, blue, red, yellow, white, shade, sunlight (*ātāpa*), light (*āloka*), darkness (*tamas*). It can be figure without being color (*varṇa-nirapekṣaṃ*)—for example, that part of long, short, etc. that constitutes the *kāya-vijñapti*, or bodily expression.[178] Or else it can be, at one and the same time, both color and figure—that is, all other varieties of the visible.[179]

The Sautrāntikas, in whose system of thought one could detect the burden of emphasis shifting from the outer to the inner, declared that color (*varṇa*) alone was real, that it alone constituted the visible, and that figure (*saṃsthāna*) was only a mental construction (*mānasaṃ*) with no corresponding objective reality (*prajñaptisat*).[180]

Their thesis is sought to be established by three main arguments. One can obtain the notion of long, short, etc. by seeing or by touching something. Therefore, if the figure were a real entity, then one should admit that it could be perceived by two sense-organs, a view that goes against the canonical definition of *rūpāyatana*, according to which it is the objective field corresponding only to one sense-organ—namely, the organ of sight.

The Vaibhāṣikas contend that when we obtain the idea of, say, "long" after having touched something, it is not that we actually perceive it by the organ of touch, but that we are reminded of the figure (long) because it is associated with the tangible. It is just as when we see the color (visible) of fire we are reminded of its heat (tangible), or when we smell the odor of a flower we are reminded of its color. The Sautrāntikas point out that this analogy is not of universal validity. Concerning the two examples cited: color reminds us of the tangible and the odor reminds us of the color because there is an invariable association (*avyabhicāra*) between the two things given in each example. But every tangible is not associated with a particular figure. Hence it is not correct to say that the perception of a given instance of tangible should necessarily and always remind us of its figure. If it were otherwise, runs the argument, then every time we touched something we should also know the color associated with it.

Second, if figure is a real *rūpa* then it has to be conceded that there could be a plurality of *rūpas* in one and the same locus (*ekadeśa*). In a variegated carpet, for instance, there are a large number of figures. If figure is a real entity, then a figure that is a part of a long line cannot, at the same time, be a part of a short line.

Third, color is a constituent element of the smallest unit of matter.[181] But the same cannot be predicated of figure.

The Vaibhāṣikas retort that if figure is nothing but a certain disposition of color, then the figure can never change if the color is the same. The Sautrāntikas meet this objection by saying that one calls something long, etc. when a number of real dharmas (elements) are placed in a certain manner or disposition.[182]

The strong opposition of the Vaibhāṣikas to interpreting figure as a mental construction with no corresponding objective reality is, in all probability, motivated by their desire to establish the reality of *kāyavijñapti* (bodily intimation). They are of the view that it is a certain figure of the body (of a living being) known as an object of visual consciousness.[183] Unlike the Sautrāntikas, they could not deprive *kayāvijñapti* of its reality because along with *vāgvijñapti* (vocal intimation) it is closely associated with *avijñapti-rūpa*.[184]

The foregoing Sautrāntika arguments against the conception of figure as a real entity cannot be overlooked if we are to understand in a broad perspective how the commentators interpreted the Dhammasaṅganī account of *rūpāyatana*. It was noted earlier[185] that in this manual some examples of figure, too, are brought under the sphere of the visible (*rūpāyatana*). But in the Atthasālinī they are interpreted in such a way that it presents a close parallelism to the Sautrāntika theory.

Commenting on the examples of figure cited in the Dhammasaṅganī, the Atthasālinī says: "The terms 'long,' etc. are accomplished by mutual reference (*aññam'aññam upanidhāya*). The terms 'circular,' etc. are accomplished by juxtaposition (*sannivesena*). Among them, with reference to what is short, 'long' is so called as being higher (*uccatara*) than that; 'short' is so called as being lower (*nīcatara*) than 'long.' With reference to what is 'big,' a thing smaller than that is 'little,' with reference to which a greater thing is 'big.'"[186]

Then it goes on to say: "Among these expressions, because it is possible to know 'long,' etc. also by touch, but not 'blue-green,' etc., therefore, in reality 'long' is not directly (*nippariyāyena*) a visible object, and neither is 'short' or similar terms."[187]

That "'long' is not directly a visible object" clearly shows that, strictly speaking, figure (*saṇṭhāna*) is not a part of the visible (*rūpāyatana*). Explaining why in the earlier account some examples of figure are enumerated under the visible, the Atthasālinī remarks that this has been done as a concession to popular usage (*vohārato*).[188]

One cannot overlook the fact that among the Sautrāntikas there was a strong tendency to interpret as nominal (*prajñaptisat*) some of the dharmas that in the Vaibhāṣika and in the Theravāda were postulated as real (*dravyatas, saccikaṭṭhaparamaṭṭhena*).

Their advocacy of the theory of representative perception (*bāhyānumeyavāda*) and their non-recognition of any of the *dharmā-*

yatana-rūpas, such as the *avijñapti-rūpa*, are indicative of their subjectivist tendencies.[189] It is very likely, therefore, that among Buddhists it was they who first advocated the theory in question before it found expression in Theravāda Buddhism.

Whether it was an introduction from an outside source or one of their own creations, the Theravādins could easily accommodate it into their system. For, unlike the Vaibhāṣikas, they did not interpret bodily intimation (*kāya-viññatti*) as a figure (*saṇṭhāna*) of the body.[190] Nor did they recognize *avijñapti-rūpa*. Hence they could conveniently relegate figure to the domain of mental constructs (*paññattis*) without thereby undermining the basis of any other established doctrine.

And it is as a logical result of this new interpretation that in the Mūlaṭīkā, the older term *rūpāyatana* (sphere of the visible) is sometimes substituted by the more specific term *vaṇṇāyatana* (the sphere of color).[191]

As for *sadda*, sound, the account given in the Dhammasaṅganī is, in the main, an enumeration of different kinds of sounds: of drums, of tabors, of chank-shells, of tom-toms, of singing, of music, etc.[192] In the post-canonical works we are presented with two different theories on the subject. Earlier is the one given in the (Sīhala) Aṭṭhakathā. Although the work is not extant now, a reference to one of its views is made in the Atthasālinī.[193]

According to this reference, sound travels in an elemental series—*bhūtaparamparā*. Of much interest is the example given in support of this view: The bodily movements of men felling trees or of washermen washing clothes are seen (quickly), although they are at a great distance. On the other hand, the sound they make is relatively slow of ascertainment (*vavatthāna*) because it comes in an elemental series (*dhātuparamparāya*) and strikes the auditory organ.[194]

The Aṭṭhakathā view, as noted by Dr. E. R. Sarathchandra,[195] is on a parallel with the one advanced by the Nyāya-Vaiśeṣikas concerning this subject: "Either sounds reach the ear in concentric circles of waves like the waves of water, or they shoot out in all directions like the filaments of a Kadamba."[196]

The Atthasālinī has alluded to the Aṭṭhakathā theory of sound only to dismiss it as unsound. The main objection raised is that such a theory cannot adequately account for our knowledge of the direction of sound: If sound comes slowly, having arisen at a distance, then it will be apprehended after some time. Coming in an elemental series and impinging on the sensitive portion of the ear, the direction it comes from might not be evident.[197] For when one hears a sound one can (fairly accurately) say whether it is a distant sound or a near sound, or whether it is a sound from the farther bank or from the hither bank.[198]

Following the Atthasālinī argument, Ācariya Dhammapāla, too, observes that if sound travels toward the ear, then there cannot be the determination of its locality and direction (*desādesa-vavatthāna*). He further notes that when sound is apprehended it remains where it has arisen. As to how an echo arises, it is said that the sound, although it remains at a distance, becomes a condition (*paccaya*) for the arising of an echo elsewhere, even as a magnet (*ayo-kanta*) for the movement of iron.[199] Then there is the observation of Ācariya Sumaṅgala: the fact that one hears the sound of thunder that arises at a distance or the sound generated within the body that is covered by the skin shows that for its apprehension sound need not travel toward the ear and strike its sensitive portion.[200]

It is significant to notice that this theory, which has been introduced in place of the earlier, is similar to the one accepted by some of the schools of Sanskrit Buddhism, according to which sound is characterized by *apravāha-vartitva*—that is, it does not exist in a series.[201]

With the development of atomism, an important problem cropped up concerning the production of sound. As we shall see in a later chapter,[202] the Vaibhāṣikas deny the possibility of atoms coming into immediate contact with one another. How, then, is the phenomenon of sound to be explained?

With the development of the theory of atomic clusters (*rūpa-kalāpas*), the Theravādins, too, had to answer a similar question.

For in their view, too, the atomic clusters, the ultimate units of matter, do not come into immediate contact.[203] If this thesis were to be maintained, the production of sound could not be attributed to an actual concussion of the atomic clusters. Hence it is that the *ṭīkā* to the Visuddhimagga, having observed that sound results from the *ghaṭṭana* (striking together) of the atomic clusters, goes on to define what this *ghaṭṭana* is: "it is the arising of material clusters in proximity to one another due to conditions."[204] The words: "arising . . . in proximity" are meant to rule out their actual contact as well as their movement. For the theory that motion is an illusion created by the genesis of momentary elements in adjacent locations (*deśāntarotpatti*) is recognized in the later works of the Theravādins, too.[205]

On the subject of *gandha*, odor, and *rasa*, savor, the treatment is mainly a matter of classifications.

The Dhammasaṅganī does not commit itself to a definite number as regards the types of odor.[206] The Atthasālinī makes a classification of all varieties into two broad groups: (a) agreeable odor (*iṭṭhagandha*), and (b) disagreeable odor (*duggandha* or *aniṭṭhagandha*). In the Vaibhāṣika each group is again considered as excessive (*utkaṭa*) or non-excessive (*anutkaṭa*).[207] Some Buddhists recognize a variety of odor that is neither agreeable nor disagreeable (*sama-gandha*).[208]

As to *rasa*, savor, the Theravāda sources do not lay down a definite number of types. The Dhammasaṅganī description is an enumeration of different types—for example, bitter, pungent, saline, alkaline, acrid, astringent, followed by the words "or whatever other savor there is."[209] The Vaibhāṣikas, on the other hand, recognize six fundamental varieties (*ṣaṇ-mūla-jāti*)—namely, sweet, sour, salt, pungent, bitter, and astringent—and admit that their mixtures could give rise to a wide variety.[210]

As for the tangible, the objective field corresponding to the organ of touch, it was already observed that, according to the Theravāda, it consists of three of the four primary elements. This subject was discussed in the course of our chapter 3 on the primary elements.

Faculties of Sex

By faculties of sex we mean *itthindriya* (faculty of femininity) and *purisindriya* (faculty of masculinity). According to the Dhammasaṅganī definition, the former means the physical appearance, marks, traits, and deportment peculiar to a female, or the state or condition of femininity (*itthatta, itthibhāva*). Likewise, the latter means physical appearance, etc., peculiar to a male, or the state or condition of masculinity (*purisatta, purisabhāva*).[211]

Two passages in the Aṅguttaranikāya show that the earlier texts, too, have understood them in the same sense.[212] But nowhere in the Nikāyas are they brought under *rūpa* (matter), let alone their being postulated as two rūpa-dhammas. The commentators seem to have been rightly aware that, in the abstract sense of femininity and masculinity, the two items could not be included in the category of *nipphanna-rūpa*. Hence it is maintained in the Atthasālinī that the physical appearance and other features that are peculiar to a female are not expressed by *itthindriya*. They are what arise because of it. Just as, because of a seed, a tree grows, replete with twigs and branches, even so because of *itthindriya* there come into being such physical features, etc., as are peculiar to a female. With the necessary adjustments, the same observation applies to *purisindriya*, too.[213]

Thus the "that" (*yaṃ*)[214] of the Dhammasaṅganī is in the commentary understood as "that through which" (*yena*).[215] This commentarial explanation falls in line with the one given by the Vaibhāṣikas. For, in their opinion, too, the two faculties of sex determine those differences between the male and the female as regards their physical form (*saṃsthāna*), tone of voice (*svara*), dispositions (*abhiprāya*), manner of being (*ācāra*), demeanor (*ceṣṭā*), etc.[216]

There is, however, this fundamental difference: The Theravādins believe that *itthindriya/purisindriya* is spread all over the body (*sakala-sarīra-byāpaka*) as *kāyendriya* (the organ of touch) is.[217] On their relative position Venerable Buddhaghosa observes that it is not correct to say that *itthindriya/purisindriya* is either "located in the space where the organ of touch is located" or "located in the space where that is not located."[218] What is attempted to show is that, although both are spread all over the body, yet the one is not an aspect or a part of the other. Those primary elements that support the organ of touch are different from those that support the faculty of sex (*bhinna-nissayatā*).[219]

On the other hand, the Vaibhāṣikas maintain that *strīndriya/puruṣendriya* is not distinct from the organ of touch but a part of it.[220] This is precisely why the Vaibhāṣikas do not count them as two separate rūpa-dharmas.[221]

Venerable Buddhaghosa says that some entertain the wrong belief that the faculty of sex is only a part of the body (*sarīrekadesavutti*). And he goes on to remark that it is partly with a view to refuting this belief that in the Visuddhimagga it is described as pervading the whole body.[222]

In consonance with their view—namely, that the two faculties of sex are not distinct from the organ of touch—the Vaibhāṣikas maintain that the two faculties have the sense of touch. That the Theravādins do not subscribe to such a view is shown from the fact that the two items are not included in the category of *rūpaṃ sappaṭighaṃ*.[223]

Since *indriya* signifies that which exercises a dominant influence, in which sense and over what do they wield their influence? The Vaibhāṣikas explain this in two ways: First, they are the determinant factor of the distribution of living beings into two groups as male and female (*sattva-bheda*). Second, they determine the differentiation of living beings (*sattva-vikalpa-bheda*); it is because of them that there are differences between the two sexes as regards the physical features, etc.[224]

From what has been observed so far, it should become clear that the Theravāda answer to the question amounts to the same.[225]

We might note in passing some interesting comments made in the Atthasālinī on some differences between the two sexes:

> The shape of a woman's hands, feet, neck, breast, etc., is not like that of a man's. The female lower body is broad, the upper body is less broad. The hands and feet are small, the mouth

> is small. The female breast is prominent. The face is without beard or moustache. The dressing of the hair, the weaving of clothes are also unlike those of a man's. The masculine features are just the opposite. For the shape of the hands, feet, neck, breast, etc., of a man is unlike the shape of those of a woman. For a man's upper body is broad, the lower body is less broad, his hands and feet are large, the face is large, the breast-flesh is less full; beard and moustache grow.

Then there are differences as to habits and deportment:

> Thus in youth women play with tiny shallow baskets, pestles and mortars, variegated dolls, and weave string with clay-fibre. There is a want of assertion in women's walking, standing, lying down, sitting, eating, swallowing. Indeed when a man of that description is seen, folk say: He walks, stands, etc., like a woman. In the case of men there is a marked difference. In youth they play with chariots and ploughs, etc., make sand-banks and dig ponds. There is assertion in their walking, etc. When a woman is seen taking long strides, etc., folk say, "she walks like a man."[226]

Coming closer to our subject, we may note here a problem that has been created by the Atthasālinī account of the two faculties of sex. The view that they are the determinant factor of the differences between the male and the female as regards their physical features, etc., does not accord with the definition of *indriya-paccaya* as given in the Paṭṭhāna of the Abhidhamma Piṭaka. In this work, with the sole exception of *itthindriya* and *purisindriya*, all the *indriyas* are postulated as *indriya-paccaya*, "condition by way of faculty."[227] The obvious implication seems to be that the two items are not interpreted as *indriya*s, although they are so designated. The situation is perfectly understandable, for, as we have seen,[228] according to the earlier texts they mean femininity (*itthatta*) and masculinity (*purisatta*), and not, as interpreted in the Atthasālinī, what are responsible for them.[229]

In all probability, it was this situation that prompted the authors of the later works to modify the Atthasālinī view on the subject. It is pointed out that, as a matter of fact, feminine features, etc., are due to the past kamma. But since they arise mostly in a continuity endowed with the *itthindriya*, *itthindriya* is to be recognized as their *kāraṇa*, "reason"—that is, a sort of supplementary cause. The same is true of *purisindriya*.[230]

Faculty of Life

It is fairly certain that the recognition of two *jīvitindriya*s, faculties of life, is a doctrinal development confined only to the Theravāda.

The first, called *arūpa-jīvitindriya* (mental), is one of the fifty-two *cetasikas* (consciousness-concomitants), and as such, is included in the *saṅkhārakkhandha*.[231] It is the factor that stabilizes and sustains every type of *citta* (consciousness) as well as those *cetasikas* that are co-nascent and co-terminous with it.[232] It is therefore counted as one of the seven "universal concomitants of consciousness" (*sabba-citta-sādhāraṇa-cetasika*).[233]

The second, called *rūpa-jīvitindriya* (material), is an *upādā-rūpa*, and as such, is included in the *rūpakkhandha*. It is the factor that stabilizes and sustains the *kamma-samuṭṭhāna-rūpa* (matter that comes into being as a result of kamma)[234]—namely, the first five sense-organs, the two faculties of sex, the physical basis of mind,[235] and all other material elements inseparably associated with them.[236] Hence it is that according to the theory of *rūpa-kalāpa*, it enters into the composition of all *kamma-samuṭṭhāna-rūpa-kalāpas*,[237] just as *arūpa-jīvitindriya* is concomitant with every kind of *citta*.

The Vaibhāṣikas, for instance, take an entirely different position: There is only one *jīvitendriya*. It is certainly not of the nature of *rūpa*. Nor is it exclusively a *caitasika* (mental) dharma, although it resembles the latter. For, unlike the *caittas* (consciousness-concomitants), it is not associated (*samprayukta*) with *cittas*.[238]

Thus, as to the faculty of life, we find two parallel developments, one recognizing two faculties and the other only one. What led to this situation becomes clear from a controversy recorded in the Kathāvatthu where the point at issue is whether there is one life-faculty or two. The arguments of the Pubbaseliyas and the Sammitīyas remind us of the Vaibhāṣika position. They contend that there is only one life-faculty, that it is common to both mind and matter, and that it is non-material. Its description as non-material suggests only its exclusion from the aggregate of corporeality and not that it is identical with any of the mental factors. For although they include the life-faculty in the aggregate of mental formations, yet they deny that any of the mental formations obtains in the attainment of cessation (*nirodha-samāpatti*). For in the attainment of cessation, the stream of consciousness and its concomitants is temporarily arrested though the physical body remains alive. The non-Theravādins' view seems to be that although the life-faculty can be assigned a place in the aggregate of mental formations, it is certainly not a pure mental factor. It may be recalled here that the Vaibhāṣikas include it in the category of "mental formations dissociated from consciousness" but make it distinct from the mental factors. In fact the commentary observes that in the opinion of the Pubbaseliyas and the Sammitīyas the life-faculty is a non-mental dhamma dissociated from consciousness (*citta-vippayutta-arūpa-dhamma*).

The Theravadins' claim for the desirability of recognizing two life-faculties is based on two main grounds. The first is that it explains satisfactorily that attainment of cessation is not identical with death, because what keeps the physical body of the person who attains "cessation" live is not the mental but the material life-faculty. The second is that the absence of mental phenomena in the material sphere does not mean that the life-principle of matter is not recognized in the material sphere (*asañña-bhava*). For in this plane of existence what operates is not the mental but the material life-faculty.[239]

As to the recognition of the life-faculty, the Sautrāntikas take a different position. In their view karma alone is sufficient and efficient to stabilize and sustain what arises as a result of karma. "Just as the destiny of an arrow and the time it will take to reach its destination are determined at the moment of its shooting, similarly the karma of an individual at the moment of rebirth fixes the destiny (*nikāya-sabhāga*) and the duration of the continuity (*santāna*) of the five aggregates." The postulation of a separate entity called "life-faculty" is not only superfluous but it gives rise to, and leaves unexplained, the question of accounting for its own stability and continuity.[240]

Material Nutriment

The Pāli expression for edible material food is *kabaḷiṅkāra-āhāra*, which literally means "food made into a ball" or "morsel-made food." In the Nikāyan terminology, it means solid material food as against sensory contact (*phassa*), volition (*mano-sañcetanā*), and consciousness (*viññāṇa*). They are all called "food" (*āhāra*), for they all nourish, sustain, and keep going the empiric individuality[241]—a process of nutriment or alimentation.

While the earlier texts understood *kabaḷiṅkāra-āhāra* in the general sense of food that all living beings take for their sustenance and growth, the Abhidhamma interpreted it in a more abstract sense to mean the nutritive aspect of matter, the "quality"of nutrition. It is of course true that the Dhammasaṅganī defines it by citing some examples of food, such as boiled rice, sour gruel, flour, fish, flesh, milk, curds, butter, cheese, etc.[242] But as the commentator observes, this is a definition given in terms of its embodiment—*vatthu-vasena*.[243]

The commentarial observation is admissible, for it is supported by the fact that *kabaḷiṅkāra-āhāra* is one of the *dhammāyatana-rūpas*. It cannot be known by any of the senses other than the mind (*mano*);[244] it is known by a process of inference. Nevertheless this definition by way of "*vatthu*" is reminiscent of its earlier meaning.

Quite in contrast is the Vaibhāṣika definition of *kavaḍīkāra-āhāra*:

it consists of three *āyatanas*—namely, *gandhāyatana* (odor), *rasāyatana* (savor), and *spraṣṭavyāyatana* (the tangible). *Rūpāyatana* (the visible) is excluded on the ground that it does not contribute to the function of alimentation.[245]

For the moment if we overlook the exclusion of *rūpāyatana*, then this interpretation does not amount to a radical departure from the earlier conception. For it may be noted here that the three *āyatanas* that make up *kavaḍīkāra-āhāra* along with *rūpāyatana* represent those material elements that are qualified as *avinirbhāga* (inseparable), and that are said to enter into the composition of all material things.[246] Hence, if what in the Nikāyas was considered as *kabaḷiṅkāra-āhāra* (food in its general sense) was sought to be explained as composed of these four *āyatanas*, then this really amounts to a case of approaching the subject from the standpoint of *āyatana*.

As regards this subject, the fundamental difference between the two schools is this: for the Theravādins *kabaḷiṅkāra-āhāra* is a separate material element, whereas for the Vaibhāṣikas it is a compound of material elements.

The Physical Basis of Mental Activity

The enumeration of *hadaya-vatthu* (the heart-basis) as a secondary material element and its recognition as the physical basis of *mano-dhātu* (mind) and *mano-viññāṇa-dhātu* (mind-consciousness) is a post-canonical development that finds mention in the Theravāda works compiled during and after the time of Ācariya Buddhaghosa. The Nikāyas are silent on the subject. Even in the Dhammasaṅganī, where we get the most exhaustive analysis of matter as far as the Pāli canon is concerned, no allusion is made to such a theory. The first canonical reference to a physical basis of mental activity is met with in the Paṭṭhāna of the Abhidhamma Piṭaka, but strangely enough the manual does not specify what it is.[247]

With their acceptance of the cardiac theory of the seat of mental activity, one question the commentators wanted to answer was why *hadaya-vatthu* was omitted in the Dhammasaṅganī. In their opinion the omission was not accidental but was due to the necessity of maintaining consistency in the method of exposition. The explanation is as follows:

> In the Vatthu-duka section of the Dhammasaṅganī, the exposition is made with reference to the bases of the first five kinds of *viññāṇa*—for example, "There is *rūpa* that is the basis of *cakkhu-viññāṇa*; there is *rūpa* that is not the basis of *cakkhu-viññāṇa*."[248] If the dyads were stated with reference to *mano-viññāṇa*, too, as "There is *rūpa* that is the basis of *mano-viññāṇa*; there is *rūpa* that is not the basis of *mano-viññāṇa*," then the Vatthu-duka section would not fall in line with the Ārammaṇa-duka section (where the dyads are stated with reference to the objects of the first five kinds of *viññāṇa*).[249] For it is not possible to establisha dyad like: "There is *rūpa* that is the object of *mano-viññāṇa*; there is *rūpa* that is not the object of *mano-viññāṇa*" (because all the *rūpa-dhammas* become the objects of *mano-viññāṇa*).[250] If there were to be inconsistency between the two sections in question, then there would not be uniformity in the method of exposition. Herein the Teacher's intention was to develop the exposition in a form that has unity (*eka-rasa*). Hence the omission of *hadaya-vatthu*, which is the basis of *mano* and *mano-viññāṇa*, was unavoidable.[251]

S. Z. Aung too suggests, but for entirely different reasons, that the omission of *hadaya-vatthu* in the Dhammasaṅganī is not accidental: "In view of the popular idea, i.e., of the cardiac theory of the seat of mental activity prevailing in his time, the Buddha preferred to be silent on the point. He did not accept the theory, but if he had expounded his own theory it would not have been acceptable to his hearers."[252]

This explanation, too, is equally unsatisfactory and equally far-fetched. To suggest that Buddhism withheld certain ideas for the simple reason that they would not "go down" with the age is to overlook the element of radicalism in Buddhist thought.

Why *hadaya-vatthu* is not mentioned in the Dhammasaṅganī, although it finds mention in the commentaries and in the kindred literature, does not seem to be a very relevant question; for what we encounter in the later texts need not necessarily find expression in the earlier. If there is a difference between the earlier and the later works as regards doctrinal tenets, this difference can be put down to a historical process at work.

Of much significance, however, is the passage in the Paṭṭhāna, which alludes to a physical basis of mental activity without specifying what it is. The interesting thing to note is the way it makes this allusion. First it specifically states that *cakkhu* is a condition by way of basis (*nissaya-paccaya*) for *cakkhu-viññāṇa* (visual consciousness). Likewise, *sota*, *ghāna*, *jivhā*, and *kāya* are instanced as basis-conditions for *sota-viññāṇa* (auditory consciousness), *ghāna-viññāṇa* (olfactory consciousness), *jivhā-viññāṇa* (gustatory consciousness), and *kāya-viññāṇa* (tactile consciousness), respectively.

But when it comes to refer to that which forms a basis-condition for *mano* and *mano-viññāṇa*, the language becomes less specific: "*Yaṃ rūpaṃ nissāya mano-dhātu ca mano-viññāṇa-dhātu ca vattanti, taṃ rūpaṃ manodhātuyā ca mano-viññāṇa-dhātuyā ca taṃsampayuttakānaṃ ca dhammānaṃ nissayapaccayena paccayo*"[253] (That material thing, based on which the mind-element and the mind-consciousness-element occur—that material thing is a condition by way of basis for the mind-element and the mind-consciousness-element and what is associated therewith).[254]

It will be seen that, in the quoted sentence, the physical basis of *mano* and *mano-viññāṇa* is not specified. It is referred to in a circuitous way as "*yaṃ rūpaṃ . . . taṃ rūpaṃ*." The term, as Mrs. Rhys Davids observes, "is guarded," but we cannot agree with her when she further observes "that the evasion is quite marked."[255] What we find here is not evasion but caution, a case of leaving the matter open. One possibility as to why the Paṭṭhāna took the above position is that the physical seat of mental activity was thought to be very complex and pervasive, and therefore its location was not limited to one particular part of the physical body.

The commentators' interpretation of "*yaṃ rūpaṃ . . . taṃ rūpaṃ*" as *hadaya-vatthu* could neither be supported nor refuted with reference to the Paṭṭhāna passage. For it is an answer to a question left unanswered.

An interesting argument in support of their interpretation is found in the sub-commentaries. The first part of this argument is an attempt to find out whether it is possible to identify the "*yaṃ rūpaṃ . . . taṃ rūpaṃ*" of the Paṭṭhāna with any of the twenty-seven rūpa-dhammas mentioned in the Dhammasaṅganī.

Attention is first drawn to the fact that *cakkhu*, *sota*, etc., which are the physical bases of the five kinds of *viññāṇas* named after them, are a variety of *nipphanna-upādā-rūpa*. Therefore—so runs the argument—the physical basis of *mano* and *mano-viññāṇa*, too, should be a rūpa-dhamma that is *nipphanna* as well as *upādā*. This eliminates the four primary elements because, although *nipphanna*, they are not *upādā*. It also eliminates the ten items that we shall examine in the next chapter because, although *upādā*, they are not *nipphanna*. Consequently the field is narrowed down to the fourteen *nipphanna-upādā-rūpas* that we have examined in this chapter.

Among them, none of the first five sense-organs can be selected because they are the physical bases of the five kinds of *viññāṇas* named after them. The four objective fields and the element of nutrition (*kabaḷiṅkāra-āhāra*) exist not only in the body of a living being but also outside of it, hence they too have to be eliminated. Since *mano* and *mano-viññāṇa* obtain even in those living beings who do not possess the faculty of sex, the two faculties of sex also have to be eliminated. The faculty of life has its own function to perform; to attribute another is not quite right, hence it should also be eliminated.[256]

So far it has been a case of elimination. And so far two things have been established: the first is that what is referred to as "*yaṃ rūpaṃ . . . taṃ rūpaṃ*" should be a *nipphanna-upādā-rūpa*; the second is that it cannot be identified with, and should therefore be distinct from, any of the (already known) thirteen *nipphanna-upādā-rūpas*. The main purpose is to show that the postulation of a separate rūpa-dhamma as the physical basis of mental activity is justifiable.

The next problem is to find out where it is located. It is said that when someone thinks of anything, bringing it to mind intently and directing his whole mind to it, he experiences exhaustion (*khijjana*) in his heart. Therefore, it is to be inferred that the location of the seat of mental activity is inside the heart (*hadayabbhantare*).[257]

What is called the "heart-basis" (*hadaya-vatthu*) is not absolutely identical with heart as such. Like the sense-organs, it is a very subtle and delicate species of matter, and is located inside the heart. Like the sense-organs, it also comes into being through the action of kamma.[258] But unlike the sense-organs,[259] it is not an *indriya*, or faculty: a thing that has domineering influence. Because of this reason, although mind and mind-consciousness have something physical as their basis (= *hadaya-vatthu*), they are not controlled by it, in the sense that the relative strength or weakness of the latter does not influence the former.[260]

In recognizing *hadaya-vatthu* as the seat of mental activity the Theravādins have followed an old Indian tradition. In a prayer in the Atharvaveda, one reads: "O Mitra and Varuna, take away the thinking power (*citta*) from the heart (*hṛd*) of this woman . . ."[261] Caraka and Suśruta, too, have recognized the cardiac theory of the seat of mental activity.[262] The question is not raised in the Nikāyas. However, as Mrs. Rhys Davids notes, the term *hadaya* finds a place in Buddhist popular psychology, but in the sense of "inmost," "inwardness," and also "thorough."[263] Thus we have "*hadaya-sukhaṃ*" (inward pleasure), "*hadayaṅgama*" (going deep into the bosom of the heart), "*dhammassa hadaya*" (the heart of the doctrine). In the Abhidhamma Piṭaka the term *hadaya* is sometimes used as synonymous with *mano* and *mano-viññāṇa*.[264] References as these, too, may have encouraged the commentators in arriving at their conclusion.

5

THE SECONDARY ELEMENTS: GROUP B

IN THIS CHAPTER we propose to examine those secondary material elements subsumed under the heading "non-concretely produced" (*anipphanna*). Though elevated to the level of material elements, they are but certain phases, qualities, or modalities of what really amounts to matter. Since they are not concretely produced by the generative conditions of matter, and since they are exempt from the characteristics of the conditioned, they do not have objective counterparts of their own. In other words, they represent a nominal category. It is this category that we intend to examine here. It consists of two modes of self-expression, three characteristics and four phases of matter, and space-element, the space bound by matter.

Modes of Self-Expression

The two *viññatti-rūpas*—namely, *kāyaviññatti* (bodily expression) and *vacīviññatti* (vocal expression)—signify bodily movements (gesture) and articulate vocal sound (speech) as two modes of self-expression or as two media for the communication of one's thought or feeling to another. This, be it noted, is only a general statement of the Buddhist conception of the two *viññattis*. Although it tends to coincide with the interpretation given by the Sāṃmitīya and the Vātsīputrīya,[265] it does not do full justice to the exact position taken by the other schools, including the Theravāda itself. The two *viññattis* are one of those subjects on which the Buddhist schools have advanced a wide variety of opinions. The initial statement should therefore be understood in a general sense.

In the Dhammasaṅgaṇī of the Abhidhamma Piṭaka, *kāyaviññatti* is defined as the state of bodily tension or excitement (*kāyassa thambhanā santhambhanā santhambhitattaṃ*) "on the part of a person who advances or recedes or fixes the gaze or glances around or retracts an arm or stretches it forth." It is said to result in response to a thought, whether wholesome (*kusala*), unwholesome (*akusala*), or morally indeterminate (*avyākata*).[266] For this reason, it is also described as invariably *citta-samuṭṭhāna*—that is, set up or given rise to by consciousness.[267]

It is called *kāyaviññatti* because it is the bodily expression or the bodily intimation of that morally qualifiable thought in response to which it arises. It makes the thought known (*viññapanā*); it is the state of having made that thought known (*viññāpitatta*).[268]

What is quite clear from this brief account is that *kāyaviññatti* is not identical with the movements of the body. It means the bodily tension, the bodily excitement, on the part of a person who moves her body or limbs.

The Sāṃmitīyas and the Vātsīputrīyas adopt a more direct approach: The bodily intimation (*kāyavijñapti*) is a movement (*gati*) given rise to by a thought that intends that particular movement.[269] The movement is that of the body (*kāya*). And it is this movement that is recognized here as the *vijñapti*, because it makes manifest or expresses that thought in response to which it arises. It is included in the *rūpāyatana*, the sphere of the visible, because it is the movement of the body, of matter that is visible. Hence it is the opinion of the Sāṃmitīyas and the Vātsīputrīyas that *kāyavijñapti* is apprehended by the organ of sight.[270]

The Vaibhāṣikas object to this interpretation on the ground that there is no movement in an ultimate sense. All elements of existence are momentary (*kṣaṇika*).[271] Wherever they come into existence, there itself they cease to exist.[272] Motion is not something that exists in reality (*dravyatas*), but is a name given to the appearance of momentary elements in adjacent locations (*deśāntarotpatti*).[273] If somebody retracted her arm or stretched it forth, in an ultimate sense, it is incorrect to say that her arm had moved. What actually happened was that the series of momentary elements that constituted what was called "the arm" arose in adjacent locations in a certain direction. Only the place of the arising of elements had changed, not a single element had moved.

Hence to identify *kāyavijñapti* with bodily movements is to deprive it of its position as a real dharma. To deprive it of its position as a real dharma is to undermine the very foundation of the *avijñapti-rūpa*, in defense of which the Vaibhāṣikas, time and again, joined issue with the Sautrāntikas.

Therefore for the Vaibhāṣikas, *kāyavijñapti* is not the movements of the body, but is such and such figure or disposition, *saṃsthāna*, of the body, given rise to, or conditioned, by a volitional thought (*cetanā*). This *kāyavijñapti-saṃsthāna* is something that is visible.[274] It can be apprehended independently of the color (of the body): "*kāyavijñapti-grahanaṃ tu varṇa-nirapekṣaṃ*."[275]

Thus, although the Vātsīputrīya-Sāṃmitīyas and the Vaibhāṣikas differ in answering what exactly constitutes *kāyavijñapti*, both agree on this point: *kāyavijñapti* comes under *rūpāyatana*, it can be apprehended by the organ of sight.

Viewed against this background, the *kāyaviññatti* of the Dhammasaṅganī raises one important problem. We saw that it could not be identified with bodily movements. Nor can it be taken as something that is apprehended by the organ of sight. For its inclusion under the heading *dhammāyatana*[276] shows that it cannot be known by any of the senses other than the mind (*mano*). It is known through a process of inference. In which way, then, does it act as a mode of self-expression? Or, to be more precise, how does it express or make known that morally qualifiable thought in response to which it arises?

It may be noted here that in the Dhammasaṅganī account, reference is made not only to the state of bodily tension or excitement (which is *kāyaviññatti*) but also to bodily movements such as retracting an arm or stretching it forth. This shows that, although bodily movements are not *kāyaviññatti*, yet they have a close connection with it. That is to say, they, too, have a part to play in the expression of thought.

This close connection would be clear if a correspondence could be established between the *kāyaviññatti* of the Dhammasaṅganī and that of the Dārṣṭāntikas as given in the Vijñaptimātratāsiddhi: "According to the Dārṣṭāntikas, there exists a certain *rūpa* that is neither color nor figure, which is produced by the thought. This *rūpa* puts in movement the hand and other members."[277] What this "certain *rūpa*" is, is not explained here in more positive terms.

In the *Karmasiddhiprakaraṇa* of Vasubandhu, an almost identical, if not the same, theory is attributed to the Sauryodayikas. According to this theory, bodily movements are due to the air-element (*vāyudhātu*), given rise to by a certain variety of consciousness (*citta-viśeṣād utpannaḥ*). And it is this air-element that is recognized as the *kāyavijñapti*.[278]

What interests us here is the fact that according to both accounts (Dārṣṭāntika-Sauryodayika) *kāyavijñapti* is the cause (*hetu*) of bodily movements. From this it may be concluded that the Dārṣṭāntikas and the Sauryodayikas do not seem to have overlooked the contention of the Vātsīputrīyas—namely, that *kāyavijñapti* occurs only when there is some kind of movement (*iñjita*) of the body and not otherwise.[279]

It may then be asked why the designation *kāyavijñapti* (that which makes known)[280] is given to the cause of bodily movements but not to the bodily movements themselves. For according to this explanation, the significance of *kāyavijñapti* as a mode of self-expression is rather indirect. This is certainly so. But like the Vaibhāṣikas, they too were committed to the theory of the denial of motion. For, although they speak of movements, they do not recognize them in an absolute sense. Strictly speaking, there is no "*deśāntarasaṃkrānti*"—that is, movement of a thing from one locus in space to another—but only "*deśāntarotpatti*"—that is, the appearance of (momentary elements) in adjacent locations.[281] It seems very probable, therefore, that it was with a view to retaining its reality that *kāyavijñapti* was sought to be identified with the cause of bodily movements.

That there is some parallelism between the *kāyaviññatti* of the

Dhammasaṅganī and that of the Dārṣṭāntikas and the Sauryodayikas is clear. The former, too, is neither color (*vaṇṇa*) nor figure (*saṇṭhāna*). For its exclusion from the *rūpāyatana* and its inclusion in the *dhammāyatana* precludes its being identified with either.

Its parallelism with that of the Sauryodayikas goes still further. As we have already noted, it is defined as "*kāyassa thambhanā santhambhanā santhambhitattaṃ.*" It may also be noted here that *thambhitattaṃ* (tension, distension) is one of the terms used in the Dhammasaṅganī in defining the air-element.[282] Does this mean that the *kāyaviññatti* of the Dhammasaṅganī, like that of the Sauryodayikas, is the air-element?

In the Dhammasaṅganī seventeen rūpa-dhammas are listed under the heading *cittasamuṭṭhāna*—that is, arising in response to, or conditioned by, consciousness. Two of them are the air-element and the *kāyaviññatti.*[283] If the latter were the same as the former, then they would not be mentioned separately and counted as two items.

On the other hand, if the *kāyaviññatti* were different from, or if it had no connection with, the air-element, then it would not be explained as (*kāyassa san) thambhitattaṃ*. The relation between them seems to be one of identity as well as difference.

The whole situation becomes clear when it is understood in light of certain observations made in the commentarial exegesis. Except for one significant fact, its interpretation tallies well with the main points brought into relief so far.

According to the commentators, what is called *kāyaviññatti* is an "*ākāra-vikāra*" or "*vikāra*" of the *cittasamuṭṭhāna* air-element. *Ākāra-vikāra* (lit. "alteration of the mode") or *vikāra* (alteration), as understood in the commentaries and in the kindred works, means a particular position, situation, or condition (of the air-element).[284] Since the air-element cannot arise or exist independently of the other three primary elements,[285] it is further observed that in reality it is the *ākāra-vikāra* of all the four (and of any other secondary element that arises and exists with them).[286] But it is called *ākāra-vikāra* of the air-element for this reason: among the primary elements (and any other secondary element that arises and exists with them) of which it is an *ākāra-vikāra*, the air-element is characterized by more intensity (*ussada*) or capability (*sāmatthiya*).[287] In the Abhidhammatthavikāsinī this *ākāra-vikāra* is said to resemble the state of effort-making (*ussahana-vikāra*) that appears in the body of a person when, with full effort, he is lifting a huge stone.[288]

We have already observed that in the Dhammasaṅganī reference is made to a list of *cittasamuṭṭhāna-rūpadhammas*, of which two are the air-element and the *kāyaviññatti*. We have also drawn attention to the close affinity between two of the words used in defining the two items in question. When these two facts are taken into consideration, the interpretation of *kāyaviññatti* as an *ākāra-vikāra* of the *cittasamuṭṭhāna* air-element (and its concomitants) seems to be quite in accord with the earlier account. It could be understood as a restatement, made in terms of elemental analysis, of the earlier general definition.

The position of *kāyaviññatti* as a mode of self-expression is explained as follows:

> *Kāyaviññatti* is a condition (*paccaya*) for the occurrence of bodily movements (*pariphandana*, *calana*). It is through the bodily movements, which are conditioned by *kāyaviññatti*, that the particular thought is expressed or intimated. The thought is known (inferred)[289] after the apprehension of the color (*vaṇṇagahanāntaraṃ*) of the body that is in movement.[290]

In recognizing *kāyaviññatti* as a condition (*paccaya*) for the occurrence of bodily movements,[291] the Theravādins are in general agreement with the Dārṣṭāntikas and the Sauryodayikas. However, there is this significant difference to be noted: according to the Sauryodayikas *kāyavijñapti* is the air-element, whereas according to the Theravādins *kāyaviññatti* is an *ākāra-vikāra* of the air-element (and its concomitants). Why the Theravādins took this position needs explanation.

It seems that *kāyaviññatti* is called so because of two reasons: The first is that it makes manifest or expresses that particular thought in response to which it arises. This manifestation or expression, as we have seen, is a certain tension or excitement of the body (*kāyassa thambhitatta*). It is not something that is visible,[292] but it is the physical representation of a mental event. In this sense it is bodily expression—that is, *kāyaviññatti*. The second is that it conditions or helps the occurrence of bodily movements through which that thought is communicated. In this sense it is that which makes known—*viññapanā*.

Now, elsewhere in the Dhammasaṅganī it is stated that the *kāyaviññatti* is *citta-sahabhū*—that is, coexistent with the thought (in response to which it arises)—and *cittānuparivatti*—that is, follows the pattern of the thought (in response to which it arises).[293] The implied reason is that, since it is the physical manifestation or representation of a thought, its duration too should be equal to the duration of that particular thought. Second, since it is brought about by being conditioned by that thought (which it makes manifest or represents), it too follows the pattern of that particular thought.

In this connection, it should be noted here that, in the view of the Theravādins, the duration of a material element is longer than that of a mental element.[294] Accordingly, although the *citta-samuṭṭhāna* air-element and its concomitants arise simultaneously with a thought-moment,[295] yet they do not cease to exist together with that thought-moment. In view of this circumstance, the air-element and its concomitants cannot be described as *citta-sahabhū*, because to describe them so is to admit that their duration is equal to that of the thought-moment. But the *kāyaviññatti* has to be *citta-sahabhū*. This explains why the designation, *kāyaviññatti*, is given not to the air-element and its concomitants, but to their *ākāra-vikāra*. Is there then no contradiction in recognizing *kāyaviññatti* as a rūpa-dhamma while describing it as *citta-sahabhū*?

What we should not overlook here is that what is called *kāyaviññatti* is not a rūpa-dhamma in its usual sense. It is not something that is distinct and separate from the air-element and its concomitants. It signifies only a particular situation or position—*ākāra-vikāra*—of the latter. It is a name given to the latter when they are in a particular position. Apart from the air-element and its concomitants, of which it is an *ākāra-vikāra*, there is no separate rūpa-dhamma called *kāyaviññatti*, just as much as there is nothing called "table" apart from a collection of rūpa-dhammas (material elements), organized and arranged in a particular order.

In other words, *kāyaviññatti* is a name given to the air-element and its concomitants when they function as bodily expression or manifestation of a thought, just as "table" is a name given to a collection of rūpa-dhammas when they function as that what we conventionally call "table." Stated otherwise: the air-element and its concomitants are called *kāyaviññatti* as long as that particular thought in response to which they arise exists, because it is during this time that they make manifest or represent that thought (= *viññatti*) and function as a condition for the occurrence of bodily movements and thereby make known that thought (= *viññāpanā*).

However, the air-element and its concomitants do not cease to exist concurrently with the cessation of that particular thought in response to which they arise, but their position and function as *kāyaviññatti* do. The sun is called "mid-sun" when it is overhead, but it does not set immediately after its position and function as mid-sun is over. A similar situation obtains here, too.

Thus it is clear that *kāyaviññatti* is not a rūpa-dhamma, distinct and separate from the air-element and its concomitants, signifying as it does only an *ākāra-vikāra* of the latter. However, in the Dhammasaṅganī not only the air-element and its concomitants but also *kāyaviññatti* are described as *cittasamuṭṭhāna*,[296] a situation that gives the impression that the latter has an arising separate from that of the former. Nevertheless, the fact that *kāyaviññatti* is described as *citta-sahabhū*, although no rūpa-dhamma can be so described, suggests that thereby the Dhammasaṅganī does not mean that it is a (separate) rūpa-dhamma. The logic that seems to have guided it in taking such a step could be that, since the air-element and its concomitants are *cittasamuṭṭhāna*, their *ākāra-vikāra* (*kāyaviññatti*), too, is *cittasamuṭṭhāna*.

The commentators clarify the whole situation when they observe that, strictly speaking, only the air-element and its concomitants are *citta-samuṭṭhāna*.[297] This is quite understandable. For, as we have already seen, *kāyaviññatti* signifies the self-same number of rūpa-dhammas when they are in a particular position or situation, and not something that is distinct from them. In other words, it is an *anipphanna-rūpa*.

As for the interpretation of *vāgvijñapti* (Pāli: *vacīviññatti*), there is general agreement among most of the schools of Sanskrit Buddhism. Voice (*vāc*) or vocal sound (*vāgdhvani*) as a mode of self-expression or as a medium for the communication of one's thought to another is *vāgvijñapti*. It is defined as sound that is discourse (*ghosoccaraṇa*), or as the distinct pronunciation of syllables (*vyaktavarṇoccarana*). Since *vāgvijñapti* means "vocal sound," it is brought under *śabda-āyatana*, the sphere of the audible.[298] It is presumably because of this general agreement on the subject that the accounts of *vāgvijñapti* occupy comparatively little space in the sources of Sanskrit Buddhism.

On the other hand, the Theravāda account of the subject takes quite a different form. The one given in the Abhidhamma Piṭaka does not present a complete picture. First, *vācā* (voice) is described as *girā* (utterance), *vyappatho* (speech, speaking), *udīrana* (vocal emission), *ghosa* (noise), *ghosa-kamma* (act of making noise), or *vacībheda* (broken or articulate voice)—which arises in response to a thought wholesome, unwholesome, or morally indeterminate. Then it is said that the manifestation (*viññatti*), the making known (*viññāpanā*), or the state of having made known (*viññāpitatta*) (of that thought) through voice is *vacīviññatti*.[299]

At first sight it might appear from this statement that *vacīviññatti* means vocal sound as a medium of thought-expression. But its exclusion from *saddāyatana*, the sphere of the audible, shows that it is not conceived as a variety of sound as such. However, the fact that vocal sound is referred to suggests that it is closely connected with *vacīviññatti*, even as bodily movements are with *kāyaviññatti*.

Third, the fact that it is also described as *citta-sahabhū*[300] shows that, like *kāyaviññatti*, it is not a discrete rūpa-dhamma.

The commentators' interpretation falls within the framework of these three fundamental facts. We may therefore take it as an explicit statement of what has been implicitly recognized in the Abhidhamma Piṭaka.

That the thought is communicated through vocal sound is admitted. But the *vacīviññatti* is not the same as vocal sound, though it is causally related to it in the same way as *kāyaviññatti* is to bodily movements.[301]

Vacīviññatti, it is said, is an *ākāra-vikāra* of the *citta-samuṭṭhāna* earth-element.[302] Although it is called so, in reality, like the *kāya-viññatti*, it is an *ākāra-vikāra* of all the four primary elements (and of whatever secondary element that arises and exists with them). In this case it is the earth-element that is characterized by more intensity and capability; hence it is called the *ākāra-vikāra* of the earth-element.[303]

This so-called *ākāra-vikāra* of the earth-element (= *vacīviññatti*) strikes against the vocal apparatus (*upādiṇṇaka, akkharuppat-tiṭṭhāna*) and produces (vocal) sound through which the thought is communicated.[304]

Why an *ākāra-vikāra* of the earth-element and its concomitants is recognized as *vacīviññatti* is because, like *kāyaviññatti*, it too has to be *citta-sahabhū*. And the position of *vacīviññatti* in relation to the earth-element and its concomitants should be understood in the same way as that of the *kāyaviññatti* in relation to the air-element and its concomitants. That is to say, apart from those elements, of which it is an *ākāra-vikāra*, there is no distinct and separate rūpa-dhamma called *vacīviññatti*—hence its inclusion in the category of *anipphanna-rūpa*.

Characteristics of Matter

By "characteristics of matter" we mean the three items—namely, *rūpassa lahutā*, *rūpassa mudutā*, and *rūpassa kammaññatā*. The first means lightness (*lahutā*) of matter, its light transformability (*lah-upariṇāmatā*), its lack of heaviness (*adandhatā*) or non-rigidity (*avithatatā*); the second, plasticity of matter (*mudutā*), its softness (*maddavatā*) or its absence of hardness (*akakkhaḷatā*); and the third, wieldiness or pliability of matter (*kammaññatā, kammaññattaṃ, kammaññabhāva*).

According to these definitions, which we have taken from the Dhammasaṅganī,[305] these three items seem to indicate some characteristics or qualities of matter in general. However, in the later works we are told that they signify certain characteristics of the matter of the body of a living being: they are not found apart from each other (*na aññam'aññaṃ vijahanti*); the triad represents a certain position of the body when it is healthy, efficient, or amenable to work.[306]

This gives an indication of why the Abhidhamma has recognized the items in question. In the Nikāyas much emphasis is laid on the desirability of bodily health or efficiency for the purposes of mental culture. A healthy body is usually described as *lahu* and *kammañña*—that is, pliable and wieldy.[307] Overeating renders the body *garu*, heavy, and *akammañña*, unserviceable; it is like a load of soaked beans. Such a state of the body is not conducive to putting forth energy in the right direction. Hence the monks are advised to have a body that is *lahu* and *kammañña*.[308] Thus it is that Khitaka of the Theragāthā exults in the thought that his body is *lahu* and that it "floats" like a piece of cotton in the air.[309] The term *mudu* occurs mostly in the references to bodily beauty.

Nevertheless, the fact that *lahu* and *kammañña* occur often in the Nikāyan allusions to bodily health and efficiency, and the fact that Buddhism attaches much importance to it, seem to confirm the statement—namely, that the three items are meant to recognize certain characteristics, not of matter in general but of the body of a living being (when it is healthy and efficient).

However, nowhere in the Nikāyas are they recognized as rūpa-dhammas, although they are so recognized in the Abhidhamma Piṭaka. Whether this means that they are understood as three separate material elements is the question that arises here.

The way they are named (note the term *rūpassa* added before each item) and the way they are defined suggest clearly that they could well be interpreted as qualities of matter (body). Their elevation to the status of rūpa-dhamma seems to have been done with a view to forestalling their being interpreted as such. But the commentators appear to have realized that by this device alone their true nature cannot be concealed. This explains why in the later works they are explained in such a way as to deprive them of their apparent position as discrete entities.

What they really amount to is stated clearly: When the body is not efficient—that is, when it is not light (*lahu*), pliable (*mudu*), and wieldy (*kammañña*)—it is said to be characterized by "*dhātukkhobha*," elemental disturbance.[310] What is called *dhātukkhobha* is either the disharmony between wind (*vāta*), bile (*pitta*), and phlegm (*semha*), or that of chyme, etc. (*rasādidhātu*).[311] In either case, in the ultimate analysis it means the same thing: it is a certain position or situation (*vikāra*) of the primary elements and of whatever other secondary element is concomitant with them.[312]

Likewise, when the body is not characterized by *dhātukkhobha*, in the ultimate analysis it also signifies a certain position or situation of the primary elements and their concomitants. It is this position or situation that is represented by the triad *lahutā-mudutā-kammaññatā*. Hence it is called *vikāra-rūpa*.[313] And since they represent a *vikāra* of the primary elements and their concomitants, apart from them there do not exist three rūpa-dhammas called *lahutā*, *mudutā*, and *kammaññatā*. Stated otherwise, they are *anipphanna-rūpa*.

Phases of Matter

The next four items—namely, *rūpassa upacaya* (growth of matter), *rūpassa santati* (continuity of matter), *rūpassa jaratā* (decay of matter), and *rūpassa aniccatā* (impermanence of matter)—are a formulation of four phases, not of matter in general but of the physical body of a living being. It is of course true that this limitation in their scope is not explicitly stated in the Abhidhamma. But the way they are described, both in the earlier and the later works, makes it clear that this was the underlying assumption. And it is only when this fact is taken into consideration that their significance as well as their mutual relation becomes increasingly clear.

Let us take the first two, first. *Rūpassa upacaya* is defined as "*yo āyatanānaṃ ācayo, so rūpassa upacayo*" (that accumulation of āyatanas is also the growth of matter), and *rūpassa santati* as "*yo rūpassa upacayo, sā rūpssa santati*" (that growth of matter is also the continuity of matter).[314] Thus, while the first is explained as "*āyatanānaṃ ācayo*," the second is identified with the first.

One immediate conclusion that can be drawn from this is that both are expressive of the same thing. On the other hand, one cannot overlook the fact that they are counted as two items and that they convey two different meanings: the first means growth or integration of matter and the second its continuity or subsistence. When both points are taken into consideration, their relation turns out to be one of identity as well as difference. In which sense are they identical and in which different?

From the (Vibhāvinī) Ṭīkā to the Abhidhammatthasaṅgaha, one gathers that the first refers to the growth of the body (embryo) from the moment of conception until the sense-mechanism is complete.[315] Although in the later works the subject under consideration has undergone much change, yet this particular statement could be supported by the data confined to the Abhidhamma Piṭaka.

We saw that *rūpassa upacaya* = *āyatanānaṃ ācayo*. We need first clarify what the term *āyatana* signifies here. It is a well-known fact that there are twelve *āyatanas*, of which six (*cakkhu*, *sota*, etc.) are qualified as *ajjhattika*, and the other six (*rūpa*, *sadda*, etc.) as *bāhira*. But usually the simple term *āyatana* is used to mean only the *ajjhattika* group. *Saḷ-āyatana* (Skt. *saḍ-āyatana*) is a case in point. In the phrase in question, too, the term appears to have been used with this restricted denotation. Further proof of this supposition is the fact that it tallies well with the rest of the data on the subject. Since *āyatanānaṃ ācayo* = *rūpassa upacayo*, we could still narrow down the field to include only the first five *ajjhattika-āyatanas*—that is, the first five sense-organs, which alone come under *rūpa* (matter).[316]

Since *ācayo* means "heaping up" or "accumulation," *āyatanānaṃ ācayo* implies that the coming into being of the five sense-organs is a graduated process. This is further confirmed by a Kathāvatthu controversy concerning the genesis of the sense-mechanism. According to some schools (the Pubbaseliya and the Aparaseliya),[317] the sixfold sense-sphere comes into being all at once (*apubbaṃ acarimaṃ*). The Theravādins reject this view on the ground that it is neither logical nor supported by the scripture. Their view is that only mind-base (*manāyatana*) and body-base (*kāyāyatana*) come into being at the moment of conception. The other four—namely, *cakkhāyatana*, *sotāyatana*, *ghānāyatana*, and *jivhāyatana*—arise subsequently in the order they are mentioned here.[318]

With this theory in mind, when one approaches the formula *āyatanānaṃ ācayo* = *rūpassa upacayo*, its significance becomes clear. The accumulation—that is, the coming into being, one after another, of the first five sense-organs—is, in other words, the growth or integration of the body (*rūpassa upacaya*). It is like saying the gathering of people is the growth of the crowd. Or to adopt a simile from the commentaries, the welling up of water is the brimming up of the well.[319]

From this it should not be concluded that the sense-organs could arise independently of some other material elements. Since they are *upādā-rūpas*, it is implied that the four *mahābhūtas* and the four *upādā-rūpas* that necessarily arise with them[320] are also present. Again, since they are *kamma-samuṭṭhāna-rūpa*, and since the stability of the *kamma-samuṭṭhāna-rūpa* is dependent on the *rūpa-jīvitindriya*,[321] the presence of the *rūpa-jīvitindriya*, too, is implied.[322]

Thus *rūpassa upacaya* means the growth of the embryo with the gradual accumulation of the sense-organs. It covers that interval from the moment of conception to the moment when the sense-mechanism is complete.

With the completion of the sense-mechanism—in other words, with the accumulation of the last sense-organ—ends what is called *rūpassa upacaya*, the growth of the body. This does not mean that there is no growth thereafter. It means that the body is not deficient in any of the sense-organs. From the point of view of the sense-organs, it is complete. Moreover, if *rūpassa upacaya* means the accumulation of the sense-organs, it follows that with the accumulation of the last sense-organ, there ends the phase called *rūpassa upacaya*.

Thereafter begins *rūpassa santati*, the continuity of the body, complete with all the sense-organs. It is not continuity in a static sense. For certainly the body grows even during this phase. It is therefore continuity (*santati*) by way of growth (*upacaya*). This explains why *rūpassa santati* is defined as *rūpassa upacaya*: *yo rūpassa upacayo sā rūpassa santati*.

Thus, both *rūpassa upacaya* and *rūpassa santati* mean "the growth of the body" (= *rūpassa upacaya*). In this sense they are identical. But they represent two phases of growth. In this sense they are different.

The third is *rūpassa jaratā*: "the decay (*jarā*) or the state of decaying (*jīraṇatā*) of the body (*rūpa*), brokenness of teeth (*khaṇḍicca*), grayness of hair (*pālicca*), the state of having wrinkles (*valittacatā*), shrinkage in the length of days (*āyuno saṃhāni*), hypermaturity of the faculties (*indriyānam paripāko*)."[323]

One question that arises here is whether *rūpassa jaratā* represents a stage in the history of the body or whether it refers to the fact of decay itself. Since brokenness of teeth, grayness of hair, etc., are symbolic of old age, it seems more appropriate if it is understood as a stage that sets in with the passage of time, when the body shows signs of decay. The use of the words "shrinkage in the length of days" does also encourage this conclusion.

Once it is understood as a stage, the next question that arises is whether it overlaps with *rūpassa santati*. What we should not overlook here is that, although *rūpassa santati* means "continuity of the body," yet it is defined as *rūpassa upacaya*, growth of the body (after the completion of the sense-mechanism). Generally speaking, when decay sets in growth ceases. And since *rūpassa santati* is defined as "the growth of the body," it seems unlikely that it was understood as covering the *jaratā* phase too. This is not to suggest that *jaratā* as a phenomenon could not take place during the *santati* (or *upacaya*) phase. But when life is young the tendency is toward growth. With the passage of time there is a plus tendency toward decay. Gradually the faculties get matured. The body begins to show signs of maturity and decay. It is these two phases that *rūpassa santati* and *rūpassa jaratā* represent. During the first the main characteristic is growth (*upacaya*); during the second it is decay (*jaratā*).

Finally we come to the final phase, or rather the moment—*rūpassa aniccatā*. This signifies the break-up of the body at the time of death.[324] It is that moment when the body becomes a (lifeless) corpse.[325]

These four *upādā-rūpas*, which amount to a formulation of four phases of the history of the body, appear to have been based on the three *saṅkhata-lakkhaṇas* referred to in the Aṅguttaranikāya. In this Nikāya it is stated that which is *saṅkhata* has three fundamental characteristics (*lakkhaṇa*)—namely, *uppāda*, *vaya*, and *ṭhitassa aññathatta*.[326]

Now, *uppāda*—that is, birth or origination—corresponds to the beginning of the first phase, *rūpassa upacaya*. *Vaya*—that is, waning away, or cessation—corresponds to *rūpassa aniccatā*. Before one could find out what corresponds to *ṭhitassa aññathatta*, one has to find out what this term really means.

As we shall soon see, different schools of Buddhism interpret *ṭhitassa aññathatta* (literally, "otherwiseness of that which is existing") in different ways, as if to justify the very meaning conveyed by the phrase. But what is common to these later-day interpretations is that they are based on the theory of moments. This theory does not find expression in the earlier texts. True, the doctrine of impermanence is constantly alluded to. But the logical implications of this doctrine were not developed on the basis of a theory of moments. And, as Mrs. Rhys Davids rightly observes, "it was inevitable that later exegesis would so develop the theme."[327]

The second point to be noted here is that although the Nikāyas recognize the rapidity of change in mental events, they assign a relative permanence to the body.

> Better were it, bhikkhus, that the uneducated worldly people should conceive this four-element-made body, rather than *citta*, to be soul. And why? The body is seen to persist

> for a year, for two, three, four, five, ten, or twenty years, for a generation, even for a hundred years or even for longer, while that which is called consciousness—that is, mind, intelligence—arises as one thing, ceases as another, both by night and by day.[328]

This difference between mind and matter as regards their duration is recognized and upheld in the Abhidhamma Piṭaka, too. A number of controversies in the Kathāvatthu suggest clearly that the Theravādins had no hesitation in recognizing the momentariness of mental elements.[329] On the other hand, they do not deny the relative permanence of the body or matter in general. In fact, the thesis (of the Pubbaseliyas and the Aparaseliyas)[330]—namely, that the duration of material things is equal to the duration of a thought-moment (*eka-cittakkhaṇika*)—is rejected as untenable.[331]

It was not the Theravādins alone who upheld this tradition. Ācārya Vasumitra records that in the view of the Mahāsāṅghikas, the material sense-organs and the primary elements "evolve" (*pariṇamati*), whereas consciousness and consciousness-concomitants do not "evolve." This has been interpreted to mean that while material elements endure for a longer time, mental elements are "*naissant-périssant en un instant*" (*kṣaṇabhaṅgura*).[332]

Ācārya Yaśomitra notes that in the opinion of the Ārya-Sāṃmitīyas, matter is of longer duration, whereas consciousness and consciousness-concomitants are characterized by instantaneous being.[333] A similar view is attributed to the Vātsīputrīyas, too: some *saṃskāras* exist for some time, while others perish at every moment.[334]

On the other hand, many other schools, notably the Sarvāstivāda, the Mahīśāsaka, the Pūrvaśaila, and theAparaśaila, disapproved of this distinction. In their view, not only mental but also material elements are of instantaneous being.[335]

It seems fairly clear that over the interpretation of the early doctrine of impermanence the Buddhist schools fell into two general groups. Some recognized the momentary duration of mental elements but assigned a relative permanence to material elements. Others objected to introducing any such distinction. As we have seen, the Theravādins of the Abhidhamma Piṭaka belong to the former group. As yet they were not prepared to admit that material elements were of momentary duration.

In view of this circumstance, as far as material elements are concerned, they seem to have understood *ṭhitassa aññathatta* in a very general sense. That is to say, material things become otherwise while they are existing. Looked at in this way, how it is represented among the four *upādā-rūpas* is easily recognizable. We have already shown that *rūpassa upacaya* and *santati* signify the gradual growth of the body, and *rūpassa jaratā* the gradual process of maturing and decay that sets in with the march of years. Since they point to the fact that the body becomes "otherwise" (*aññathatta*) while it is "existing" (*ṭhitassa*), they could be understood as representative of *ṭhitassa aññathatta*.

The position of the three *saṅkhata-lakkhaṇas* in relation to the four *upādā-rūpas* could then be graphically illustrated, as follows:

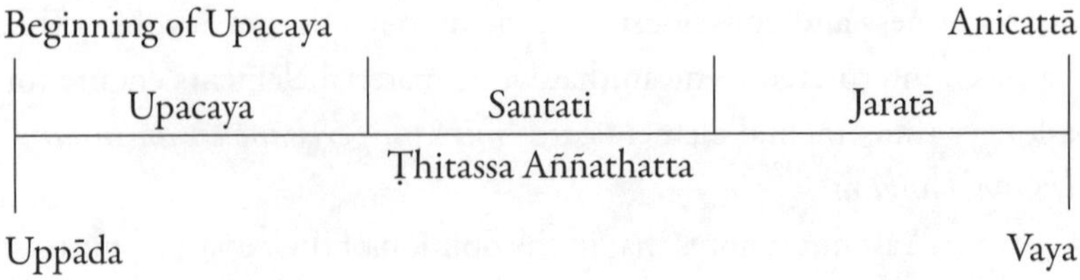

When the Aṅguttaranikāya refers to the three *saṅkhata-lakkhaṇas*, the purpose is to show that all mental and material things are impermanent. The fact that in the earlier texts the impermanence of both groups is not explained in equal terms is a different question. The Abhidhamma Piṭaka has not deviated from this fundamental principle. It may then be asked why it has made a special attempt to show the "*saṅkhata*-ness" of the body, in particular.

Moral edification seems to be the reason behind this device. True, some relative permanence could be assigned to the body. Yet it is not something that is everlasting. It has a beginning all right, but it has an end, too. It has a phase of growth all right, but it has a phase of decay, too. "This corporeal frame of mind is made up of the four elements, starts from parents, is sustained by rice and other foods, is impermanent and subject to attrition, abrasion, erasion, dissolution and disruption, and this consciousness of mine is tied and bound up therewith."[336] This is how one is expected to approach one's own body so that one's own attachment to it, let alone to any other instance of materiality, should cease thereby. When one remembers that the scope as well as the approach of the Buddhist analysis of matter is mainly determined by ethical factors, one need not be surprised why the Abhidhamma Piṭaka has deemed it necessary to enumerate the four items that we have so far discussed.

When the doctrine of impermanence, which in the earlier texts was described in simple and general terms, came to be explained with greater precision, attempts were also made to reinterpret the *saṅkhata-lakkhaṇas.*

The Vaibhāṣikas interpreted *sthityanyathātva* (*ṭhitassa aññathatta*) as *jaratā*, postulated another item, *sthiti*,[337] and thus increased the number to four: (1) *jāti*, origination; (2) *sthiti*, existence; (3) *jaratā*, decay; and (4) *anityatā*, extinction. All dharmas (elements of existence), mental as well as material, characterized by them are *saṃskṛta*. Only *ākāśa* (space) and the two kinds of *nirodha* (cessation) escape from their inexorable sway.[338] At every *kṣaṇa* (moment), all (*saṃskṛta*) dharmas are affected by them. A *kṣaṇa* is the time during which the four *saṃskṛta-lakṣaṇas* accomplish their operation. The Vaibhāṣikas also maintained that the characteristics were not only distinct from, but also as real as, the dharmas they characterize—showing thereby a strong predilection to naïve realism. And in consonance with this thesis, it was also claimed that they were in turn characterized by *anulakṣaṇas*, secondary characteristics.

The Sautrāntikas made a prolonged polemic against this Vaibhāṣika interpretation. They pointed out that the *saṃskṛta-lakṣaṇas* were mere characteristics, mere designations, with no objective reality, and argued that the recognition of *anulakṣaṇas* would lead to the problem of infinite regress (*anavasthā*). In their view, they apply not to one but to a series of momentary elements. "The series or stream itself is called subsistence (*sthiti*), its origin is called *jāti*, its cessation is *vyaya*, and the difference in its preceding and succeeding moments is called *sthityanyathātva*."[339] A momentary element, so they argued, cannot have a phase called *sthiti* or *jaratā*, for whatever that originates has no time to subsist or decay, but can only perish.[340]

How the Theravādins of the Abhidhammic commentaries and the kindred works developed the doctrine of impermanence and how they interpreted the *saṅkhata-lakkhaṇas* can be understood clearly when the subject is unfolded against this background. We have already shown that although the Abhidhamma Piṭaka recognizes the momentariness of mental elements, it does not extend the same principle to material elements. The new development is to be seen in the formulation of a theory of moments, replacing the early doctrine of momentariness. It applies to both groups of elements equally, but for one significant difference: the earlier tradition that matter is of longer duration is recognized, but of course not in the same form.[341] On some technical points the Theravāda theory differs from those of the Vaibhāṣikas and the Sautrāntikas. However, in the *ṭīkās* where the subject is dealt with in more detail, it has come very close to that of the Sautrāntikas.

The most striking thing about the Theravāda theory is that the fact of momentariness is explained in quite a different way: Each dhamma has three moments—namely, *uppādakkhaṇa*, the moment of origination; *ṭhitikkhaṇa*, the moment of subsistence; and *bhaṅgakkhaṇa*, the moment of cessation. The three moments do not correspond to three different dhammas. On the contrary, they represent three phases (*avatthā*)—the nascent, the static, and the cessant of one "momentary" dhamma. Hence the statement "the dhammas are momentary" means that a given dhamma has three momentary phases or stages. It arises in the first moment, subsists in the second moment, and perishes in the third moment.[342]

Commenting on the three *saṅkhata-lakkhaṇas* of the Aṅguttara Nikāya,[343] the commentary says that *uppāda* is *jāti* (birth, origination), *vaya* is *bheda* (destruction), and *ṭhitassa aññathatta* is *jaratā* (decay).

And it goes on to say that these three are represented by *uppādakkhaṇa*, *bhaṅgakkhaṇa*, and *ṭhitikkhaṇa*, respectively.[344] The fact that *jāti* and *bheda* are said to be represented by *uppādakkhaṇa* and *bhaṅgakkhaṇa*, respectively, does not pose a very significant problem. But the fact that *jaratā* is said to be represented by *ṭhitikkhaṇa* shows that the so-called moment of subsistence is also the moment of decay.

In contrast, the Vaibhāṣikas take *jaratā* as distinct from *sthiti* and accordingly count them as two separate *saṃskṛta-lakṣaṇas*. Since the Theravādins explain *ṭhiti (kkhaṇ*a) as *jaratā*, it may be concluded that there is some kind of change or modification in a given dhamma during the moment of its subsistence.

That this is so is shown by two comments made by Ācariya Buddhaghosa and Ācariya Buddhadatta. In almost identical words, they observe that *jaratā* is manifested as the loss of *navabhāva*, newness, of a dhamma (*navabhāvāpagama*), and not as the loss of its *sabhāva*, or intrinsic nature (*sabhāvānapagama*). It is like (new) paddy becoming old (*vīhipurāṇabhāvo viya*).[345] Since *jaratā*= *ṭhiti (kkhaṇ*a), this means that a dhamma is new and fresh at the moment of its origination, but is old, matured, changed, or modified at the moment of its subsistence—though its intrinsic nature remains the same.

Of much significance is the fact that both commentators took special care to point out that *jaratā* does not signify the loss of *sabhāva*, but only the loss of *navabhāva*. Thereby they were intent to show that during the *jaratā* phase the identity of a dhamma is not completely lost. If it were otherwise, then it would mean that the dhamma that subsists is not the same as the dhamma that originates. There would be two dhammas corresponding to the two moments, *uppādakkhaṇa* and *ṭhitikkhaṇa*—a situation that would undermine the very foundation of the theory of moments.

However, this explanation raises one significant problem. If a dhamma becomes different without, however, losing its intrinsic nature, then this situation approaches the doctrine of *pariṇāmavāda* (theory of evolution), according to which the essence, the substance, remains the same while its modes undergo change. Change, as it came to be finally interpreted in the schools of Buddhist logic, is not the transformation of one and the same dharma from one stage to another, but the replacement of one momentary dharma by another.[346] The following polemic in the Abhidharmakośa, directed against the Vaibhāṣikas who admitted *jaratā* of one momentary dharma, applies equally to the Theravāda explanation.

"But how can we attribute to a dharma the fact of change? What is called change is transformation. Transformation is the dissimilitude between two stages. Now, can one say that a dharma becomes different from itself? If it remains the same, it is not something different. If it transforms, it is not the same thing. Therefore the transformation of a dharma is impossible."[347]

The authors of the *ṭīkās*, notably Ācariya Sumaṅgala, seem to have taken notice of the whole problem stemming from the recognition and definition of *jaratā*. This explains why an attempt has been made to foist a new interpretation into *jaratā*—an interpretation that really amounts to its denial.[348]

It may be recalled here that according to the earlier account *jaratā* is manifested as the loss of newness (*navabhāva*) of a dhamma, and not as its complete loss of identity. According to Ācariya Sumaṅgala's interpretation, *navabhāva* or newness is only a figurative expression for *uppādakkhaṇa*, the moment of origination—so called because of its chronological priority in relation to *ṭhitikkhaṇa*, the moment of subsistence. That is to say, since *uppādakkhaṇa* of a dhamma precedes its *ṭhitikkhaṇa*, in this sense the former is its newness (*navabhāva*). Understood in this way, the loss of newness is nothing but the lapse of the moment of origination (*uppādakkhaṇa*), and the (immediate) lapse of the moment of origination means the succession of the moment of existence (*ṭhitikkhaṇa*). Now, just as *uppādakkhaṇa* is called *navabhāva*, "newness," because it comes before *ṭhitikkhaṇa*, even so *ṭhitikkhaṇa* is called *jaratā*, "oldness," because it comes after *uppādakkhaṇa*.[349]

There is another reason—this of course is only implied—why *ṭhitikkhaṇa* could be designated as *jaratā*. Sometimes *ṭhitikkhaṇa* is defined as "*nirodhābhimukhāvatthā*" or "*bhaṅgassa abhimukhāvatthā*"[350]—

that is, that phase (moment) when a dhamma is facing its destruction. The obvious implication is that since *bhaṅgakkhaṇa* is the immediate and unavoidable successor to *ṭhitikkhaṇa*, during its moment of subsistence a dhamma can only face its own destruction, its own death. Generally speaking, death is preceded by old age (*jaratā*). And since *bhaṅgakkhaṇa* is always (immediately) preceded by *ṭhitikkhaṇa*, on the above analogy, but as a figure of speech, the latter could well be designated as "old age" (*jaratā*).

Ācariya Sumaṅgala is rightly aware that in the context of this new interpretation the "oldness-of-the-paddy simile" (*vīhipurāṇabhāvo viya)*[351] is not relevant, if not misleading. Accordingly, he observes that when a paddy becomes old there is at least a change in its savor, etc. On the other hand, when a dhamma becomes old—that is, when it comes to the moment of subsistence—it abandons nothing else but its own moment of origination.[352]

To sum up the difference: according to Ācariya Buddhaghosa and Ācariya Buddhadatta, *ṭhitikkhaṇa* is also called *jaratā* because at this moment a dhamma has undergone a change, although it has not lost its complete identity. According to Ācariya Sumaṅgala, although *ṭhitikkhaṇa* is called *jaratā*, the latter term is not to be understood as decay or as implying any idea of change, modification, or transformation of a dhamma. In other words, there is no *jaratā* when it is understood in its usual sense. According to the former, *ṭhiti (kkhaṇa)* is really *jaratā*; according to the latter, *ṭhiti (kkhaṇa)* is really *ṭhiti* in the true sense of the term.

This new interpretation, though it has successfully eliminated the problem stemming from the earlier definition of *jaratā*, upsets the correspondence between the three *khaṇas* (moments) and the three *saṅkhata-lakkhaṇas*. We saw[353] that according to the earlier account, *ṭhitikkhaṇa* represented the third *saṅkhata-lakkhaṇa*—that is, *ṭhitassa aññathatta*. However, since *ṭhiti (kkhaṇa*) was explained as *jaratā*, one cannot say that some justice was not done to the idea of "change" or "becoming otherwise" conveyed by the phrase *ṭhitassa aññathatta*. But in the later account *ṭhiti (kkhaṇa*) is not understood as *jaratā*, although it is (figuratively) called so. As such, has it any claim to represent *ṭhitassa aññathatta*?

From a passing comment[354] made by Ācariya Sumaṅgala, one gathers that he did not take *ṭhitikkhaṇa* as corresponding to *ṭhitassa aññathatta*. In view of this circumstance, the third *saṅkhata-lakkhaṇa*, *ṭhitassa aññathatta*, remains unrepresented by any of the three *khaṇas*.

Nevertheless the denial—namely, that it does not apply to a momentary dhamma—carries the implication that it applies to a series of momentary dhammas.

This brings the position of the Theravādins another step closer to that of the Sautrāntikas.[355] However, there is this fundamental difference to be noted: unlike the Sautrāntikas, Ācariya Sumaṅgala (and others) do not deny the *ṭhiti* phase of a momentary dhamma. If this too could be denied, then the difference would become almost negligible. In fact, among some Theravādins there was a movement toward such a direction.

For Ācariya Sumaṅgala himself refers to one Ācariya, named Ānanda, who objected to the recognition of the *ṭhitikkhaṇa* under any guise, whether it was interpreted as *jaratā* or not. According to the latter, a dhamma has only two phases, one of origination and the other of cessation. *Ṭhiti* is recognized, but as applying only to a series. This is called *pabandha-ṭhiti*, the series itself as subsistence. *Ṭhitassa aññathatta* is interpreted as *pubbāpara-visesa*, the difference between the preceding and the succeeding dhammas that constitute a series (*pabandha*).[356]

It hardly needs mention that the above interpretation is an attempt to introduce wholesale the Sautrāntika theory into the Theravāda. From what we can gather from the *ṭīkās*, it does not seem to have had a great following among the Theravādins. The counterargument of Ācariya Sumaṅgala and others amounts to this:

> True, a dhamma that originates should also cease to exist. But before it could cease to exist, there should be at least a moment when it turns toward its own cessation (*nirodhābhimukhāvatthā*). It is this moment when a

> dhamma is facing its own cessation that we call "the moment of subsistence" (*ṭhitikkhaṇa*). The underlying assumption of this counterargument seems to be that a dhamma that arises cannot cease to exist at one and the same time, for otherwise existence and non-existence would become coexistent—an extremely difficult situation even to imagine.

This brings us to an end of our survey of how the Abhidhammic commentaries and *ṭīkās* have explained the early doctrine of impermanence on the basis of a formulated theory of moments. Our purpose in giving this account is to show how and why they differ from the Abhidhamma Piṭaka in interpreting the four *upādā-rūpas*—namely, *rūpassa upacaya*, *rūpassa santati*, *rūpassa jaratā*, and *rūpassa aniccatā*—with which we are concerned in this section.

How they are defined in the Abhidhamma Piṭaka has already been examined. We have shown that these four items, which amount to a formulation of some phases in the history of the body, are based on the three *saṅkhata-lakkhaṇas*. We have also shown that in explaining how the body is *saṅkhata*, the Abhidhamma Piṭaka does not go so far as to say that the rūpa-dhammas that constitute it are of momentary duration. Therefore, and quite understandably, the later scholiasts could not retain the earlier account of the subject in the same form. For, in their view, the three *saṅkhata-lakkhaṇas* represent three momentary phases—the nascent, the static (decay), and the cessant—of a "momentary" dhamma. It is to be expected, therefore, that their interpretation of the subject should fall in line with this development.

That *rūpassa upacaya* and *rūpassa santati* are expressive of the same phenomenon is recognized by the later scholiasts, too. (That there is some kind of difference between them is not denied, but this can be overlooked for the moment.) But in their view, it is *jāti* or *uppāda* of *rūpa*—that is, genesis or origination of matter.[357] With the recognition of this fact the four *upādā-rūpas* get reduced to three—namely, (1) *rūpassa jāti* (= *upacaya* and *santati*), (2) *rūpassa jaratā*, and (3) *rūpassa aniccatā*. These three items, it may be noted here, correspond to the three *khaṇas* (moments)—namely, (1) *uppādakkhaṇa*, (2) *ṭhitikkhaṇa* (*jaratā*), and (3) *bhaṅgakkhaṇa*. Once this correspondence is established it is easy to approach the subject from the point of view of the theory of moments.

According to a post-canonical theory of the Theravāda,[358] the body consists of an enormous number of *rūpa-kalāpas*—that is, the ultimate or the smallest clusters of rūpa-dhammas. The rūpa-dhammas of each *rūpa-kalāpa* are not separable, one from another. They form a unity having a common origin, a common existence, and a common cessation. Hence the three momentary phases of one *rūpa-kalāpa* mean the three momentary phases of all those rūpa-dhammas that make up that particular *rūpa-kalāpa*. The continuity of the body-series is due to the circumstance that when some *rūpa-kalāpas* perish they are immediately succeeded by others. It is a process of continual succession, projecting a picture of a relatively static existence.

The nascent phase, in other words, the *uppādakkhaṇa* of all those rūpa-dhammas that enter into the composition of the body-series, is *rūpassa jāti* (= *upacaya* and *santati*); their static phase, in other words, the *ṭhitikkhaṇa*, which is also called *jaratā*, is *rūpassa jaratā*; their cessant phase, in other words, the *bhaṅgakkhaṇa*, is *rūpassa aniccatā*.

Although both *rūpassa upacaya* and *rūpassa santati* are said to signify *rūpassa jāti*, yet this difference between them is recognized: The nascent phase of those rūpa-dhammas that constitute the body-series from the moment of conception until the sense-mechanism is complete is *rūpassa upacaya*. The nascent phase of those that constitute it thereafter up to the time of death (*cuti-pariyosānaṃ*) is *rūpassa santati*.[359]

The latter statement needs some explanation. We have already shown[360] that, according to the Abhidhamma Piṭaka, *rūpassa santati* signifies that phase of the body (growth) that comes before *rūpassa jaratā*. But according to the new interpretation, *rūpassa jāti* (= *upacaya* and *santati*), *rūpassa jaratā*, and *rūpassa aniccatā* signify three momentary phases of a *rūpa-dhamma/rūpa-kalāpa* that enters into the composition of the body-series. As such, strictly speaking, *rūpassa jaratā*, as understood by the Abhidhamma Piṭaka, has no place in the context of this new interpretation. This explains why *rūpassa santati* (= *rūpassa jāti*) is said to continue up to the moment of death.

Nevertheless *jaratā*, as understood by the earlier texts, is also recognized, but is given a different interpretation. It is called *pākaṭa-jarā*,[361] "evident decay," and is distinguished from *jarā* or *jaratā* as a momentary phase.[362] The latter is called *avici-jarā*, because it takes place incessantly, without interruption.[363] Brokenness of teeth (*khaṇḍicca*) is an instance of *pākaṭa-jarā*. In terms of elemental analysis, *pākaṭa-jarā* is only a *vikāra*.[364] That is to say, it merely signifies a peculiarity of the position, situation, or arrangement of the momentary[365] *rūpa-dhammas/rūpa-kalāpas* that constitute the body-series.

In the course of our discussion of the theory of moments we noticed that Ācariya Ānanda (as represented by Ācariya Sumaṅgala) objected to the recognition of *ṭhitikkhaṇa*, the moment of subsistence, under any guise.[366] When approached from this point of view, the four items would get reduced to two: *rūpassa jāti* (= *upacaya* and *santati*) and *rūpassa aniccatā*.

Why the items under consideration are brought under the heading *anipphanna* may now be considered. These items signify certain phases or, as the commentators say, certain characteristics (*lakkhaṇa*) of the *nipphanna-rūpa*. As such, they are not real rūpa-dhammas. When a rūpa-dhamma originates, it is called *rūpassa jāti*; when it subsists (decay),[367] it is called *rūpassa jaratā*; when it perishes, it is called *rūpassa aniccatā*. In addition to the rūpa-dhamma that originates, subsists (decay), and perishes, there are no rūpa-dhammas answering to the names *rūpassa jāti*, *rūpassa jaratā*, and *rūpassa aniccatā*.

If these characteristics, too, were postulated as real entities, then it would be necessary to postulate another set of (secondary) characteristics to account for their own origination, subsistence, and cessation. And these (secondary) characteristics would, in turn, require another set of (secondary-secondary) characteristics to account for their origination, etc. In this way it would lead to a process ad infinitum.

And it is in order to avoid this problem of infinite regress that the characteristics are not recognized as entities distinct from, and as real as, the dhammas that they characterize. This is the significance of the statement made in the Mohavicchedanī: "It is not correct to assume that origination originates, decay decays, and cessation ceases, because such an assumption leads to the (fallacy) of infinite regress (*anavaṭṭhāna*)."[368]

Element of Space

We have drawn attention to the fact that, although in the Nikāyas *ākāsa* is sometimes enumerated immediately after *paṭhavī*, *āpo*, *tejo*, and *vāyo*, it is not recognized as a *mahābhūta*.[369] As far as its exclusion from the category of *mahābhūtas* is concerned, the post-Nikāyan works agree with the Nikāyas. However, when we come to the Dhammasaṅganī and the Vibhaṅga we find an item called *ākāsa-dhātu*, element of space, recognized as one of the *upādā-rūpas*.[370] Its recognition as an *upādā-rūpa* carries the implication that it is dependent on the *mahābhūtas*.

In explaining why in the Dhammasaṅganī *ākāsa-dhātu* is recognized as an *upādā-rūpa*, Professor Keith observes that it is intimately connected with matter. It is pointed out that, since it is necessary for the movement of matter, it can well be placed under secondary matter.[371]

That *ākāsa-dhātu* is that which affords room for the movement of material things is of course one of the ways in which it is described in the Vibhaṅga.[372] But it is very doubtful whether this was the sole or rather the main factor that was taken into consideration in placing it under matter. For if it were the reason, then it ought to have been given a position at least on par with the four *mahābhūtas* rather than being recognized as dependent on, and therefore secondary to, them.

The whole situation becomes clear when it is understood in light of the Vaibhāṣika conception of *ākāśa*: Two kinds of *ākāśa* are distinguished. One is elevated to the status of an *asaṃskṛta-dharma*—that is, something that transcends all laws of causation and conditionality, and is referred to by the simple term *ākāśa*. The other is brought under matter and is referred to by the compound *ākāśa-dhātu*.[373]

Dr. McGovern tells us that in the Chinese sources the former is rendered as *hsuk'ung* and the latter as *k'ung*. *K'ung*, he says, "agrees more or less with the Sthaviravādin (= Theravādin) conception of *Ākāśa*."[374] To this correspondence, Professor Louis de la Vallée Poussin too has drawn attention.[375] The fact that both are included in matter does certainly show that there is a close parallelism between them. Of equal significance is the fact that both are referred to not by the simple term *ākāśa*, but by the compound *ākāśa-dhātu*.

This is only a part of the story. There is much evidence to show that the Theravādins too have recognized another kind of *ākāsa*. This they have never included in *rūpa*; and except for one significant fact, it corresponds to the a*saṃskṛta-ākāśa* of the Vaibhāṣikas.[376]

First let us consider what Buddhism means by *ākāśa-dhātu* and examine why it is brought under matter. In the Abhidharmakośa the Vaibhāṣika *ākāśa-dhātu* is defined as follows: the cavity or the void of the door, of the window, etc., this is external *ākāśa-dhātu*; the cavity of the mouth, the cavity of the nose, etc., are internal *ākāśa-dhātu*.[377] The Theravāda definition is more or less the same; the distinction between internal (*ajjhattika*) and external (*bāhira*) is also recognized: The cavities of the ear (*kaṇṇacchidda*), of the nose (*nāsacchidda*), the mouth-door (*mukhadvāra*), that through which what is eaten, drunk, or chewed is swallowed, that where it is deposited, and that through which it is evacuated are internal *ākāsa-dhātu*. Likewise, the cavities and interstices that obtain outside of the body—(the cavities in the wall, of the door-spaces, etc.)[378]—are external *ākāsa-dhātu*.[379]

It will thus be seen that according to both schools, *ākāśa-dhātu* means cavities, holes, apertures, interstices, etc. It could therefore be understood as bounded or delimited space. The Chinese rendering, *k'ung*, is said to mean "lack of *rūpa*, or interstices between *rūpa*."[380]

The later works of the Theravāda, too, recognize this meaning when they refer to *ākāsa-dhātu* by the technical term *pariccheda-rūpa*.[381]

Pariccheda signifies not only that which delimits (*paricchindati*) but also that which is delimited (*paricchijjati*).[382] The implication is that, since *ākāsa-dhātu* means cavities, interstices, etc., it sets limits to, and is itself limited by, the surrounding matter.

Once *ākāsa-dhātu* is understood as bounded or delimited space, why it is recognized as dependent on the *mahābhūtas* is not far to seek. Holes, cavities, etc., have an intimate connection with matter in the sense that they obtain owing to the peculiar position or situation of the latter. In this sense they can well be conceived as dependent on matter. And since the four *mahābhūtas* should necessarily enter into the composition of all material things, on further analysis, they are dependent on the *mahābhūtas*.

This explanation is further confirmed by Ācariya Buddhaghosa's statement that *ākāsa-dhātu* is manifested as the confines of matter (*rūpa-mariyāda-paccupaṭṭhānā*) and that it has its proximate cause in matter delimited by it (*paricchinnarūpa-padaṭṭhānā*).[383] The same idea is implied in Ācārya Yaśomitra's comment that it is established (*vyavasthāpitaṃ*) with reference to (*apekśya*) walls, etc.[384]

Insofar as the Vaibhāṣikas are concerned, one cannot, however, say that this was the only factor that was taken into consideration. In their view, *ākāśa-dhātu* is either light (*āloka*) or darkness (*tamas*), and as such is visible (*sanidarśana*). For this reason it is considered as part of *rūpāyatana*.[385] That the Theravādins do not admit the visibility of *ākāśa-dhātu* is shown not only by its inclusion in the *dhammāyatana* but also by a Kathāvatthu controversy. Some Buddhists argue that it is visible on the ground that one can see the interval between two trees or two posts, the space in a keyhole or in a window. The Theravāda reply is that in the case of an interval between two trees, for instance, one sees with his eye only the color of the two trees and that the interval as such is known only by the mind.[386]

The Vaibhāṣikas, as stated above, distinguish *ākāśa-dhātu* from *ākāśa*. The latter, like *pratisaṅkhyā-* and *apratisaṅkhyā-nirodha*, is an *asaṃskṛta-dharma*. As such, the *saṃskṛta-lakṣaṇas*[387] do not apply to it. It is omnipresent (*sarvagata*) and eternal (*nitya*). Its nature is non-obstruction (*anāvaraṇa-svabhāva*). That is to say, it does not obstruct (*āvṛṇoti*) matter that freely exists therein; nor is it obstructed (*āvriyate*) by matter, for it cannot be dislodged by the latter. However, it is not the mere absence of obstruction (*anāvaraṇa-bhāvamātra*), but is something positively real.[388] Thus what is called *asaṃskṛta-ākāśa* may be understood as space, considered as absolutely real and as constituting a receptacle for the existence and movement of matter.

In the Milindapañha we are introduced to an *ākāsa* that is quite different from the *ākāsa-dhātu* of the Dhammasaṅganī. Its fundamental characteristics are as follows: In no way can it be grasped (*sabbaso agayho*); it inspires terror (*santāsaniyo*); it is infinite (*ananto*), boundless (*appamāno*), and immeasurable (*aparimeyyo*); and it does not cling to anything (*alaggo*), is not attached to anything (*asatto*), rests on nothing (*appatiṭṭhito*), and is not obstructed by anything (*apalibuddho*).[389]

Elsewhere in the same work we are told that two things in this world are not born of kamma (*akammajā*) or of causes (*ahetujā*) or of season (*anutujā*)—namely, nibbāna and *ākāsa*.[390]

With reference to this *ākāsa* of the Milindapañha, Professor Keith observes that "it is certainly a more philosophic view than is found in the Dhammasaṅganī of the Abhidhamma Piṭaka, where it is classified as a material derivate."[391] According to this observation, the *ākāsa-dhātu* of the Dhammasaṅganī and the *ākāsa* of the Milindapañha represent two different views on the same subject, and the latter is a more refined version of the former.

It is of course true that the Milindapañha is later than the works of the Abhidhamma Piṭaka. However, as we shall see fairly soon, the type of *ākāsa* referred to therein is known to the Abhidhamma Piṭaka. Moreover, when one considers the fundamental characteristics of the Milindapañha *ākāsa* one cannot fail to notice its strong similarity with the *asaṃskṛta-ākāśa* of the Vaibhāṣikas. Of much significance is the statement that only nibbāna and *ākāsa* are not born of kamma (*akammajā*) or of causes (*ahetujā*) or of season (*anutujā*).

This is a clear attempt to bring *ākāsa* on a par with nibbāna. The Vaibhāṣikas, too, elevate *ākāśa* to such a position by recognizing *ākāśa* and the two kinds of nirodha as *asaṃskṛta*. And we have already shown how the *ākāsa-dhātu* of the Dhammasaṅganī (and the Vibhaṅga) corresponds to the *ākāśa-dhātu* of the Vaibhāṣikas. In view of these circumstances, we could quite justifiably assume that, as the Vaibhāṣikas do, the Theravādins too distinguish between two kinds of *ākāsa*. As such, the type of *ākāsa* referred to in the Milindapañha should be understood not as a different (later) version of the same kind of *ākāsa* (*-dhātu*) of the Dhammasaṅganī (and the Vibhaṅga), but as the Theravāda counterpart of the Vaibhāṣika *asaṃskṛta-ākāśa*.

It is not in the Milindapañha alone that we get reference to the Theravāda counterpart of the Vaibhāṣika *asaṃskṛta-ākāśa*. One of the controversies in the Kathāvatthu of the Abhidhamma Piṭaka concerns the question whether *ākāsa* is *asaṅkhata*. In one of his answers the Theravādin admits that *ākāsa* is not *saṅkhata*.[392]

This admission shows that the *ākāsa* at issue here is not the same as the *ākāsa-dhātu* of the Dhammasaṅganī, because the latter is *saṅkhata*. On the other hand, it points to the close correspondence between the *ākāśa* of the Kathāvatthu controversy and that of the Milindapañha. It may be recalled here that, according to the latter work, both nibbāna and *ākāsa* are not born of kamma or of causes or of season. This is another way of saying that both are not *saṅkhata*.[393] For all *saṅkhata-dhammas* arise and exist because of causes. Since the *ākāsa* of the Kathāvatthu and that of the Milindapañha are not *saṅkhata*, it is fairly certain that both works refer to the same kind of *ākāsa*.

There is, however, this significant problem to be considered: Although the Theravādins of the Kathāvatthu controversy deny that *ākāsa* is *saṅkhata*, they do not admit that it is *asaṅkhata*.[394] Thus, in their view, it cannot be described either as *saṅkhata* or as *asaṅkhata*.

The commentator says that this is because *ākāsa* is a mere *paññatti* (*paññatti-mattaṃ*)[395]—that is, a nominal dhamma. As far as the data are concerned this conclusion is certainly correct. For that which is neither *saṅkhata* nor *asaṅkhata* should be a *paññatti*.[396]

There is, however, the following situation to be considered. The definition of *ākāsa* in the Milindapañha does not give any indication of its being recognized as a *paññatti*. On the other hand, as already stated, it bears a strong resemblance to the *ākāśa* of the Vaibhāṣikas, which is an *asaṃskṛta-dharma*. It has also been noted that according to this work both nibbāna and *ākāsa* are not *saṅkhata*. Now if *ākāsa* is not a *paññatti* and if it is not *saṅkhata*, it should be an *asaṅkhata-dhamma*. But what is significant to note here is that, although the Milindapañha applies the term *asaṅkhata* to nibbāna,[397] it (carefully) avoids applying the same term to *ākāsa*. On this point, as we have seen, the Kathāvatthu is more positive, for it categorically says that *ākāsa* should not be described as *asaṅkhata* (although of course it denies that it is *saṅkhata*).

When the above situation is taken into consideration, it is difficult to follow the commentator. As we have already observed, it is of course true that his conclusion is supported by the data in the Kathāvatthu. But there are some good reasons to believe that the problem at issue here is on quite a different level. As such, the commentator's conclusion does not seem to represent the actual situation that obtains in the Kathāvatthu.

The Theravādins, it should be noted here, never object to nibbāna being qualified as *asaṅkhata*. What is more, they seem to have deemed it improper to extend the term to something else even if it is not *saṅkhata*, lest this should give the impression that it is as exalted and as noble as nibbāna—the highest ideal of Buddhism. This seems to be the reason why the Milindapañha and the Kathāvatthu do not apply the term *asaṅkhata* to *ākāsa*, although according to both it is not *saṅkhata*. In other words, *ākāsa*, as conceived in these two works, is not a *paññatti*; it is a real dhamma that is not *saṅkhata*, but that is not designated as *asaṅkhata*.

On the one hand, this suggestion explains the peculiar situation that obtains in the Milindapañha. On the other, it gets more positive support from the nature of the Theravāda arguments as represented in the Kathāvatthu controversy.

To the statement of the opponent—namely, that *ākāsa* is *asaṅkhata*—the immediate reaction of the Theravādins is: "Does this mean to say that *ākāsa* is Nibbāna, the Shelter, the Cave, the Refuge, the Goal, the Past-Decease, the Ambrosial?"[398] When the opponent denies this, the Theravādin says in that case one has to recognize two nibbānas. Even his other arguments are mainly based on the assumption that the extension of the term *asaṅkhata* to *ākāsa* would necessarily amount to a confusion, if not identity, between nibbāna and *ākāsa*. The main argument of the opponent is: "If you deny that *ākāsa* is *saṅkhata*, you should admit that it is *asaṅkhata*."[399]

From what we have observed so far it should become clear that the Theravādins, too, distinguish between two kinds of *ākāsa*, and that, except for some minor details, they correspond to the two kinds of *ākāśa* recognized by the Vaibhāṣikas. One sometimes reads that while the Vaibhāṣikas elevated *ākāśa* to the status of an *asaṃskṛta-dharma*, the Theravādins brought it under matter.[400] Such a contrast is not justified. It overlooks the fact that both schools have recognized two kinds of *ākāśa*, one of which (= *ākāśa-dhātu*) is included in, and the other (= *ākāśa*) excluded from, matter.

We might also note in passing that parallel situations are met with in other systems of Indian thought, too. The Sāṃkhya-Yoga, for instance, distinguishes between two kinds of *ākāśa*—namely, *kāryākāśa* and *kāraṇākāśa*. The former is derivative because it is produced from *śabda-tanmātra*, the sound-potential; the latter is original because it is associated with *prakṛti*, the uncaused first cause of the world of not-self.[401] Similarly certain Jaina works, too, recognize two varieties of *ākāśa*. One is *logāgāsa*, the space that gives room for the existence of all extended substances (*astikāya*). The other is *alogāgāsa*, the infinite space beyond the cosmos, where the two conditions of motion (*dharmastikāya*) and rest (*adharmastikāya*) do not have their influence.[402]

Of course, the correspondence between these theories does not go very far, because each of them has been formulated according to the metaphysical assumptions of the particular system of thought to which it belongs. But what is striking is the similarity in the pattern of development.

What made the Buddhists draw such a distinction could be traced to the Nikāyas themselves. Therein sometimes *ākāsa* is described particularly with reference to holes, cavities, apertures, etc.[403] Such descriptions suggest the beginning of *ākāsa-dhātu* that is brought under matter.

Sometimes it is described as the ultimate basis, a sort of fulcrum or receptacle, of the whole physical world. Thus in the *Mahāparinibbāna Sutta*, the Buddha is represented as saying: "This great earth, O Ānanda, rests on water, water on air, and air on *ākāsa*."[404] And in the *Rāhulovāda Sutta* it is said that *ākāsa*, for its part, does not rest on anything (*ākāso na kattha ci patiṭṭhito*).[405] In fact, Sage Nāgasena (Milindapañha) cites this same canonical statement after enumerating the fundamental characteristics of *ākāsa*,[406] implying thereby that it is such statements in the earlier texts that paved the way to the conception of *ākāsa* that we find in the Milindapañha and the Kathāvatthu. Equally significant is an observation made by Ācārya Yaśomitra: When the Vaibhāṣikas argue that *ākāśa* is real they base this argument on a (sūtra) passage where the Buddha declares to a brāhmin that the earth rests on the circle of water, the circle of water on air, air on *ākāśa*, and that *ākāśa* for its part does not rest on anything, does not cling to anything.[407]

When we come to the commentaries and the subsequent works, the whole subject has undergone a notable change. The *ākāsa* of the Kathāvatthu and the Milindapañha, which, as we have seen, is the Theravāda counterpart of the Vaibhāṣikas' *asaṃskṛta-ākāśa*, came to be designated as *anantākāsa*, infinite space, or *ajaṭākāsa*, unbounded space.[408] Although the two terms are reminiscent of its earlier realistic conception, the use of another term, *tucchākāsa*,[409] false or empty space, indicates an attempt to deprive it of its reality. As a matter of fact, it is clearly stated that it is only a *paññatti*,[410] a nominal dhamma with no corresponding objective reality.

Understandably the same fate fell on the *ākāsa-dhātu* by its being subsumed under the heading *anipphanna-rūpa*. For this is another way of saying that it is neither *rūpa* (matter) nor a *dhamma* (element of existence) in the true sense of the terms. As such, its description as that which delimits (*paricchindati*) or that which is delimited (*paricchijjati*)[411] should not be understood in a realistic sense. For it is nothing but the mere limitation of matter—*rūpa-pariccheda-mattaṃ*.[412]

6

CLASSIFICATION OF MATERIAL ELEMENTS

Section A

IN THE COURSE of our discussion of the twenty-eight rūpa-dhammas,[413] we saw how they were subjected to certain classifications, such as the one into primary and secondary. In addition to those, an earlier discussion of which was necessitated for a better understanding of the subject so far covered, there are others, no less important. And it is these remaining classifications that we propose to examine in this chapter.

Divisions and classifications play a significant part in the Abhidhammic systematization. They are the stock-in-trade of its methodology, the fundamental means whereby the import and the implications of the terms representing the various elements of existence (*dhammā*) are sought to be unfolded. In the seven *pakaraṇas* of the Abhidhamma Piṭaka it is very rarely indeed that one finds a direct enumeration of all the rūpa-dhammas; oftener than not they are presented under various classifications. Hence it is that the Rūpavibhatti[414] of the Dhammasaṅganī consists, to a great extent, of an enormous number of classifications, arranged into ten sections in an ascending numerical order.

The first[415] section consists of 104 classifications,[416] each being an arrangement of rūpa-dhammas into two groups. The last 90 are developed in a rather "mechanical" way. In each, the distribution of rūpa-dhammas into two groups is made in such a way that only one rūpa-dhamma constitutes the first "group," whereas all the others constitute the second group. The first is described by a positive term and the second by its negative, formed with the addition of the negative particle *na*. The last 90 should, therefore, be understood as a device to show the characteristics peculiar to a given rūpa-dhamma. In each such arrangement the contrast between a given rūpa-dhamma, on the one hand, and the rest, on the other, is brought into relief. Two methods are adopted for this purpose.

a. Sometimes a characteristic or a function peculiar to a given rūpa-dhamma is taken as the basis of the arrangement—for example, "There is matter that is the basis of visual consciousness (= *cakkhu*, the organ of sight) and there is matter that is not the basis of visual consciousness (= all the remaining rūpa-dhammas)."[417] What results from such an approach is obvious: that rūpa-dhamma, the peculiar characteristic or function of which is taken as the basis of the arrangement, comes under the positive category and all the rest under the negative. This is a method with wide scope, for what is recognized as peculiar to one rūpa-dhamma cannot be predicated of another. However, only the five sense-organs and the corresponding objective fields are subjected to such a treatment. And this results in as many as forty arrangements. It is only a different way of describing the oft-recurrent thesis that the first five sense-organs are the bases (*vatthu*, *nissaya*) and that the five objective fields corresponding to them are the objects of the first five kinds of consciousness (*viññāṇa*) and their concomitants (*cetasikas*).[418]

b. Sometimes a given rūpa-dhamma itself is taken as the basis of the arrangement—for example, "There is matter that is *kabaḷiṅkāra-āhāra* and there is matter that is not *kabaḷiṅkara-āhāra* (= the remaining rūpa-dhammas)."[419] According to this method, matter in its totality can be dif-

> ferentiated in as many ways as there are rūpa-dhammas. However, the actual number of the arrangements exceeds the number of rūpa-dhammas, because of this reason: some items such as the sense-organs are repeated under *dhātu*, *āyatana*, and *indriya*. There are, in all, forty such arrangements: each sense-organ as *dhātu*, *āyatana*, and *indriya* is distinguished thrice from the rest of the rūpa-dhammas (15); each objective field as *dhātu* and *āyatana* is distinguished twice (10); and the remaining fifteen are each distinguished only once (15).[420]

The fourteen classifications that occur at the beginning of the first section are more important in the sense that they form the nucleus of a great majority that come in the next nine sections. They are the arrangement of rūpa-dhammas into two groups as (1) *upādā* and *anupādā*, (2) *upādiṇṇa* and *anupādiṇṇa*, (3) *upādiṇṇ'upādānīya* and *anupādiṇṇ'upādānīya,* (4) *sanidassana* and *anidassana*, (5) *sappaṭigha* and *appaṭigha*, (6) *indriya* and *na indriya*, (7) *mahābhūta* and *na mahābhūta*, (8) *viññatti* and *na viññatti*, (9) *cittasamuṭṭhāna* and *na cittasamuṭṭhāna*,(10) *citta-sahabhū* and *na citta-sahabhū*, (11) *cittanuparivatti* and *na cittanuparivatti*, (12) *ajjhattika* and *bāhira*, (13) *oḷārika* and *sukhuma*, and (14) *dūre* and *santike*.

The implications of a great majority of these fourteen classifications have already been examined. No. 1 refers to the distinction between primary and secondary matter,[421] and no. 7 indicates the type of material elements that constitute each group.[422] No. 4 points to a characteristic peculiar to *rūpāyatana*. Since *rūpāyatana* represents the visible, it alone comes under the positive heading *sanidassana* (visible).[423] As far as the contents are concerned, there is no difference between nos. 5, 13, and 14: the sense-organs and the objective fields are *sappaṭigha*, *oḷārika*, and *santike*; the remaining rūpa-dhammas are *appaṭigha*, *sukhuma*, and *dūre*. We have discussed their significance and shown how they testify to a recognition, on the part of the Theravāda Abhidhamma, of the difference between what early Buddhism and what most of the Buddhist schools in common recognize as matter on the one hand and the later accretions on the other hand.[424] No. 6 is an attempt to classify all the rūpa-dhammas into two groups as *indriya* and non-*indriya*. The five sense-organs, the two faculties of sex, and the material faculty of life constitute the first group,[425] and the rest the second. No. 8 draws attention to the fact that two rūpa-dhammas—namely, *kāya-* and *vacī-viññatti*—are *viññattis*,[426] and that the rest are not *viññattis*. Nos. 10 and 11 are based on two characteristics (= *citta-sahabhū* and *cittānuparivatti*)[427] peculiar to the two *viññattis*. As such these two items alone come under the positive terms and all the rest under the negative.

The classification into *upādiṇṇ'upādānīya* and *anupādiṇṇ'upādānīya* (no. 3) is the same as that into *upādiṇṇa* and *anupādiṇṇa* (no. 2), except for this difference: in the former the term *upādānīya* is added to qualify both the positive and the negative subclasses of the latter. Thus *upādānīya*[428] signifies a characteristic common to all the rūpa-dhammas. No. 3 cannot, therefore, be taken as a separate classification. Most probably it was made in order to avoid any possible confusion between the apparently similar *upādānīya* and *upādiṇṇa*.[429] As the former qualifies all the rūpa-dhammas, and the latter only some, the distinction in their meaning is not to be overlooked.

We are thus left with only three classifications—that is, those into (a) *upādiṇṇa* and *anupādiṇṇa*, (b) *cittasamuṭṭhāna* and *na citta-samuṭṭhāna*, and (c) *ajjhattika* and *bāhira*. Before we come to a discussion of them, let us survey the other nine sections that contain more complex classifications.

The second section consists of 103 classifications, each being an arrangement of rūpa-dhammas into three groups. Each such arrangement has the classification into *ajjhattika* and *bāhira* of the first section as its invariable basis.

It is transformed into one with three classes by classifying either the *ajjhattika-rūpas* or the *bāhira-rūpas* (but not both concurrently) into two groups. For example,

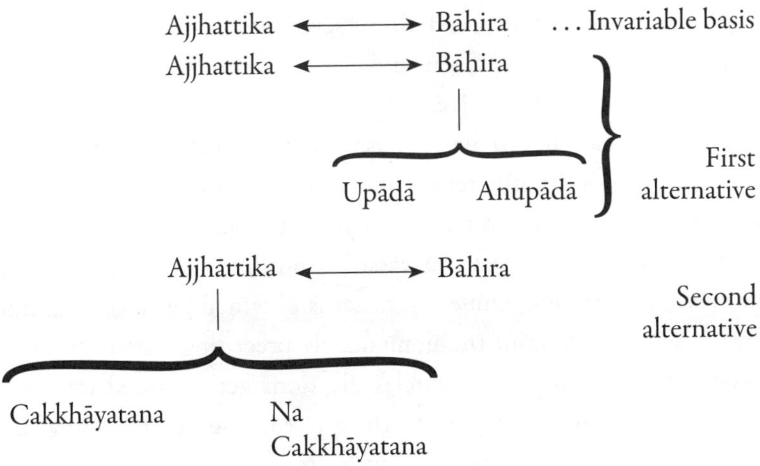

The characteristics with reference to which either the *ajjhattika* or *bāhira-rūpas* are classified into two groups are all taken from the first section. Hence the second section is only a complex arrangement of all the classifications given in the first. Its purpose is to show the position of the classification into *ajjhattika* and *bāhira* vis-à-vis the remaining 103 of the preceding section.

In the third section there are twenty-two classifications, each into four groups. All of them are traceable to the first fourteen classifications of the first section. A selected classification into two groups is made into one with four, by arranging into two groups the items included in the first as well as in the second groups of the former. For example,

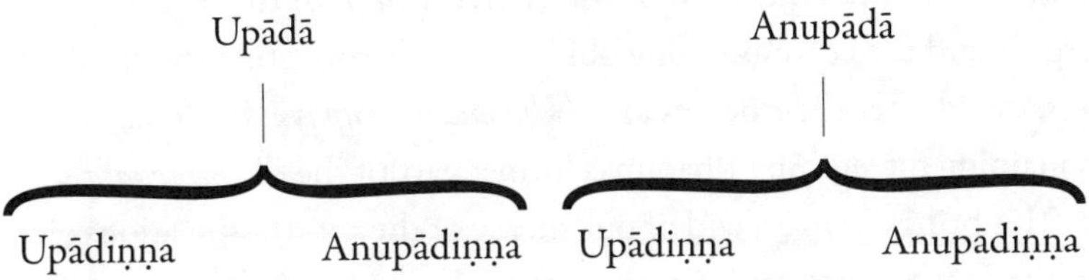

All the characteristics involved in these twenty-two classifications are taken from the first section. As such, they are an attempt to establish some kind of relation between the different groups in the first fourteen classifications of the first section.

The next seven sections, containing seven classifications in order into five, six, seven, eight, nine, ten, and eleven groups, are more repetitive and therefore less informative.

The classification into five groups is the same as that into *upādā* and *anupādā*, but for this difference: since *anupādā* consists of the four primary elements, it is accordingly arranged into four "groups."

In the case of the next three classifications into six, seven, and eight groups, the ascending numerical order is obtained by classifying into two a selected group of the immediately preceding classification—a process whereby the first two classifications get absorbed into, and thus represented by, the third. Their purpose is to show how the rūpa-dhammas can be classified according to the way they become objects of consciousness. Color (*rūpa*), for instance, differs from sound (*sadda*) in that while the former is known by visual consciousness (*cakkhuviññeyya*), the latter is known by auditory consciousness (*sotaviññeyya*).[430]

The classification into nine groups is the same as that into *indriya* and *na indriya*, except for this difference: since *indriya-rūpa* counts eight rūpa-dhammas, the positive group is accordingly arranged under eight headings.

This same classification is next made into one with ten groups by classifying the items that come under the negative heading—that is, *na indriya*—into two groups as *sappaṭigha* and *appaṭigha*.

The last with eleven headings shows how the rūpa-dhammas are distributed in the older list of the twelve *āyatanas*: the first five sense-organs and the corresponding objective fields constitute the ten *āyatanas*, called after their names as *cakkhāyatana*, *rūpāyatana*, etc., and the remaining fifteen rūpa-dhammas form a part of the *dhammāyatana*.[431]

This brings us to an end of our survey of the 230 classifications given in the Dhammasaṅgaṇī. From what we have observed in its course, it should appear that it is not necessary to go into each and every one of them separately. We noticed that all the classifications given in the second and third sections, and three of the seven given in the next seven sections, are all traceable to the first section, which consists of classifications into two groups. The few exceptions were noted, and we have indicated in the relevant places that any data they yielded were discussed in more appropriate contexts. Our aim is not only to elicit some important classifications for discussion but also to give a conspectus of the Abhidhammic methodology as revealed from the Abhidhammic exposition of matter.[432]

The ensuing discussion will therefore be confined to an examination of those classifications of the first section that came under our final selection.

Section B

First let us examine the implications of the classification into *upādiṇṇa* and *anupādiṇṇa*.[433] The positive term *upādiṇṇa* literally means "that which has been appropriated or laid hold of," but in order to understand what it exactly connotes in the Abhidhammic terminology, we have to get at the agency behind this act of appropriation or laying hold of.

Professor Louis de la Vallée Poussin is of the opinion that the pair of terms *upādiṇṇa* and *anupādiṇṇa* of the Pāli Abhidhamma conveys the same sense as *upātta* and *anupātta* as explained in the Abhidharmakośa.[434]

The Kośa defines *upātta* as "that which the mind and mental factors get hold of and self-appropriate (*svīkṛta*) by way of support (*adhiṣṭhāna*)."[435] The five sense-organs (with the exception of those that were and those that will be) and those other material elements that are inseparable from, or integrated with, the sense-organs (*indriyābhinna, indriyāvinirbhāga*)—namely, *rūpa* (color), *gandha* (odor), *rasa* (taste), and *spraṣṭavya* (the tangible)—are called *upātta*. The relation between this kind of matter and mind is one of close connection: "there is a reciprocal reaction between mind and this kind of matter, and this is what in common language is called *sacetana* or *sajīva*."[436]

It should also be noted here that, as explicitly stated in the Kośa,[437] and also as is clearly implied by the very definition given to the term in question, the mental elements are not *upātta*.

With this background in mind, if we proceed to examine the meaning assigned to *upādiṇṇa* in the Dhammasaṅganī and also the meaning revealed from its usage in different contexts, its identification with *upātta* presents some difficulties.

The Dhammasaṅganī makes it abundantly clear that what is called *upādiṇṇa-rūpa* comes into being through the action of kamma (*kammassa kaṭattā*).[438] However, this statement does not in itself constitute a serious difficulty in identifying it with *upātta-rūpa*. For the Kośa, too, refers to a category of matter said to be the result of karma (*vipākaja*), the contents of which are the same as those enumerated under *upātta*.[439] It could therefore be argued that when the Dhammasaṅganī says that *upādiṇṇa-rūpa* comes into being through the action of kamma, this has to be understood not as a definition as such, but as an explanation on the origin of the matter so designated.

There is, however, some positive evidence that suggests that *upādiṇṇa* is not used in the same sense as *upātta*. The evidence comes from another passage of the Dhammasaṅganī purporting to give the complete denotation of the term *upādiṇṇa*. To the question "What dhammas are *upādiṇṇa*?" it provides the following answer:

> The results of tainted skillful and nonskillful actions belonging to the sense sphere, form sphere, and formless sphere, which are associated with the aggregates of feelings, perceptions, mental formations, and consciousness, and with any materiality that arises owing to kamma—it is these states that are upādinna.[440]

This statement makes it abundantly clear that not only matter but also the other four aggregates (*khandhas*) that come into being through the action of kamma (*vipāka*, *kammassa kaṭattā*) are considered as *upādiṇṇa*. On the other hand, as stated in the Kośa, mental elements (*vedanā*, *saññā*, etc.,) are not called *upātta*, a fact implied by the very definition given to it: "that which the mind and mental factors grasp by way of their support."

To sum up the difference: whereas the Dhammasaṅganī uses *upādiṇṇa* to denote all resultant states of kamma, mental as well as material, the Kośa uses *upātta* to designate those rūpa-dhammas that the mind and the mind-factors take as their support.

It could, however, be said that the original meaning of *upādiṇṇa* is the same as that of *upātta*, and that when the Dhammasaṅganī uses it to include mental elements as well, it has illegitimately extended the meaning of the term. Herein we are concerned with the meaning of *upādiṇṇa* as used in the Dhammasaṅganī. Whether it represents a subsequent development or not is another question.

Such a view could, however, be maintained if there were evidence in the earlier texts, the suttas for instance, which would lend support to the meaning assigned to *upātta* in the Kośa. In a number of suttas the term *upādiṇṇa* occurs in a stock formula where the four *mahābhūtas* are described. Each *mahābhūta* is said to exist either internally (*ajjhattaṃ, paccattaṃ*)—that is, as part of the complex that makes the individual—or externally (*bāhira*)—that is, in the nonsentient world. The distinction in question is sought to be established by designating the former as *upādiṇṇa*. Such bodily constituents as teeth, hair, nails, bones, blood, etc. are cited as *upādiṇṇa*.[441] Although the negative term *anupādiṇṇa* does not occur, yet we may say that the matter that enters into the composition of trees, hills, rocks, etc. is *anupādiṇṇa*.

In the *Mahāhatthipadopama Sutta* where this distinction is extended to the *ākāsa-dhātu* as well, *upādiṇṇa* is explained as that which is appropriated by craving—*taṇhūpādiṇṇa*.[442]

Thus in the suttas *upādiṇṇa* is used to distinguish the matter that enters into the composition of a living being from other instances of matter. Since *upādiṇṇa* is further explained as *taṇhūpādiṇṇa*, it may be asked why only the matter of the body is so designated. The answer is provided in the same passage where the term is explained: One appropriates one's own body with craving (*taṇhā*), which manifests itself in such thoughts as, "This am I" (*ahanti*), "This is mine" (*mamanti*), and "I am (this)" (*asmīti*).[443] Accompanied by craving, such thoughts can be directed to other things too. But in the main, it is one's own body that one appropriates with craving, with it one identifies oneself. It is *upādiṇṇa* par excellence. And in this sense the term is used to qualify only the body (so as to distinguish it from other instances of matter).

Ācariya Buddhaghosa's remarks in this connection are quite significant. Commenting on *upādiṇṇa*, as used in the suttas, he observes that it means: "*daḷhaṃ ādinnaṃ ahaṃ mamanti evaṃ daḷhaṃ ādinnaṃ, gahitaṃ, parāmaṭṭhaṃ.*"[444] In fact, the commentators were quite aware that in the earlier texts *upādiṇṇa* was used in a sense different from the sense in which it came to be used in the Abhidhamma. For instance, the commentator of the Majjhimanikāya observes that *upādiṇṇa* (as used in the Majjhimanikāya) refers to all matter, irrespective of the distinction as to whether it is kamma-caused or not, that enters into the composition of the body (*sarīraṭṭhaka-rūpa*).[445]

That the earlier meaning of *upādiṇṇa* is different from either of the meanings given to it by the Dhammasaṅganī and the Kośa is further confirmed by the difference in the items brought under the term. Since the suttas understand *upādiṇṇa* as referring to the matter that constitutes the body, they bring under it such things as hair, bones, blood, urine, excreta, etc.[446] For the Dhammasaṅganī, since *upādiṇṇa-rūpa* means the matter that arises by way of kammic fruition, it eliminates from the category so designated such rūpa-dhammas as the triad of *lahutā*, etc., because they are *cittasamuṭṭhāna*.[447] For the Kośa, since *upātta* means "that which the mind and mental factors take by way of support (*adhiṣṭhāna*)," it eliminates from the category so designated such things as head hair, bodily hair, nails, and teeth.[448]

Professor Louis de la Vallée Poussin has drawn attention to the fact that the "Majjhima III 240, reproduced in the Pitāputrasamāgama, gives hair . . . the excrements as *ajjhattaṃ paccattaṃ kakkhalaṃ upādinnaṃ.*" Since the hair is not *upādinna*,[449] he is inclined to believe that one has confused the *ajjhattika-rūpa* with *upātta-rūpa*.[450] It appears to us that it is not necessary to explain away the anomaly in question by putting it down to a confusion between *upādiṇṇa* and *ajjhatta*. The anomaly persists because it is concerned with a term that has two meanings, the earlier and the later. If in the suttas a term occurs in a sense different from what it has assumed subsequently, this is understandable. For when a term acquired a different meaning subsequently, attempts were not always made to change the contexts in which the self-same term had been used in the original sense so as to bring all in line with the later meaning. Sometimes even in the same work both meanings do occur. In the Vibhaṅga,[451] for instance, *upādiṇṇa* is used in the Nikāyan sense as well as in the sense in which it is used in the Dhammasaṅganī.

Since the meaning of *upādiṇṇa* in the Dhammasaṅganī is different from that of *upātta* in the Kośa, and both from that suggested by its usage in the suttas, we may reasonably assume that the first two cases are two separate developments of the original idea. It may, however, be noted here that, since the Kośa does not bring mental elements under *upātta*, to that extent it is more faithful to the earlier.

The term is explained in a similar way in the Abhidharmāmṛta of Ācārya Ghoṣaka, where also all the mental elements are excluded from the category of *upātta*.[452] Even the Pāli commentaries and the *ṭīkās* do not lend any support to the interpretation of the *upādiṇṇa* of the Dhammasaṅganī in light of the *upātta* of the Kośa. They all agree in maintaining that the matter so designated is *kammaja* or *kamma-samuṭṭhāna*[453]—that is, given rise to by karma. The Visuddhimagga observes that it is called so because it is grasped by *kamma-taṃ kammena upādiṇṇattā upādiṇṇam.*[454] The explanation given in the Vibhāvinī Ṭīkā, although almost the same, seems to combine the two meanings given to it in the suttas and in the Dhammasaṅganī: "*taṇhā-diṭṭhihi upetena kammunā attano phalabhāvena ādiṇṇattā*,"[455] "(so termed) because it has been grasped at by the karma that is closely attended with craving and erroneous opinion, by way of its own fruit."[456] However, it should not be overlooked here that in the commentarial works the Nikāyan explanation of *upādiṇṇa* is also recognized.

The items brought under *upādiṇṇa* may be considered now. On the basis of *upādiṇṇa* and its negative, *anupādiṇṇa*, the Dhammasaṅganī arranges the rūpa-dhammas into three groups.[457]

The first group is invariably *upādiṇṇa*. It consists of the eight *indriya-rūpas*—namely, the five physical sense-organs, the two faculties of sex, and the material faculty of life.

The second group is sometimes *upādiṇṇa* and sometimes *anupādiṇṇa*. It consists of eleven items—namely, the four *mahābhūtas*, *rūpa*, *gandha*, *rasa*, *āhāra*, *ākāsadhātu*, *upacaya*, and *santati*. These items represent the type of matter with which the *indriya-rūpas* are associated. Since the *indriya-rūpas* are a variety of *upādā-rūpa*, they cannot exist without being supported by the *mahābhūtas*. And the *mahābhūtas* cannot exist independently of four of the *upādā-rūpas*—namely, *rūpa*, *gandha*, *rasa*, and *āhāra*.[458] This explains the presence of the first eight items in the second group. The inclusion of *ākāsa-dhātu* seems to have been necessitated by the need to account for any cavities or holes involved in the constitution of the sense-organs. The inclusion of *upacaya* and *santati*, which signify the growth of the body in this group, shows that according to the Dhammasaṅganī the growth of the *upādiṇṇa-rūpa* is itself *upādiṇṇa*. In other words, the growth of the kamma-caused *rūpa* is also considered as kamma-caused.

It is not difficult to understand why the items included in this (second) group are not always *upādiṇṇa*. When they exist in association with the *indriya-rūpas* they are *upādiṇṇa*, and when they exist otherwise they are *anupādiṇṇa*.

It will be seen that in this (second) group there are some items that in the commentaries are brought under the heading *anipphanna*. We have already noted that according to the commentators, strictly speaking, none of the *anipphanna-rūpas* can be described as *kamma-samuṭṭhāna* (= *upādiṇṇa*), although they can be so described in an indirect way (*pariyāyato*) or in a conventional sense.[459] Hence from their point of view, strictly speaking, *ākāsa-dhātu*, *upacaya*, and *santati* are not *upādiṇṇa*.

The third group is always *anupādiṇṇa*. It consists of eight items—namely, the two *viññattis*; the triad of *lahutā*, *mudutā*, and *kammaññatā*; *jaratā* and *aniccatā*; and *sadda*. Elsewhere in the Dhammasaṅganī the first five items are brought under the heading *cittasamuṭṭhāna*.[460] This explains why they are completely excluded from the category of *upādiṇṇa*, which is "*kammasamuṭṭhāna*." The Kathāvatthu shows that although the authors of the Abhidhamma Piṭaka had no objection to assigning causes to *jāti* (genesis) and *upacaya-santati* (growth), they were not prepared to treat *jaratā* and *aniccatā* in the same way.[461] It is in keeping with this tradition that *jaratā* and *aniccatā* are included in this group. For, to have included them in either of the first two groups is to recognize that they are brought about by kamma.

Closely connected with the theory that the sense-organs are *kammasamuṭṭhāna* is the problem arising from the definition of *vipāka*. In four of the Kathāvatthu controversies the Theravādins maintain that what is material can never be *vipāka*. Since *vipāka*, as it is generally understood, means the results of kamma, this denial at first sight seems to contradict what we have been saying so far—namely, that some rūpadhammas come into being through the action of kamma. The Theravāda arguments, however, point to a different conclusion. Against the assertion of the Mahāsāṅghikas[462]—namely, that the sense-organs are *vipāka*—the following objection is raised: "The *vipāka* is a matter of feeling, pleasant, painful or neutral; it is conjoined with feeling of these three kinds; it is conjoined with mental contact, feeling, perception, volition and thought; it goes with a mental object; with it go adverting, attention, volition, anticipation and aiming. Are the five sense-organs anything of this kind?"[463] This counterargument is meant to show that, in the view of the Theravādins, the term is applicable only to the mental states resulting from kamma. In other words, for the Theravādins *vipāka* is essentially a subjective experience. But this does not mean that they object to the recognition of the sense-organs as the results of kamma. It only means that, in the terminology of the Abhidhamma Piṭaka, the term *vipāka* is given a restricted denotation. The controversy concerns a question relating to the use of terms. In actual fact both parties agree with the view that the sense-organs are kamma results. In fact, the commentator observes that the Theravāda argument is meant to show that the usage (*vohāra*) of *vipāka* does not apply to the rūpa-dhammas resulting from kammic fruition.[464] This explains why no objection is raised against the Mahāsāṅghikas' assertion that the *manāyatana* could be *vipāka*.[465] It is also in keeping with this circumstance that in the Dhammasaṅganī passage we have quoted above,[466] while the four *khandhas* that represent the mental elements are described as *vipāka*, the rūpa-dhammas are separately mentioned with the qualification: *kammassa kaṭattā*. Most probably it is this phrase that later gave rise to *kaṭattā-rūpa*, which in the Paṭṭhāna[467] became the standard term for *kamma-samuṭṭhāna-rūpa*.

Whether the sense-organs are the result of one kamma or of a multiplicity of kammas is another question that drew the attention of the Buddhists. Sage Nāgasena confirms the latter alternative. Just as—so runs the illustration—five different seeds sown in a field later yield five different kinds of fruits, even so the five sense-organs result from diverse kammas and not from one kamma.[468]

Ācariya Buddhaghosa, too, seems to have had the same theory in mind when he says that the difference between the sense-organs is due to *kamma-visesa*, the difference in the kammas of which they are the results.[469]

However, his commentator interprets "*kamma-visesa*" not as referring to a multiplicity of kammas, but as referring to a single kamma having the potentiality of differentiating the sense-organs. In explanation it is said that although the kamma is one, arising as it does from the desire for a mode of existence (*attabhāva*) complete with five sense-bases, yet since it is the cause of the differentiation of the sense-organs, it is described as "*kamma-visesa*."[470] It is further observed that the difference of this kamma by which it is a condition (*paccaya*) for the organ of sight, by that same difference it is not a condition for the organ of hearing and so on, for otherwise there will not be any difference between the sense-organs.[471]

It is very unlikely that Ācariya Buddhaghosa had used the term *kamma-visesa* in the same sense as his commentator interpreted it. The probability is rather that he meant a multiplicity of kammas, as was recognized by Sage Nāgasena. Since "*bhūta-visesa*," which occurs in the same sentence,[472] means the difference between the primary elements (plural), it seems more proper that *kamma-visesa*, too, should be similarly interpreted.

What interests us more here is the fact that both explanations attempt to show that the difference between the sense-organs is due to the kamma or kammas of which they are the results. The reason for this is not far to seek. We saw how certain Buddhists, adopting a Vaiśeṣika theory, maintained that the difference between the sense-organs was due to the difference in their supporting primary elements. We also noticed what prevented the Theravādins from accepting that theory.[473] This explains why both explanations insist on the fact that the difference between the sense-organs is due to the kamma or kammas of which they are the results.

Finally a fact that has been implicit in the foregoing account of *kammasamuṭṭhāna-rūpa* should be made explicit here. The matter that comes into being through the action of kamma does not obtain outside of the body of a living being. This is only an implication arising from the fact that only the *indriya-rūpas*, the *hadayavatthu*,[474] and what is inseparably associated with them are recognized as *kammasamuṭṭhāna*.

The arrangement of rūpa-dhammas on the basis of *cittasamuṭṭhāna* and its negative may be considered now. The term *cittasamuṭṭhāna*, as observed by Mrs. Rhys Davids, does not imply creation of matter by mind.[475] In our account of the two *viññattis*, it was stated that some rūpa-dhammas arise in response to a thought, wholesome (*kusala*), unwholesome (*akusala*), or neutral (*avyākata*).[476] The implication is not that they are created but that they are set up or prompted by mind. It is precisely for this reason that in the Paṭṭhāna, consciousness (*citta*) and its concomitants (*cetasika*) are instanced as a condition by way of co-nascence (*sahajāta-paccaya*) in relation to all rūpa-dhammas qualified by *cittasamuṭṭhāna*.[477]

As in the case of *upādiṇṇa* and its negative, on the basis of *cittasamuṭṭhāna* and its negative, too, all rūpa-dhammas are made into three groups.[478] The first is recognized as invariably *citta-samuṭṭhāna*, and it consists of the two *viññattis*. We have already shown that these two items are not two discrete rūpa-dhammas in the sense that each signifies an *ākāra-vikāra* (a particular position or situation) of a set of (other) rūpa-dhammas.[479] We have also drawn attention to the fact that, since the set of rūpa-dhammas in question is *cittasamuṭṭhāna*, the Dhammasaṅganī has thought it proper to extend the same description to the two *viññattis* too.[480] And once the two *viññattis* are described as *cittasamuṭṭhāna*, it is but proper that this description should be further qualified as "invariably." For each of them represents an *ākāra·vikāra* of only those rūpa-dhammas that are *cittasamuṭṭhāna*.

The second group comes under both headings—that is, *cittasamuṭṭhāna* and its negative. It includes the four *mahābhūtas*, *rūpa*, *gandha*, *rasa*, *āhāra*, *sadda*, *ākāsa-dhātu*, the triad of *lahutā*, etc., *upacaya*, and *santati*. Their inclusion under the negative heading is because of the simple reason that they do not always arise in response to, or conditioned by, consciousness (*citta*). Their inclusion under the positive heading is because of the fact that they are the kinds of rūpa-dhammas, the *ākāra-vikāras* of which are represented by the two *viññattis*. In this case they are *cittasamuṭṭhāna*. As to the selection of the items included in this group, the following facts may be noted here. The first eight items are the basic elements present in every instance of matter. The ninth, *sadda*, refers to vocal sound associated with *vacīviññatti*. *Akāsa-dhātu*, which in this case represents the cavities and holes in the body, is also connected with the *viññattis*. In the production of vocal sound the cavity in the mouth, for instance, has its part to play. The triad of *lahutā*, etc., which represents bodily efficiency, could facilitate bodily movements involved in *kāya-viññatti*. These, it seems to us, are the reasons for recognizing the first thirteen items as (sometimes) *cittasamuṭṭhāna*. The inclusion of *upacaya* and *santati* need not deter us here. What we have said about their inclusion under *upādiṇṇa* applies here, too.

In the above (second) group we find certain items, which in the commentarial exegesis are recognized as *anipphanna*. Hence from its point of view, strictly speaking, all such items are not *cittasamuṭṭhāna*.

The third group is never *cittasamuṭṭhāna*. It consists of the eight *indriya-rūpa*s, *jaratā*, and *aniccatā*. The first eight, as we have seen, are invariably *upādiṇṇa*—that is, *kammasamuṭṭhāna*. Hence they must be included in this group. The inclusion of the next two items is because no cause or condition is assigned to them.[481]

The two headings that we have considered so far, *upādiṇṇa* (*kamma-samuṭṭhāna*) and *citta-samuṭṭhāna*, imply two generative conditions (*samuṭṭhāna-paccaya*) of matter—namely, kamma and *citta*. To this the commentators add *utu* and *āhāra*.

Utu (temperature or season) is another name for *tejo-dhātu*, which is one of the *mahābhūtas*, and which represents the phenomenon of heat and cold. *Āhāra* is the same as *kabaḷiṅkāra-āhāra*, which is one of the *upādā-rūpas*, and which represents the nutritive aspect of matter, the "quality" of nutrition. Both are recognized as two generative conditions of matter. The kinds of matter conditioned by *utu* and *āhāra* are called *utusamuṭṭhāna* and *āhārasamuṭṭhāna*, respectively.[482] Whereas *āhārasamuṭṭhāna-rūpa* is confined to the body of a living being, *utusamuṭṭhāna-rūpa* obtains both internally and externally—that is, as part of the matter that constitutes the body and is also outside of it.[483]

Finally there remains to be considered the classification of the rūpa-dhammas into two groups as *ajjhattika* and *bāhira*.[484] While the five sense-organs are brought under *ajjhattika-rūpa*, the remaining items are brought under *bāhira*.[485] This arrangement is not an Abhidhammic innovation, for it is implied in the classical list of twelve *āyatanas*, arranged in the same way, into two groups.

With reference to what are some items *ajjhattika* (internal) and the others *bāhira* (external)? Buddhist exegesis gives more than one explanation, and they all purport to show that no implication of *ātmavāda* (the belief in a soul, self) should be associated with the term *ajjhattika*, "belonging to the self."

According to one explanation, frequently repeated, *ajjhattika* means that which belongs to the *atta*. And the term *atta* is interpreted not as referring to soul, but as synonymous with *attabhāva*—that is, the empiric individuality as composed of mental and physical factors. Since the sense-organs such as *cakkhu*, *sota*, etc. exist only as a part of the complex that makes the living being, they are called *ajjhattika*, "belonging to the *attabhāva*."[486]

There are, however, other rūpa-dhammas that also go to make the living being.

Therefore one may ask why they are not brought under the heading *ajjhattika-rūpa*. The exclusion of such items as the four *mahābhūtas* is understandable, for unlike the sense-organs they do not exist exclusively as a part of the complex that makes the living being. But the same is not true of *itthindriya*, *purisindriya*, *rūpa-jīvitindriya*, and *hadaya-vatthu*. Along with the sense-organs they, too, are recognized as invariably *kammasamuṭṭhāna*. Because of this very fact[487]—not to mention any other—they never exist outside of the body of a living being.

Ācariya Sumaṅgala, the author of the Vibhāvinī Ṭīkā, seems to have taken notice of this situation when he observes that, as a matter of fact, rūpa-dhammas other than the sense-organs also go to make up what is called *attabhāva*, but as a matter of convention the latter alone are designated as *ajjhattika-rūpa*.[488] As an alternative explanation it is said that the sense-organs alone are *ajjhattika* par excellence (*visesato*), because they are so helpful to the *attabhāva* that they seem to say: "If it were not for us you would be like unto a log of wood!"[489]

The Abhidharmakośa, on the other hand, takes *ātman* as a synonymous term for *citta*, consciousness. Consciousness is the object of the notion of "self" (*ātman*); it is that which the people falsely take to be their self. Hence, by way of metaphor, it receives the name ātman. Then it observes that the sense-organs (including the *mano-dhātu*) are proximate (*pratyāsanna*, *abhyāsanna*) to consciousness because they are in fact its "point d'appui" (*āśraya*). For this reason the sense-organs are described as *ādhyātmika*, whereas *rūpa*, *rasa*, etc., which become the objects of consciousness, are described as *bāhya*, external (to consciousness).[490]

What all these explanations attempt to show is that the dichotomy between *ajjhattika* (*ādhyātmika*) and *bāhira* (*bāhya*) has no reference to a self (*atta*, *ātman*), because the Buddhist attitude to *ātmavāda* is one of emphatic denial.

However, in understanding why in the Dhammasaṅganī only the sense-organs are brought under the heading *ajjhattika-rūpa*, the explanation given in the Abhidharmakośa is more helpful than any other. If, as is suggested by the other explanations, *attabhāva* is the center with reference to which the distinction between "internal" (*ajjhattika*) and "external" (*bāhira*) is established, then this raises the question as to why such items as the two faculties of sex are excluded from the category of *ajjhattika-rūpa*. The question does not arise if, as is suggested by the Abhidharmakośa, consciousness (*citta*) is taken as the point of reference. That is to say, the bases or supports (*vatthu*, *nissaya*) of consciousness (*citta*) are internal to it, whereas the things that become the objects are external to it.

It is true that no consciousness can arise without reference to an object too. However, since the sense-organs are the very bases of consciousness, in this sense they are more proximate to it. This idea seems to be implied by the fact that the consciousnesses are named after their bases as *cakkhu-viññāṇa* (eye-consciousness), *sota-viññāṇa* (ear-consciousness), etc. The statement made in the commentary to the Paṭṭhāna—namely, that when consciousness arises, it seems to spring forth from within the sense-organs[491]—is based on the same idea.

Ācariya Sumaṅgala's statement—namely, that the use of the term *ajjhattika* to qualify only the sense-organs is mostly a matter of convention[492]—becomes more meaningful if it is understood in the context of an observation made by Sthavira (= Śrīlāta), a celebrity of the Dārṣṭāntika school. The latter rightly points out that the distinction between *ādhyātmika* and *bāhya* is not a hard and fast one but is of relative application (*pāryāyikaṃ*): as bases of consciousness the sense-organs alone are *ādhyātmika*, but since the sense-organs, too, can become the objects of consciousness, they become *bāhya* as well.[493]

Sthavira's observation could be confirmed from another point of view. From a Vibhāṣā passage, cited by Louis de la Vallée Poussin, one gathers that the difference between the two terms is established from two other points of view: (a) the dharmas that are found in the person proper (*svātmabhāva*) are personal; those that are found in another and those that are not integrated with living beings (*asattvākhya*) are external; (b) the dharmas integrated with living beings are personal; the others are external.[494]

A similar situation obtains in the Vibhaṅga and the Dhammasaṅganī: The two terms in question are used in the adverbial as *ajjhattaṃ* and *bahiddhā* to signify another distinction. *Rūpaṃ ajjhattaṃ* denotes the matter that makes up one's own person and *rūpaṃ bahiddhā* that which makes up all other living beings.[495] The point of reference differs from person to person. To A his own body is *ajjhattaṃ*, but to B it is *bahiddhā*. As such, it cannotbe identified with either (a) or (b) of the Vibhāṣā. Nor does it fall in line with the Nikāyas, where the two terms are often used in the adverbial to establish the dichotomy between the matter that constitutes the body of the living being and the matter that obtains outside of it. In the Vibhaṅga and the Dhammasaṅganī the same pair of terms is applied to the other four *khandhas*, too.[496] Perhaps for the sake of uniformity a stock formula is used in respect of *rūpakkhandha* as well as the other four *khandhas*. This explains why *rūpaṃ ajjhattaṃ* and *rūpaṃ bahiddhā*, as understood by these two works, do not represent matter in its totality.

CLASSIFICATION OF THE MATERIAL ELEMENTS

Classification Headings

A = upādā	a = anupādā
B = upādiṇṇa	b = anupādiṇṇa
C = upādiṇṇ'upādānīya	c = anupādiṇṇ'upādānīya
D = sanidassana	d = anidassana
E = sappaṭigha	e = appaṭigha
F = indriya	f = na indriya
G = mahābhūta	g = na mahābhūta
H = viññatti	h = na viññatti
I = cittasamuṭṭhāna	i = na cittasamuṭṭhāna
J = cittasahabhū	j = na cittasahabhū
K = cittānuparivatti	k = na cittānuparivatti

L = ajjhattika	l = bāhira
M = oḷārika	m = sukhuma
N = santike	n = dūre

Material Elements

1 = paṭhavī	10 = rūpa	19 = ākāsa
2 = tejo	11 = sadda	20 = lahutā
3 = vāyo	12 = gandha	21 = mudutā
4 = āpo	13 = rasa	22 = kammaññatā
5 = cakkhu	14 = itthindriya	23 = upacaya
6 = sota	15 = purisindriya	24 = santati
7 = ghāna	16 = jīvitindriya	25 = jaratā
8 = jivhā	17 = kāyaviññatti	26 = aniccatā
9 = kāya	18 = vacīviññatti	27 = āhāra

(*Hadaya-vatthu* is not known to the Dhammasaṅganī)

I. Classification of the 1st Section

I	A 5–27	a 1–4
II	B 5–9, 14–16, (1–4, 10, 12, 13, 19, 23, 24, 27)*	b 11, 17, 18, 20–22, 25, 26, (1–4, 10, 12, 13, 19, 23, 24, 27)*
III	C 5–9, 14–16, (1–4, 10, 12, 13, 19, 23, 24, 27)*	c 11, 17, 18, 20–22, 25, 26, (1–4, 10, 12, 13, 19, 23, 24, 27)*

*= The items indicated by this mark come under *upādiṇṇa* as well as under *anupādiṇṇa* (see above, 99–100) or under *cittasamuṭṭhāna* as well as under *na cittasamuṭṭhāna* (see above, 104–5).

	D	d
IV	10	1–9, 11–27
	E	e
V	1–3, 5–13	4, 14–27
	F	f
VI	5–9, 14–16	1–4, 10–13, 17–27
	G	g
VII	1–4	5–27
	H	h
VIII	17, 18	1–16, 19–27
	I	i
IX	17, 18, (1–4, 10–13, 19–24, 27)*	5–9, 14–16, 25, 26, (1–4, 10–13, 19–24, 27)*
	J	j
X	17, 18	1–16, 19–27
	K	k
XI	17, 18	1–16, 19–27
	L	l
XII	5–9	1–4, 10–27
	M	m
XIII	1–3, 5–13	4, 14–27
	N	n
XIV	1–3, 5–13	4, 14–27

II. Classification of the 2nd Section

	LA	1A	1a
i	5–9	10–27	1–4
	LB	lB	lb
ii	5–9	14–16, (1–4, 10, 12, 13, 19, 23, 24, 27)*	11, 17, 18, 20–22, 25, 26, (1–4, 10, 12, 13, 19, 23, 24, 27)*
	LC	lC	lc
iii	5–9	14–16, (1–4, 10, 12, 13, 19, 23, 24, 27)*	11, 17, 18, 20–22, 25, 26, (1–4, 10, 12, 13, 19, 23, 24, 27)*

iv	Ld 5–9	lD 10	ld 1–4, 11–27
v	LE 5–9	lE 1–3, 10–13	le 4, 14–27
vi	LF 5–9	lF 14–16	lf 1–4, 10–13, 17–27
vii	Lg 5–9	lG 1–4	lg 10–27
viii	Lh 5–9	lH 17, 18	lh 1–4, 10–16, 19–27
ix	Li 5–9	lI 17, 18, (1–4, 10–13, 19–24, 27)*	li 14–16, 25, 26, (1–4, 10–13 ,19–24, 27)*
x	Lj 5–9	lJ 17, 18	lj 1–4, 10–16, 19–27
xi	Lk 5–9	lK 17, 18	lk 1–4, 10–16, 19–27
xii	LM 5–9	lM 1–3, 10–13	lm 4, 14–27
xiii	LN 5–9	lN 4, 14–27	ln 1–3, 10–13

Classification of the 3rd Section

i	AB 5–9, 14–16 (10, 12, 13, 19, 23, 24, 27)	Ab 20–22, 25, 26, (10, 12, 13, 19, 23, 24, 27)*	aB (1–4)*	ab (1–4)*

ii	AC 5–9, 14–16, (10, 12, 13, 19, 23, 24, 27)*	Ac 11, 17, 18, 20–22, 25, 26, (10, 12, 13, 19, 23, 24, 27)*	aC (1–4)*	ac (1–4)*
iii	AE 5–13	Ae 14–27	aE 1–3	ae 4
iv	AM 5–13	Am 14–27	aM 1–3	am 4
v	AN 5–13	An 14–27	aN 1–3	an 4
vi	BD 10*	Bd 5–9, 14–15, (1–4, 12, 13, 19, 23, 24, 27)*	bD 10*	bd 11, 17, 18, 20–22, 25, 26, (1–4, 12, 13, 19, 23, 24, 27)*
vii	BE 5–9, (1–3, 10, 12, 13)*	Be 14–16, (4, 19, 23, 24, 27)*	bE 11, (1–3, 10, 12, 13)*	be 17, 18, 20–22, 25, 26, (4, 19, 23, 24, 27)*
viii	BG (1–4)*	Bg 5–9, 14–16, (10, 12, 13, 19, 23, 24, 27)*	bG (1–4)*	bg 11, 17, 18, 20–22, 24, 26, (10, 12, 13, 29, 23, 24, 27)*
ix	BM 5–9, (1–4, 10, 12, 13)*	Bm 14–16, (4, 19, 23, 24, 27)*	bM 11, (1–3, 10, 12, 13)*	bm 17, 18, 20–22, 25, 26, (4, 19, 23, 24, 27)*
x	BN 5–9, (1–3, 10, 12, 13)*	Bn 14–16, (4, 19, 23, 24, 27)*	bN 11, (1–3, 10, 12, 13)*	bn 17, 18, 20–22, 25, 26, (4, 19, 23, 24, 27)*

xi	CD 10*	Cd 5–9, 14–16, (1–4, 10, 12, 13, 19, 23, 24, 27)*	cD 10*	cd 11, 17, 18, 20–22, 25, 26, (1–4, 10, 12, 13, 19, 23, 24, 27)*
xii	CE 5–9, (1–3, 10, 12, 13)*	Ce 14–16, (4, 19, 23, 24, 27)*	cE 11, (1–3, 10, 12, 13)*	ce 17, 18, 20–22, 25, 26, (4, 19, 23, 24, 27)*
xiii	CG (1–4)*	Cg 5–9, 14–16, (10, 12, 13, 19, 23, 24, 27)*	cG (1–4)*	cg 11, 17, 18, 20–22, 25, 26, (10, 12, 13, 19, 23, 24, 27)*
xiv	CM 5–9, (1–3, 10, 12, 13)*	Cm 14–16, (4, 19, 23, 24, 27)*	cM 11, (1–3, 10, 12, 13)*	cm 17, 18, 20–22, 25, 26, (4, 19, 23, 24, 27)*
xv	CN 5–9, (1–3, 10, 12, 13)*	Cn 14–16, (4, 19, 23, 24, 27)*	cN 11, (1–3, 10, 12,13)*	cn 17, 18, 20–22, 25, 26, (4, 19, 23, 24, 27)*
xvi	EF 5–9	Ef 1–3, 10–13	eF 14–16	ef 4, 17–27
xvii	EG 1–3	Eg 5–13	eG 4	eg 14–27
xviii	FM 5–9	Fm 14–16	fM 1–3, 10–13	fm 4, 17–27
xix	FN 5–9	Fn 14–16	fN 1–3, 10–13	fn 4, 17–27
xx	GM 1–3	Gm 4	gM 5–13	gm 14–27
xxi	GN 1–3	Gn 4	gN 5–13	gn 14–27

7

CORRELATION OF MATERIAL ELEMENTS

THE BUDDHIST VIEW of the nature of reality is based on the two complementary methods of analysis and synthesis (*bheda-saṅgaha-naya*). The task of analysis is to show that the objects of our ordinary conceptual thought are not substantial entities or irreducible realities. The task of synthesis is to show that the ultimate factors into which they are resolvable (*dhammas*) are not distinct entities existing in themselves but interdependent nodes in a complex web of relationships. It is in order to accomplish this latter task that Buddhism proposes two versions of conditionality. Earlier is the one called *paṭiccasamuppāda*, the doctrine of dependent origination. The other is the *paccayākāra-naya*, the system of correlation introduced by the Theravāda Abhidhamma. Its purpose is not to substitute for the earlier one but to supplement it. Hence in the Visuddhimagga we find used a combined version of both methods of conditionality.

The Abhidhamma doctrine of conditionality is an integral part of the dhamma theory and therefore it assumes significance within its framework. Its purpose is not to explain the absolute origin of the mental and material factors into which our world of experience is analyzed. This situation is in full consonance with the early Buddhist doctrine of causality whose purpose is not to explain the absolute origin and the ultimate direction of the world but to describe the uninterrupted continuity of the saṃsāric process. According to Buddhist teachings, no temporal beginning of the universe is conceivable. Accordingly Buddhism dissociates itself from all cosmogonical causal theories that seek to trace the absolute origin of the world-process from some kind of uncaused transempirical reality.

There are three postulates that the Abhidhamma theory of conditionality recognizes as axiomatic:

1. Nothing arises without the appropriate causes and conditions. This is to rule out the theory of fortuitous origination (*adhicca-samuppanna*), the theory that rejects all principles of causality and conditionality.[497]
2. Nothing arises from a single cause. This is to rule out all theories of singular causes (*ekakāraṇavāda*).[498] Their rejection means that the Abhidhamma dissociates itself from all monistic theories that seek to explain the origin of the world from a single cause, whether it is conceived as a personal God or impersonal Godhead.
3. Nothing arises as a single, solitary phenomenon (*ekassa dhammassa uppatti paṭisedhitā hoti*).[499] This amounts to saying that on the basis of a single cause, or on the basis of a multiplicity of causes, or purely due to fortuitous circumstances, there can never be a single effect or a solitary phenomenon.
4. It is on the rejection of these three views that the Abhidhamma doctrine of conditionality is founded. Their rejection means: from a plurality of causes a plurality of effects takes place.

Applied to the Abhidhamma analysis of mind and matter, this means that a multiplicity of dhammas brings about a multiplicity of other dhammas.

One clear conclusion emerging from this situation is that the dhammas always arise not as solitary phenomena, but as combinations or clusters. This is true of both mind and matter. Hence whenever consciousness arises, together with it arise at least seven mental factors—namely, contact, feeling, perception, volition, one-pointedness, psychic life, and attention.[500] Thus even the smallest psychic unit or moment of consciousness turns out to be a complex corelational system.

In the same way, the smallest unit of matter, called the "basic octad" (*suddhaṭṭhaka*), is in the final analysis a cluster of eight material factors—namely, the four great elements of matter and four material elements dependent on them: color, odor, taste, and nutritive essence. None of these eight material dhammas arise singly because they are necessarily coexistent and positionally inseparable.[501]

There are two other basic factors to be noted here. The first is that no mental or material factor can propel itself into existence by its own power. By their very nature the dhammas are completely devoid of own-power or own-sway (*dhammānaṃ savasavattitābhimāno paṭisedhito hoti*).[502] This is rule out the possibility of self-causation. The other is that no mental or material dhamma can be brought into being by a power external to the dhamma either. This is to rule out the possibility of external causation. The rejection of these two theories means that only dhammas help other dhammas to arise and persist in being. There is another thing that merits our attention here. Buddhist exegesis warns us that the cause should not be understood as some kind of potential effect. "The cause is not pregnant with the effect" (*na phalena sagabbho*) as the *prakṛti*, the primordial cause of the Sāṃkhya philosophy (*pakativādīnaṃ pakati viya*). The allusion is to the evolutionary theory of causation (*satkāryavāda*), according to which the effect remains in a latent form in the cause, and therefore the effect is some kind of evolute of the cause. Hence the Buddhist commentaries insist that "the cause is not in the effect" (*phale hetu natthi*), "the effect is empty of the cause" (*hetu-suññaṃ phalaṃ*).[503]

It is with reference to the system of correlation (*paccayākāra-naya*) that the Abhidhamma seeks to explain the interdependence and the conditionality of all dhammas (elements of existence). It is said to provide an explanation as to the causal relation of all dhammas, not only in their temporal sequence but also in their spatial concomitance. In regard to this subject there are two things that should be noted at the very outset—namely, (a) *paccaya*, the condition or the relating thing, and (b) *paccayuppanna-dhamma*, the conditioned or the related thing. In a given relation between two dhammas, if one constitutes a necessary ground for the existence of the other, then it is designated as *paccaya*, and the other—that is, what is conditioned thereby—*paccayuppanna*. In the words of Ācariya Buddhaghosa, whatever dhamma that is a support for the persistence or origination of another is to be taken as the *paccaya* of the latter. It is to be understood, he says, in the sense of assisting in the arising or coming to be of the conditioned (*paccayuppanna*) dhamma.[504]

In all there are twenty-four *paccayas*, that is, twenty-four ways in which one dhamma is a condition for another—namely, *hetu* (moral root), *ārammaṇa* (object), *adhipati* (dominance), *anantara* (contiguity), *samanantara* (immediate contiguity), *sahajāta* (co-nascence), *aññamañña* (reciprocity), *nissaya* (basis), *upanissaya* (inducement), *purejāta* (pre-nascence), *pacchājāta* (post-nascence), *āsevana* (habitual recurrence), *kamma* (volitional action), *vipāka* (retribution), *āhāra* (nutriment), *indriya* (faculty), *jhāna* (absorption), *magga* (path), *sampayutta* (association), *vippayutta* (dissociation), *atthi* (presence), *natthi* (absence), *vigata* (disappearance), and *avigata* (non-disappearance).[505]

The schools of Sanskrit Buddhism postulate six kinds of *hetu* (cause) and four kinds of *pratyaya* (condition) as factors responsible for the origination of all dharmas. *Kāraṇa-hetu* (the raison d'être), *sahabhū-hetu* (coexistent cause), *sabhāga-hetu* (identical cause), *saṃprayukta-hetu* (associated cause), *sarvatraga-hetu* (universal cause), and *vipāka-hetu* (cause of retribution) are the six kinds of *hetu*. *Hetu-pratyaya* (cause-condition), *samanantara-pratyaya* (immediate contiguity-condition), *ālambaṇa-pratyaya* (object-condition), and *adhipati-pratyaya* (dominance-condition) are the four kinds of *pratyaya*.[506]

Ācārya Yaśomitra says that no distinction is drawn between *hetu* and *pratyaya* and that both are synonymous.[507] We may then ask why some items are brought under *hetu* and the others under *pratyaya*. The answer given is that the exposition of *hetu* is based on an examination of causes by way of non-obstacle (*avighna-bhāva*), coexistence (*sahabhūtva*), identity (*sadṛśatva*), etc., whereas that of the *pratyayas* is based on an examination of causes by way of immediate contiguity (*samanantara*), etc.[508] That there is, however, an element of redundancy involved here is shown by the explanation given as to the relation between the two groups.

What one can gather from the different explanations as to the relation between the six *hetus* and the four *pratyayas* is that the two groups have not been considered as completely exclusive of each other. In other words, the two items in question are understood as more or less convertible. This is in keeping with the terminology of the Nikāyas where *hetu* and *paccaya* are used in apposition,[509] but is quite in contrast to the Pāli Abhidhamma Piṭaka where the use of *hetu* is restricted to denote only those factors (*lobha*, *dosa*, *moha*, etc.) that determine the ethical quality of volitional acts.[510]

This is a brief résumé of the Theravādins' *paccayākāra-naya* and of the *hetus* and *pratyaya*s of the schools of Sanskrit Buddhism.[511] We are interested in the subject only insofar as it bears some relevance to the analysis of matter. In regard to this subject, too, there are many points of contact between the Theravāda and the other schools of Buddhist thought. In this connection there are two main things to be noted.

One is that the Theravādins have postulated a comparatively large number of *paccayas*. However, an examination of the list should show that sometimes an item is repeated under different names; sometimes a group of (already mentioned) items are brought under a new heading. That the Theravādins were not unaware of this situation is shown by Ācariya Anuruddha's observation—namely, that the twenty-four *paccayas* are reducible to six.[512]

Second, as we have already observed, in the schools of Sanskrit Buddhism the two terms *hetu* and *pratyaya* are recognized as more or less convertible. Therefore, in finding out what corresponds to (Pāli) *paccayas* one need not confine oneself to (Sanskrit) *pratyayas*, but may take into account the *hetus*, too. Third, as Louis de la Vallée Poussin remarks, certain differences concern the nomenclature but not the interpretation.[513] For example, the *aññamañña-sahajāta-paccaya* of the Theravādins is the same as the *sahabhū-hetu* of the Sarvāstivādins.[514] To this should be added: sometimes the nomenclature remains the same but the interpretation differs. For example, the *hetu-paccaya* of Pāli Buddhism has practically no correspondence with the *hetu-pratyaya* of the Sanskrit schools.[515]

Taking all these points into consideration, we may examine how material dhammas enter into the system of correlation of the Theravādins. Wherever possible we may also observe the parallel cases as found in the other systems of Buddhist thought. In the main, we are interested in those relations where what is material constitutes either a *paccaya* or a *paccayuppanna-dhamma*. In other words, the following discussion is an attempt to unfold the implications of the phrase *rūpaṃ sappaccayaṃ*, which occurs in the *Dhammasaṅgaṇi*.[516]

Ārammaṇa-paccaya

Ārammaṇa-paccaya (= *ālambaṇa-pratyaya*) can mean anything that, as object, constitutes a condition for the arising of consciousness (*citta*) and its concomitants (*cetasika*).[517] We have already indicated how all rūpa-dhammas fall under six different headings according to the way they become the objects of consciousness.[518] *Rūpa*, *sadda*, *gandha*, *rasa*, and *phoṭṭhabba* are known as objects of the five kinds of *viññāṇa* named after the corresponding sense-organs (= *cakkhu-viññāṇa*, *sota-viññāṇa*, etc.), and the remaining rūpa-dhammas as the objects of *mano-viññāṇa*. Hence, while the first five items are instanced as *ārammaṇa-paccayas* in relation to the first five kinds of *viññāṇa*, the remaining rūpa-dhammas are instanced as *ārammaṇa-paccayas* in relation to the sixth.

Adhipati-paccaya

Adhipati-paccaya, the condition by way of dominance, is of two varieties: *ārammaṇādhipati* and *sahajātādhipati*.

The former is the same as *ārammaṇa-paccaya*, but for this difference: only those objects that exert a dominant influence on the consciousness and its concomitants are recognized as *ārammaṇādhipati*.[519]

The latter applies only to the four kinds of *iddhipāda*—namely, *chanda-samādhi* (concentration of intention), *viriya-samādhi* (concentration of energy), *citta-samādhi* (concentration of consciousness), and *vīmaṃsa-samādhi* (concentration of investigation).[520] These four factors alone are recognized as *sahajātādhipati* because they exert an overwhelming influence on the mental states that arise simultaneously with them. They are so powerful that at a given moment only one of them can arise.[521] If a particular consciousness and its concomitants, which are influenced by one of these *iddhipādas*, give rise to *cittasamuṭṭhāna-rūpa*, then this *cittasamuṭṭhāna-rūpa* is also recognized as influenced by that *iddhipāda*.[522] This is the position of matter in relation to *sahajātādhipati-paccaya*. In this particular relation the position of matter is only that of the *paccayuppanna-dhamma* (conditioned).

The *adhipati-paccaya* of the Theravādins should not be confused with the *adhipati-pratyaya* of the Abhidharmakośa. According to the latter work, it is the same as *kāraṇa-hetu*. As such its scope is greater than that of any other *pratyaya*. For what is called *kāraṇa-hetu* applies to all *saṃskṛta-dharmas* but for one exception: a dharma is not the *kāraṇa-hetu* of itself. The function of *kāraṇa-hetu* is to be understood not in a positive sense, that is, as a *kāraka* (agent), but in a negative sense, that is, as offering no obstacle.[523] Its universal application is based on the contention that no dharma constitutes an obstacle (*avighna-bhāvāvasthā*) to the origination of those other dharmas which are destined to be originated (*uppattimant*).[524] The implication is that "it does not directly make any disturbance in the causal nexus."[525]

There are two reasons why *kāraṇa-hetu* is also called *adhipati-pratyaya*: the first is that it applies to the largest number of dharmas (*adhikaḥ pratyayaḥ*); the second is that it constitutes a condition in relation to the largest number of dharmas (*adhikasya pratyayaḥ*).[526]

That there is a big difference between the *adhipati-pratyaya* of the Abhidharmakośa and that of the Theravādins is obvious. Stated briefly, for the Abhidharmakośa, *adhipati* signifies dominance mainly by way of quantity, whereas for the Theravādins, *adhipati* signifies dominance solely by way of quality.[527]

In view of the fact that *kāraṇa-hetu* (= *adhipati-pratyaya*) applies to all dharmas, it goes without saying that each and every rūpa-dharma constitutes a *kārana-hetu*, not only in relation to the other rūpa-dharmas but also in relation to all *arūpa-dharmas* (mental elements).

Sahajāta-paccaya

In the case of two dhammas, if one cannot arise unless simultaneously with the arising of the other, then the latter is recognized as a *sahajāta-paccaya* (co-nascence condition) in relation to the former. If the relation between A and B is such that B always arises simultaneously with A, then A is the *paccaya* and B is the *paccayuppana-dhamma*. This does not necessarily mean that A cannot arise independently of B. It only means that under no circumstances can B arise independently of A. The two are not on a par.[528]

When they are on a par, the relation between them is described as *aññamañña*, reciprocal. It is one of mutual support. In this case, while A is a *sahajāta-paccaya* in relation to B, B too is a *sahajāta-paccaya* in relation to A. What is true of one is equally true of the other.[529] Accordingly, in such a relation each becomes at one and the same time the *paccaya* as well as the *paccayuppanna-dhamma*.[530]

The latter variety of *sahajāta-paccaya*, which is distinguished from the former by being qualified as *aññamañña*, is the same as the *sahabhū-hetu* of the Sarvāstivādins. For in the case of *sahabhū-hetu*, too, the related things are considered not only as causes but also as effects in relation to each other.[531]

The Sautrāntikas take strong exception to this principle of reciprocal conditionality or causation. They concede, however, that between two coexistent things one could become the cause of the other, and cite the relation between the visual organ and the visual consciousness as a case in point. But they refuse to believe that two coexistent things could be related in such a way that one becomes at one and the same time the cause as well as the effect of the other.[532] The counterargument of the Sarvāstivādins amounts to this: There are certain things that always arise simultaneously; when one is present the others are also present, and when one is absent the others are also absent. Therefore, it is to be concluded that the relation between such things is one of reciprocal causation.[533]

The well-known example cited in this connection is that of three sticks set upright, all leaning against one another at their upper ends.[534] The Sautrāntikas contend that there is a complex of anterior causes that is responsible for this peculiar position of the sticks (because of which position the three sticks do not fall to the ground).[535]

The objection of the Sautrāntikas to recognizing the *sahabhū-hetu* is not without significance, for it shows that their general policy of reducing the lists[536] was applied to the list of *hetus* and *pratyayas* as well.

How the two kinds of *sahajāta-paccaya* apply to matter may be considered now.

Two cases were noted in two previous chapters: (a) The four *mahābhūtas* are a *sahajāta-paccaya* (non-reciprocal) in relation to the *upādā-rūpas*. (b) Each of the *mahābhūtas* is a *sahajāta-paccaya* (*aññamañña* = reciprocal) in relation to the other.[537] The first establishes the necessary dependence of the *upādā-rūpas* on the *mahābhūtas*, and the second the coordinate position of the *mahābhūtas*.

There are two more cases to be noted: (a) Consciousness and consciousness-concomitants are a *sahajāta-paccaya* (non-reciprocal) in relation to *cittasamuṭṭhāna-rūpa*.[538] Here the conditionality is not recognized as reciprocal because of the simple reason that a consciousness and its concomitants can arise without necessarily giving rise to *cittasamuṭṭhāna-rūpa*. (b) The other refers to the relation between *nāma* (mind) and *rūpa* (matter) at the moment of conception (*paṭisandhi*). Here the conditionality is recognized as reciprocal, with a view to showing that both come into being simultaneously and that the one cannot come into being independently of the other.[539]

Nissaya-paccaya

This refers to something that aids something else in the manner of a base or foundation. Consequently, all the examples given with reference to *sahajāta-paccaya* are repeated as *nissaya-paccaya*s, too. Again, since the first five sense-organs are the physical bases of the first five kinds of consciousness named after them, the former are instanced as *nissaya-paccayas* in relation to the latter. Similarly is explained the position of *hadaya-vatthu* (i.e., *yaṃ rūpaṃ taṃ rūpaṃ* of the Paṭṭhāna)[540] in its relation to *mano* and *mano-viññāṇa*.[541]

Purejāta- and Pacchājāta-paccaya

Purejāta-paccaya (pre-nascent condition) refers to something that, having arisen first, becomes a support to something else that arises later; and *pacchājāta-paccaya* (post-nascent condition) refers to something that, having arisen later, becomes a support to something else that has arisen earlier.[542] In the first as well as in the second, that which becomes the *paccaya* (condition) and that which becomes the *paccayuppanna* (conditioned) are not co-nascent. The first is like the father who supports his son. The second is like the son who supports his father.

The first five sense-organs (*cakkhu*, *sota*, etc.) and the corresponding sense-objects (*rūpa*, *sadda*, etc.) are recognized as *purejāta-paccayas* in relation to the first five kinds of consciousness (*cakkhu-viññāṇa*, *sota-viññāṇa*, etc.).[543] Their recognition as such is because of the circumstance that by the time, say, visual consciousness arises, the organ of sight and the visible have been existing. The organ of sight and the visible do not come into existence simultaneously with the visual consciousness, in relation to which they become *paccayas*. This statement is true enough from the point of view of the Abhidhamma Piṭaka and the earlier works where the relative duration of matter is recognized.[544] But as we have already seen, the early doctrine of impermanence later gave rise to a formulated theory of moments.[545]

It may be recalled here that according to the theory in question, each element of existence, mental or material, has three momentary phases—namely, the nascent (*uppāda*), the static (*ṭhiti*), and the cessant (*bhaṅga*). There is, however, this difference to be noted: the static phase (*ṭhiti*) of a material element is longer than that of a mental element.[546] Therefore, if a material element and a mental element come into existence simultaneously, they will not cease to exist simultaneously. The former will continue to exist (for some time) even after the cessation of the latter. Thus, the principle—namely, that matter is of longer duration than mind—is not abandoned even after the development of the theory of moments.

From this it follows that a material element, which arises earlier, can become a condition in relation to a mental element, which arises later. In other words, the former can become a *purejāta-paccaya* in relation to the latter. We have already noted that the first five sense-organs and the corresponding sense-objects are *purejāta-paccayas* for the first five kinds of consciousness. The time-difference involved here is explained by the commentators as follows: When consciousness arises, say, with the organ of sight as its basis and the visible (*rūpa*) as its object, then both the organ of sight and the visible (*rūpa*), are in their static phase (*ṭhiti*).[547] That is to say, at this time both the organ of sight and the visible (*rūpa*) have passed their nascent phase (*uppāda*). It is because of this chronological priority that they are described as *purejāta*, and it is because they become the basis and the object, respectively, of visual consciousness that they are considered as *paccayas*.

The other item that is considered as *purejāta-paccaya* is the *hadaya-vatthu*—that is, in relation to *mano* and *mano-viññāṇa*.[548] At the moment of conception, however, the relation is not of this kind. For, as we have already indicated,[549] at this moment *hadaya-vatthu* and *manāyatana* come into being simultaneously.

In the case of the relation by way of *pacchājāta*, the *paccaya* is always mental.

Consciousness (*citta*) and its concomitants (*cetasika*) constitute a *pacchājāta-paccaya* for (the preservation of) the body.[550] This too is based on the principle that matter is of longer duration than mind. Since the static phase (*ṭhiti*) of a material element is longer than that of a mental element, there is the possibility of the matter of the body being conditioned by post-nascent (*pacchājāta*) consciousness and its concomitants.

It will be seen that *purejāta-* and *pacchājāta-paccaya* do not apply to those relations where both *paccaya* (condition) and *paccayuppanna* (conditioned) are mental. This is because of the following reason: Mental elements arise either simultaneously or in immediate contiguity. If they arise simultaneously, they must perish simultaneously. If they arise in immediate contiguity, then the immediately preceding one has to perish before the immediately succeeding one could appear. Hence a mental element cannot become either a *purejāta-* or a *pacchājāta-paccaya* in relation to another mental element.[551]

Kamma-paccaya

As a *paccaya* in the system of correlation, kamma is of two kinds: If what is conditioned thereby arises simultaneously with it, it is known as *sahajāta*. If what is conditioned thereby is asynchronous, it is known as *nānākhaṇika*. In both cases the reference is to *cetanā*, volition.

Concerning the first, it is said that *cetanā*, whether wholesome (*kusala*) or unwholesome (*akusala*), forms a *paccaya* for those mental states that arise together with it. If these mental states give rise to (*cittasamuṭṭhāna*) *rūpa*, then the latter too is considered as conditioned by that *cetanā*. The implication is that the mental states and the matter in question are determined, fashioned, and impelled by the force of *cetanā*.[552]

Cetanā (volition), it may be noted here, is one of those *cetasikas* that arise with every kind of consciousness. Hence it is described as *sabba-citta-sādhāraṇa*.[553] From this it follows that *citta-samuṭṭhāna-rūpa* is always conditioned by *cetanā*. And, if kamma is another name for *cetanā*, it may be asked why *cittasamuṭṭhāna-rūpa* is not described as "*kammasamuṭṭhāna-rūpa*." This calls for a consideration of the Buddhist theory concerning the fruition of kamma.

The Buddhists maintain that the effect of kamma never takes place concurrently with the kamma.[554] It is argued that if kamma fructifies at the very moment of its occurrence, then a person who performs a kamma that is conducive to birth in heaven will be born a *deva* at that very moment.[555] This view—namely, that the effect of kamma is not synchronous with the kamma itself—is maintained in the Abhidharmakośa, too. This work goes on to say that the fruition of karma does not take place even immediately after (*anantara*) the occurrence of the karma.[556]

In view of the fact that kamma and kammic fruition do not take place simultaneously, the *cittasamuṭṭhāna-rūpa* that arises together with, and conditioned by, *cetanā* cannot be understood as the fruition of that *cetanā* (*kamma*). In other words, the relation between *cetanā* and *cittasamuṭṭhāna-rūpa* is not the same as that between kamma (*cetanā*) and its fruit (*phala*). This does not mean that *cetanā* is not partly responsible for the arising of the matter in question. For otherwise the former would not have been recognized as a *paccaya* in relation to the latter.

Consequently the second variety of *kamma-paccaya*, which is described as *nānākhaṇika*, is the *kamma-paccaya* par excellence. The relation involved here is that between kamma (*cetanā*) and its *phala* (fruit, effect), because the qualification, *nānākhaṇika*, signifies a difference in time in their occurrence. It is in order to account for all those mental and material elements that come into being as the result (*phala*) of kamma that this variety of *paccaya* is established. As for matter, we have already stated that the first five sense-organs, the two faculties of sex, the physical basis of mental activity, and all other material elements that are inseparably associated with them are results of kamma (*kammasamuṭṭhāna*).[557] Suffice it to note here that it is in relation to the above kinds of matter that kamma (*nānākhaṇika*) constitutes a *paccaya*.

Vipāka-paccaya

In the previous chapter we drew attention to the fact that in the Abhidhamma Piṭaka the use of the term *vipāka* is restricted to denote only those results of kamma that are mental.[558] It is in keeping with this tradition that only mental elements are instanced as examples of *vipāka-paccaya*. This does not mean that matter cannot become the *paccayuppanna* (the conditioned) in relation to *vipāka-paccaya*.

Vipāka (results of kamma that are mental) is considered to be of a very delicate and tranquil nature (*santabhāva*). For, it comes into being as if it were not impelled by any effort (*nirussāha*). Hence, in the capacity of a *paccaya*, *vipāka* exerts a tranquilizing influence on its *paccayuppanna-dhamma*.[559]

At the time of conception (*okkantikkhaṇe*), all the mental elements are *vipāka*.

As such, at this time they all form a *paccaya* by way of *vipāka* for the matter that comes into being simultaneously with them.[560] Again, the (*cittasamuṭṭhāna*) *rūpa* that arises in response to a consciousness, and its concomitants that are *vipāka*, is also recognized as conditioned by *vipāka-paccaya*.[561] These are the two occasions when matter comes under the influence of *vipāka*.

The *vipāka-paccaya* of Pāli Buddhism does not correspond to the *vipāka-hetu* of the schools of Sanskrit Buddhism.

In the case of the former, as we have seen, *vipāka* itself is the *paccaya*. As such, *vipāka-paccaya* does not mean condition in relation to *vipāka*. It means condition by way of *vipāka*. The kind of relation involved here applies to things that arise simultaneously.

In contrast, the latter refers to the cause (*hetu*) of *vipāka*: "*vipākasya phalasya hetur vipāka-hetuḥ*."[562] The cause (*hetu*) of *vipāka* is karma. Therefore the *vipāka-hetu* of the schools of Sanskrit Buddhism corresponds to the *kamma-paccaya* (i.e., *nānākhaṇika*) of Pāli Buddhism. The kind of relation involved here is between the antecedent karma and the subsequently arising karma-result (*phala*).

Āhāra-paccaya

In its technical sense, *āhāra* (food, nutriment) means not only *kabaḷiṅkāra-āhāra*, which is one of the material elements, but also *phassa* (sensory or mental impression), *cetanā* (volition), and *citta* (consciousness), for they all nourish, sustain, and keep going the empiric individuality as composed of mental and material factors. Each of them is therefore cited as *āhāra-paccaya*, condition by way of nutriment. In their capacity as *paccayas*, they nourish their related things so as to enable them to endure long, to develop, to flourish, and to thrive.[563]

Of the last three items, *phassa* and *cetanā* are two of the *cetasikas* that arise with every kind of consciousness.[564] And the other—that is, *citta*—means consciousness itself. As such, whenever *cittasamuṭṭhāna-rūpa* arises, it is always conditioned by these three *āhāra-paccayas*. And, as stated above,[565] at the moment of conception all the mental elements are a condition in relation to all the material elements. Therefore matter at the time of conception is also similarly conditioned.[566]

The last—that is, *kabaḷiṅkāra-āhāra*, which stands for the material "quality" of nutrition—nourishes and sustains the body. Hence the former is postulated as *āhāra-paccaya* in relation to the latter.[567]

Indriya-paccaya

Indriya-paccaya, the condition by way of faculty, is like *adhipati-paccaya*, the condition by way of dominance, in the sense that it exercises a dominating influence over the things related to it.[568]

In all there are twenty-two *indriyas*. Of them, fourteen are *arūpino*, mental (one is *mano* and the other thirteen are *cetasikas*). They become *indriya-paccayas* in relation to *cittasamuṭṭhāna-rūpa*.[569]

The remaining eight *indriyas*—namely, the first five sense-organs, the two faculties of sex, and the (material) faculty of life—are *rūpino*, material. The two faculties of sex, though designated as *indriya*, are not postulated as *indriya-paccayas*.[570]

Over what and what things the first six items wield a dominating influence has already been indicated: The sense-organs are *indriya-paccayas* in relation to the five kinds of consciousness named after them, in the sense that if the former are weak the latter too become weak, and if the former are strong the latter too become strong.[571] The uninterrupted continuity of the *kammasamuṭṭhāna-rūpa* depends on the presence of the material faculty of life.[572] It is in this sense that the latter wields a dominating influence on the former.

As to the non-recognition of the two faculties of sex as *indriya-paccayas*, the commentators give the following explanation: At the initial stages of the embryonic development, although the faculty of masculinity and the faculty of femininity are present, they do not perform their respective functions—that is to say, they do not bring about the manifestation of sex distinctions. Since they remain dormant and inactive at this stage, it is to be concluded that they are not *indriya-paccayas*. This conclusion is based on the contention that at no time does an element of existence, whether mental or material, which can rightly be called an *indriya-paccaya*, remain inactive or dormant.[573]

From the point of view of the Abhidhamma Piṭaka, the above explanation does not arise. For, as we have seen,[574] according to the Abhidhamma Piṭaka, the two faculties of sex mean femininity and masculinity, and not their raison d'être as interpreted in the commentaries.

Jhāna- and *Magga-paccaya*s

The seven *jhāna* factors (e.g., thought-conception, discursive thinking, etc.) and the twelve path factors (e.g., right view, right intention, etc.) influence those mental states that arise in association with them. And, if such mental states give rise to (*cittasamuṭṭhāna*) *rūpa*, the latter too is considered as influenced accordingly.[575]

Hetu-paccaya

We have already indicated how *hetu-pratyaya* is explained in the Abhidharmakośa: every dharma is a *hetu-pratyaya* in relation to all other dharmas. The implication is that no dharma constitutes an obstacle (*avighnabhāvāvasthā*) to the origination of those other dharmas that are destined to be originated. Hence *hetu-pratyaya* is not a *kāraka*—that is, it is not something that helps something else positively. Its function is negative, that is, non-obstruction.[576]

According to the Theravādins, on the other hand, *hetu-paccaya* signifies those factors that determine the ethical quality of volitional acts. The factors in question are *lobha* (covetousness), *dosa* (hatred), *moha* (delusion), and their opposites. It is on the basis of these factors that a particular thought is judged as wholesome (*kusala*) or unwholesome (*akusala*).[577]

They form *paccayas* by way of *hetu*, "moral root," in relation to those mental states that arise together with them. And if such mental states give rise to (*cittasamuṭṭhāna*) *rūpa*, the latter too is considered as conditioned thereby.[578]

This does not mean that material elements too become morally qualifiable as wholesome (*kusala*) or unwholesome (*akusala*). For it is a well-established thesis that no ethical quality can be predicated of matter.[579] In this connection it should be noted that the function of *lobha*, *dosa*, etc., is not limited to determining the ethical quality of mental states. Those mental states that are conditioned by them are said to be firm and well-fixed like firmly rooted trees.[580] Consequently the (*cittasamuṭṭhāna*) *rūpa* that arises in response to such mental states does also become firm and well-fixed. It is in this sense that *lobha*, *dosa*, etc., are instanced as *hetu-paccayas* in relation to *cittasamuṭṭhāna-rūpa*.

Atthi- and *Avigata-paccayas*

As two *paccayas*, *atthi* (presence) and *avigata* (non-abeyance) are completely identical. They need not deter us here, for they are two names given to a combination of four *paccayas*—namely, *sahajāta* (co-nascence), *aññamañña* (reciprocity), *nissaya* (basis), and *purejāta* (pre-nascence).[581] We have already examined their implications with reference to matter.[582]

Upanissaya-paccaya

The Paṭṭhāna does not include any of the material elements in the relation based on the *upanissaya-paccaya*, the condition by way of inducement. In the commentaries, however, the sense-objects are cited as constituting *ārammaṇa-upanissaya-paccaya*s, object-inducement-conditions, in relation to consciousness and its concomitants. What is called *ārammaṇa-upanissaya* need not be examined here, for it corresponds to *ārammaṇādhipati*.[583]

So far we have been considering those relations with reference to which matter becomes either a *paccaya* or a *paccayuppanna-dhamma*. There are certain varieties of relation into which matter does not enter. They are based on the following *paccayas*: *āsevana*, *sampayutta*, *anantara*, *samanantara*, *natthi*, and *vigata*. We may consider, as briefly as possible, why such relations are not obtainable in the domain of matter.

The function of *āsevana-paccaya*, the condition by way of habitual recurrence, is that of causing its *paccayuppanna-dhammas* to accept its inspiration for them to gain greater and greater proficiency. It is just as in learning by heart through constant repetition the later recitation becomes gradually easier and easier.[584] Now, this so-called energy or proficiency that each succeeding event comes to acquire is interpreted and evaluated entirely in ethical terms.[585] But, as stated earlier,[586] no ethical quality can be predicated of material phenomena—hence its exclusion from this kind of relation.

Consciousness (*citta*) and its concomitants (*cetasika*) are said to be related by way of *sampayutta*, association, when they have the following four characteristics: the same sense-organ as their basis (*ekavatthu*), the same object (*ekārammaṇa*), simultaneous origination (*ekuppāda*), and simultaneous cessation (*ekanirodha*).[587] Material elements cannot be so related because of the simple reason that they cannot share the above-mentioned four characteristics in toto. For although the last two characteristics apply to them—for example, the four *mahābhūtas* that come into being simultaneously and cease to exist simultaneously—the first two do not. Nor can mind (*nāma*) and matter (*rūpa*) be so related. For a mental element and a material element can have in common only one of the above four characteristics—that is, either simultaneous origination (*ekuppāda*) or simultaneous cessation (*ekanirodha*): If they arise simultaneously—for example, at the moment of conception—then they do not cease to exist simultaneously. If they cease to exist simultaneously, then they could not have arisen simultaneously. This is based on the theory that the duration of a material element is longer than that of a mental element.[588]

It is for these reasons that the relation between mind and matter is described as one of *vippayutta*, dissociation, and not *sampayutta*. All mental elements are *vippayutta* in relation to all material elements, and vice versa.[589] However, only the physical bases of consciousness—namely, the first five sense-organs and the heart-basis (*hadaya-vatthu*)—are considered as *vippayutta-paccaya*s.[590] It is said that when consciousness springs up, it springs up as if it were "issuing forth" (*nikkhantā viya*) from within its physical basis. Thus there is some kind of close association between the consciousness and the physical basis—an association not observable between the consciousness and the sense-object. Hence the physical basis alone is said to constitute a *vippayutta-paccaya* in relation to the consciousness.[591] This conclusion seems to be based on the idea that when something is related to something else by way of *vippayutta-paccaya*, there should exist a close connection between them—an idea that reminds us of the definition given to *citta-viprayukta-saṃskāras* in the schools of Sanskrit Buddhism.[592]

Anantara (contiguity) and *samanantara* (immediate contiguity) are but two names given to the same kind of *paccaya*. All classes of consciousness (*citta*) and their concomitants (*cetasika*), which have just ceased to exist, are *anantara*-or *samanantara-paccaya*s in relation to all classes of consciousness and their concomitants, which arise in the immediately succeeding moment.[593] The schools of Sanskrit Buddhism, too, understand *samanantara-pratyaya* in a similar way, and like the Theravāda they, too, apply it only to mental elements.[594]

What concerns us here is why *samanantara-paccaya* is excluded from the domain of matter. It is stated that only those phenomena that are capable of giving rise to other phenomena, immediately after their cessation, are reckoned as *samanantara-paccayas*, conditions by way of immediate contiguity.[595] Since *samanantara-paccaya* is applied only to mental elements, it is implied that the succession of elements in a regular order is not always true of material elements.

As two *paccayas*, there is no difference between *natthi* (absence) and *vigata* (abeyance).[596] The definitions and the examples given in respect of them show that they are identical with *samanantara-paccaya*. The Paṭṭhāna says: "*Samanantara-vigatā cittacetasikā dhammā paccuppannānaṃ cittacetasikānaṃ vigata-paccayena paccayo.*"[597] (Those consciousnesses and their concomitants that have just ceased to exist are a condition by way of disappearance to those consciousnesses and their concomitants that have just arisen.) This is the same as *samanantara-paccaya* stated differently. The immediately preceding dhamma is a condition for the immediately succeeding dhamma, in the sense that the disappearance of the former affords an opportunity for the origination of the latter. Since these two *paccayas* represent only a restatement of the *samanantara-paccaya*, what has been observed as to the exclusion of matter from the relation by way of *samanantara* applies equally to these two cases, too.

8

ATOMIC CLUSTERS

ONE OF THE Theravāda theories, without, apparently, any antecedent history in the Pāli canon itself, is the theory of *rūpakalāpas*. A post-canonical development in all its essentials, it makes its first appearance in the Visuddhimagga and in the Abhidhammic commentaries. In its fully developed form, however, it occurs in the manuals and commentaries of the twelfth century and later, notably the Abhidhammatthasaṅgaha of Ācariya Anuruddha, its Siṃhala *sannē* by Ācariya Sāriputta, its Pāli *ṭīkā* by Ācariya Sumaṅgala, and such Abhidhammic compendiums as the Nāmarūpasamāsa and the Saccasaṃkhepa.

An examination of the fundamental principles of the theory of *rūpakalāpas* would show that it is the Theravāda counterpart of the atomic theory of the schools of Sanskrit Buddhism. Much has been done by modern scholarship to critically examine the atomism of the Vaibhāṣikas and the Sautrāntikas.[598] Very little, however, is known about the close analogy that the theory of *rūpakalāpas* presents to the atomic theory of Sanskrit Buddhism.

There are valid reasons to believe that in developing the theory in question the Theravādins were much influenced by the Sanskrit Buddhist scholasticism. Louis de la Vallée Poussin and McGovern have drawn attention to the fact that atomism as a subject is discussed in the Mahāvibhāṣā.[599] The allusion therein to the opinions of Vasumitra, Bhadanta, and Buddhadeva on the question whether the atoms come into contact or not[600] shows clearly that in its time the atomic theory had become a well-established tenet of Sanskrit Buddhism.[601]

It is true that the (earlier) Pāli commentaries, where we meet with the theory of *rūpakalāpas* in an undeveloped form, are based on the Sīhaḷa Aṭṭhakathās that are not extant now. It is also true that, in view of this circumstance, it is not easy to ascertain how much of the Abhidhamma was developed in the latter before the compilation of the former. However, since the Theravāda commentarial exegesis developed in comparative isolation in Sri Lanka, it is very unlikely that it influenced the Buddhist schools that flourished in the mainland. Therefore, and in view of the close parallelism that exists between the Theravādins' theory of *rūpakalāpas* and the atomic theory of the schools of Sanskrit Buddhism, it seems very probable that the former was formulated on the basis of the latter. In the manuals and the commentaries of the twelfth century and later, where the theory under consideration is presented in its fully developed form, the signs of external influence are more marked and therefore more unmistakable.

This is not to suggest that the theory of *rūpakalāpas* is a complete replica of the atomic theory of Sanskrit Buddhism. As we shall soon see, there are certainly some differences. But most of them are unavoidable, stemming as they do from the fundamental differences as to the way the Theravādins and the non-Theravādins have conceived the various elements of matter. For instance, since the Theravādins have postulated comparatively a large number of material elements, it is but natural that this numerical discrepancy should reflect itself in the theory of *rūpakalāpas* as well. It is also worth noting here that between the Vaibhāṣikas and the Sautrāntikas there had been some major differences of opinion concerning certain aspects of the theory, which have their parallels in the theory of *rūpakalāpas* as well.

The Vaibhāṣikas have postulated two kinds of *paramāṇu* (atom)—namely, the *dravya-paramāṇu* (the unitary atom) and the *saṃghāta-paramāṇu* (the aggregate-atom, i.e., the molecule).

The former is the smallest unit of matter: it is the most subtle (*sarva-sūkṣma*);[602] it is partless (*niravayavat*) and therefore no spatial dimensions (*dig-bhāga-bhedatva*) can be predicated of it.[603] Ācārya Saṃghabhadra, one of the celebrities of the neo-Vaibhāṣika school, defines it as follows: Among the material things (*rūpas*) susceptible to resistance (*sapratigha*), the most subtle that is not susceptible to being divided again is the atom. That is to say, the atom is not divisible by another material thing or by mind—just as the moment that is the smallest unit of time is not divisible into half-moments.[604]

A *dravya-paramāṇu* never arises or exists in isolation. It always arises and exists in combination with other *dravya-paramāṇus*. A collection of them, forming a unity and having a simultaneous origination and a simultaneous cessation, is called *saṃghāta-paramāṇu*, "aggregate-atom"—that is, molecule.[605] The smallest *saṃghāta-paramāṇu* is an octad consisting of the four primary elements and four of the secondary elements—namely, *rūpa*, *gandha*, *rasa*, and *bhautika-spraṣṭavya*.[606] That the four primary elements always arise simultaneously and that the secondary elements cannot arise independently of the primary are the two fundamental principles involved in the conception of the *saṃghāta-paramāṇu*.

This is a brief statement of the two kinds of *paramāṇu* postulated by the Vaibhāṣikas. We have given it in brief outline with a view to finding out whether the two varieties are represented in the atomic theory of the Theravādins, too.

At the outset it should be noted that, as far as the medieval manuals and the commentaries, wherein the theory of *rūpakalāpas* appears in its developed form, are concerned, there is no evidence to suggest that the Theravādins have incorporated the Vaibhāṣika conception of the *dravya-paramāṇu*. However, two intriguing passages in the Visuddhimagga seem to contain an allusion to such a conception.

In the first passage it is stated that the bodily constituents such as head hair, bodily hair, and so on should be understood by way of *kalāpas*, groups: what in common parlance is called head hair is only a collection of eight material elements—namely, the four primary elements and four of the secondary elements: *rūpa*, *rasa*, *gandha*, and *āhāra*. Therefore, the passage goes on to say, from the point of view of the ultimate analysis, head hair is an "*aṭṭha-dhamma-kalāpa-matta*"—that is, merely a collection of eight elements.[607]

The second passage enjoins another way of looking at the matter that enters into the composition of the body—that is, by way of *cuṇṇa*, particles. "In this body the *paṭhavī-dhātu* taken as reduced to fine dust and pounded to the size of *paramāṇu* might amount to an average *doṇa*-measure full, and that is held together by the *āpo-dhātu* measuring half as much."[608]

In the medieval works of the Theravādins the term *kalāpa* is used in a technical sense, that is, as referring to the smallest unit of matter, which is a collection of material elements.[609] In this technical sense, *kalāpa* corresponds to the *saṃghāta-paramāṇu* of the Vaibhāṣikas. If one were to understand the *kalāpa* of the first passage (see *aṭṭha-dhamma-kalāpa*) in this technical sense, then one could suggest that *aṭṭha-dhamma-kalāpa* corresponds to the *saṃghāta-paramāṇu* and that *cuṇṇa* or *paramāṇu* of the second passage corresponds to the *dravya-paramāṇu*. However, a close examination of the implications of the two passages along with a consideration of the contexts in which they occur would lead to a different interpretation.

That in the Visuddhimagga passage the term *kalāpa* is not used in the same sense as it came to be used in the medieval works is easily seen. What the Visuddhimagga says is that the head hair, for instance, is an *aṭṭha-dhamma-kalāpa*, a collection or group of eight elements. If it had used the term *kalāpa* in the technical sense, then it should say that the head hair is a collection of *kalāpas* (each consisting of eight elements). The term should be put in the plural and not in the singular. For, in its technical sense, *kalāpa* means the smallest unit of matter, and as such, the head hair should consist of a large number of *kalāpas*. It is clear therefore that when the Visuddhimagga says that the head hair is an *aṭṭha-dhamma-kalāpa*, it is referring to the eight kinds of material elements that enter into its composition.[610]

As yet, there is no implication here that, in the "ultimate" analysis, material things consist of atoms. Nor is there any contradiction between the two usages of the term, for a given material thing can be described in either sense of the term. From the Buddhist point of view, one can say that the hair on one's head is a *kalāpa* of eight material elements, because it consists of the four primary elements and four of the secondary elements—namely, *rūpa*, *gandha*, *rasa*, and *āhāra*.[611] One can also say that the hair on one's head consists of an enormous number of *kalāpas*, each consisting of the above-mentioned eight material elements.[612] It is in the former sense that Ācariya Buddhaghosa, the author of the Visuddhimagga, uses the term *kalāpa*. On the other hand, Ācariya Anuruddha, the author of the Abhidhammatthasaṅgaha, uses the term *kalāpa* to mean the smallest unit of matter. For the former, it means a group (the general sense); for the latter, the smallest group (the technical sense).

On the other hand, it can be shown that what the medieval works call *kalāpa* (i.e., in the technical sense) corresponds to what the Visuddhimagga in the second passage calls *cuṇṇa* or *paramāṇu*.

We have already shown that in the Buddhist works the names of the four primary elements are used in two distinct senses: one in the sense of *lakkhaṇa* (characteristic) and the other in the sense of *ussada* (intensity). In the first sense, *paṭhavī* is *kakkhaḷatta* (solidity). In the second, what is *kakkhaḷa* (solid) is *paṭhavī*, for whatever material thing wherein the characteristic of *kakkhaḷatta* is most intense (*ussada*, *sāmatthiya*) is also called *paṭhavī*, although in fact it consists of all the four primary elements and their concomitants.[613]

When the Visuddhimagga refers to the atomization of *paṭhavī-dhātu*, it uses *paṭhavī-dhātu* in this second sense. In fact, at the beginning of the passage concerned, it is said that head hair, bodily hair, etc., are *paṭhavī*, and that blood, mucus, etc., are *āpo*. It is also said that they are called so on account of the respective prominence of each primary element—*ussada-vasena pana paṭhavī-dhātu āpo-dhātūti saṅgahaṃ gato*.[614] Thus in the statement—namely, that the *paṭhavī-dhātu* of the human body is reducible to *paramāṇu* (atoms)—the term *paṭhavī-dhātu* refers to the head hair, bodily hair, etc.

Next, it may be noted that according to the theory of *avinibhoga-rūpa*,[615] the four primary elements and four of the secondary elements—namely, *rūpa*, *rasa*, *gandha*, and *āhāra*—are necessarily coexistent (*niyata-sahajāta*) and positionally inseparable (*padesato avinibhoga*).[616] From this it follows that those parts of the human body that, on account of the intensity of the *paṭhavī-dhātu*, are conventionally called *paṭhavī-dhātu*, consist of the above-mentioned eight material elements. And, since these eight elements are positionally inseparable (*padesato avinibhoga*), even when the head hair, bodily hair, etc. are reduced to *paramāṇus*, each of the *paramāṇu* should in turn consist of the same number of elements. Thus what the Visuddhimagga calls *cuṇṇa* or *paramāṇu* turns out to be an aggregate of eight material elements. It is the same as *kalāpa* in its technical sense and does correspond to the *saṃghāta-paramāṇu* of the Vaibhāṣikas.

Our interpretation of *cuṇṇa* or *paramāṇu* in this way is also confirmed by the statement that the *paṭhavī-dhātu*, when reduced to the size of *paramāṇus*, might amount to an average *doṇa*-measure and that the *āpo-dhātu* to half as much. In a given instance of matter there is no quantitative difference between the primary elements that enter into its composition; the only difference is one of intensity (*ussada*). If the Visuddhimagga had used *paṭhavī* and *āpo* in the philosophical sense (in the sense of *lakkhaṇa* only), then it would not say that, when reduced to the size of *paramāṇus*, the former might amount to a *doṇa*-measure and the latter to half as much.

From the foregoing observations it should appear that, in the two passages of the Visuddhimagga, there is no allusion to the *dravya-paramāṇu*. Even in the subsequent Abhidhammic compendiums and the commentaries, the situation remains unchanged. For the Theravādins, the ultimate unit of matter is an aggregate—a collection of material elements forming a unity and having a simultaneous origination (*ekuppāda*) and a simultaneous cessation (*ekanirodha*).[617]

In the Visuddhimagga, where the theory in question is introduced for the first time, this ultimate unit is called *paramāṇu* or *cuṇṇa*. In the subsequent works, *kalāpa* became the standard term. While the first two terms are indicative of the fact that what is indicated thereby is the smallest unit of matter, the other brings into relief that, although it is the smallest, yet in the ultimate analysis, it is but a plurality of different material elements. The preference shown by the authors of the medieval works for the use of *kalāpa* instead of *paramānu* and *cuṇṇa*, the two earlier terms, is itself indicative of their desire to emphasize this fact. The use of the term *piṇḍa* in the Abhidhammatthasaṅgaha and its paraphrase as *rūpa-samudāya* in the Sinhalese *sannē* of Ācariya Sāriputta are also suggestive of the same fact.[618]

The fundamental principle underlying this theory is not far to seek. What are called secondary elements (*upādā-rūpa*s) are always dependent on the primary elements (*mahābhūtas*), for they cannot arise independently of the latter. Nor can a single primary element arise independently of the other three and at least four of the secondary elements.[619] Thus there is no material element, whether it is primary or secondary that can have an independent existence. Hence material elements always arise by way of groups (*piṇḍa-vasena*).[620] Consequently, when a given instance of matter, say, a piece of stone, is reduced to smaller pieces—whatever be the number of pieces or whatever be the size of each piece—the fact remains that each of them is a group or plurality of material elements. The smallest unit of matter, whether we call it *cuṇṇa*, *paramāṇu*, *piṇḍa*, *kalāpa*, or *rūpa-samudāya*, is no exception to this universal law.

The nearest Theravāda term to the *dravya-paramāṇu* of the Vaibhāṣikas is *kalāpaṅga*, literally, "the limb of the group"—that is, a constituent of a *kalāpa*.[621] The very term *aṅga* (*kalāpa* + *aṅga*) suggests that it has no independent existence and implies a whole. But is not the part smaller than the whole? Therefore is it not more logical to postulate the *kalāpaṅga* as the smallest (*sabba-pariyantima*) unit of matter?

The Vaibhāṣikas would answer this question in the affirmative. For, in their view, the constituent—that is, the so-called *dravya-paramāṇu*—though it cannot exist independently (it always arises in combination with seven others), is the most subtle (*sarva-sūkṣma*).[622] They seem to have argued that, since the *saṃghāta-paramāṇu* is an aggregate of *dravya-paramāṇus*, it admits divisibility. To describe as *sarva-sūkṣma* what admits divisibility is a contradiction in terms.

The Theravādins, on the other hand, seem to have followed a different line of argument. It is true that, since the *kalāpa* is an aggregate, each of the constituents (*kalāpaṅga*) that make up this aggregation is smaller (subtler) than the aggregate itself. But this is only logically so. In reality, the *kalāpaṅga* does not exist by itself; it is in inseparable association with other *kalāpaṅgas*. With this view, the Vaibhāṣikas too agree. The Atthasālinī observes that although it is possible, for the sake of defining the characteristics (*lakkhaṇato*), to speak of *rūpa*, *rasa*, etc. as separate elements, yet positionally (*padesato*) they are not separable, one from another. *Rūpa*, *rasa*, etc.—so runs the argument—cannot be dissected and separated like particles of sand.[623] The color (*rūpa*) of the mango, for instance, cannot be separated from its hardness (*paṭhavī*) or from its taste (*rasa*). This situation is true of the *kalāpaṅgas* of a *kalāpa*, too. Hence there is no necessity, other than merely logical, to postulate the *kalāpaṅga* as the *sabba-pariyantima*, for in actual fact it is not positionally (*padesato*) separable from the other *kalāpaṅgas* of the same *kalāpa*.

This, it appears to us, is the line of argument that led the Theravādins to observe silence on the question of the *dravya-paramāṇu* and to define the *rūpakalāpa* as the *sabba-pariyantima*. In taking up this position, they seem to have been influenced by the Sautrāntikas.

For, it may be noted here, the Vaibhāṣika conception of the *dravya-paramāṇu* came in for severe criticism on the part of the Sautrāntikas. As a matter of fact, it was the most significant issue that divided the two schools over the atomic theory.

What made the Sautrāntikas join issue with the Vaibhāṣika conception of the *dravya-paramāṇu* was that it was sought to be defined as devoid of parts (*niravayavat*) and exempt from resistance or impenetrability (*pratighāta*), which is the fundamental characteristic of matter.[624] The Vaibhāṣikas did not want to define the *dravya-paramāṇu* as possessing parts, because this implied the divisibility of the atom. Its exemption from *pratighāta*, according to Ācārya Yaśomitra, is a corollary arising from the first thesis: when there are no parts there cannot be *pratighāta*.[625] To the objection that if the *dravya-paramāṇu* is of this nature, it escapes the definition of matter, the Vaibhāṣikas reply: "Certainly, the atom is exempt from resistance (*rūpana*); but an atom never exists in complete isolation. In a state of agglomeration (*saṃghātastha, saṃcita*) it is susceptible to deterioration and resistance."[626]

But this way of defining the atom led to further complications. The Abhidharmakośa and the Vyākhyā rightly point out that, if the *dravya-paramāṇu* is devoid of parts and exempt from *pratighāta*, then even the aggregate will be devoid of parts and exempt from *pratighāta*, because the aggregate is ultimately constituted of the atoms. What is lacking in the latter cannot be predicated of the former.[627]

In this connection one cannot also forget the severe diatribes launched by the Buddhist Idealists (Vijñānavādins) against the definition of the atom as devoid of spatial division. In order to have a basis for their polemics they provisionally agreed with the objection of the Sautrāntikas that the aggregates are ultimately constituted of, and therefore not different from, the atoms, the difference between one atom and an aggregate being only one of quantity.

It was the failure, on the part of the Vaibhāṣikas of Kāśmīr, to take notice of this fact that gave rise to the fallacy of their assumption that, although the atoms do not touch, the same situation is not true of the aggregates.[628] Once this oneness (*ekatva*) is overlooked, it leads to many mutually incompatible conclusions and fails to give a rational explanation to many a phenomenon of day-to-day experience: It is a matter of common experience, for instance, that when the sun rises a given aggregate is found to be illuminated at its eastern direction and dark at its western direction, or when one sees or touches, say, a wall, one does not see or touch its opposite side—two situations that unmistakably point to the conclusion that the aggregates have spatial divisions. This characteristic cannot be predicated of them if the atoms that constitute them do not severally possess it.[629]

It is supposed (by the neo-Sarvāstivādins) that the combination of atoms takes place in such a way that six different atoms occupy six points of space—east, west, north, south, above, and below—of another atom. This law of atomic aggregation carries with it the implication that the atom has at least six sides. On the other hand, if it be contended that the locus occupied by one atom is common to all the six, then the atom being devoid of parts and exempt from resistance (*pratighāta*), all the six would coalesce into one; the difference between the magnitude of one atom and that of six would vanish.[630]

These objections and counterobjections between the Buddhist schools show that when it came to the question of defining the atom, the atomists were caught in the horns of a big dilemma. On the one hand, to admit the spatial dimensions (*digbhāga-bhedatva*) of the atom is to admit its divisibility—a contradiction in terms if the atom is defined as the smallest unit of matter and not amenable to further division. On the other hand, to deny the spatial dimensions of the atom is to deny the spatial dimensions of the aggregate—a situation contradicted by common experience. The Vaibhāṣikas followed the first line of argument and the Sautrāntikas the second, each party tenaciously clinging to its own view without attempting a solution to the resulting paradox.

This gave a good opportunity for the Buddhist Idealists to refute both alternatives and to establish their theory that matter is "logically inadmissible": If, as the Sautrāntikas say, the atoms "are extended, they are divisible, and as a consequence they are not real. If, as the Vaibhāṣikas say, the atoms are not extended, they cannot constitute material things with mass. If anything, the atom should be "extended," but what is "extended" is divisible, and what is divisible cannot be a real entity (*dravyasat*). The inescapable conclusion, they contended, is that matter is "logically inadmissible."[631] Thus the paradox was solved, but the solution offered was not in favor of either of the contending parties. The intervention of the umpire, in this case, is not to judge who is right but to show that both are equally wrong. However, there was no possibility for the Theravādins to accept the conclusion of the Vijñānavādins, because, being realists, they were not prepared to subscribe to the idealistic metaphysic underlying that conclusion.

That spatial dimensions can be predicated of the *kalāpa* is clearly suggested by an isolated reference in the Viśuddhimārgasannaya that says that *ākāsa*, the intervening space between two *kalāpas*, "has the function of delimiting the *kalāpa* as: this is the lower side (*yaṭa*) of the *kalāpa* and that is the upper side (*uḍa*) of the *kalāpa*."[632]

This is further confirmed by a theory advanced as to the size of the *kalāpa* in relation to a (cubic) inch (*aṅgula*). It occurs in the Vibhaṅga Aṭṭhakathā.[633] The term used is *paramāṇu*. We propose to interpret the *paramāṇu* of the Theravādins as identical with the *rūpakalāpa*, on the strength of the observations made in the course of this chapter. The table runs as follows:

36 *paramāṇus*	= 1 *aṇu*
36 *aṇus*	= 1 *tajjāri*
36 *tajjāris*	= 1 *ratharenu*
36 *ratharenus*	= 1 *līkhā*
7 *līkhās*	= 1 *ūkā*
7 *ūkās*	= 1 *dhaññamāsa*
7 *dhaññamāsas*	= 1 *aṅgula*, "finger-breadth," i.e., (cubic) inch.

Thus the size of the *paramāṇu* in relation to the cubic inch will be:

$$1 / (36 \times 36 \times 36 \times 36 \times 7 \times 7 \times 7) = 1 / 576{,}108{,}288$$

That this table, which gives the size of the *paramāṇu* in relation to the cubic inch, is one that is arbitrarily assumed goes without saying. For, there were no physical data for a mathematical calculation of infinitesimal units. A somewhat similar table, perhaps the original source of the above, is given by Varāhamihira.[634] Yamakami Sōgen[635] and Takakusu[636] have referred to similar tables adopted by the schools of Sanskrit Buddhism. At best, they all may be described as attempts to emphasize how infinitesimally small the *paramāṇu*, the ultimate unit of matter, is.

For the *paramāṇu* is so small that in the *Vibhaṅga Aṭṭhakathā* it is (figuratively) described as a particle of space (*ākāsa-koṭṭhāsa*).[637] The *Visuddhimagga Ṭīkā* observes that it comes only within the province of the divine eye (*dibba-cakkhu*).[638] This is similar to the view expressed in some Jaina works—namely, that the *paramāṇu* can be known only by those who have realized *kaivalya-jñāna*.[639]

Another problem that was hotly debated by the schools of Sanskrit

Buddhism that adopted atomism was whether the atoms came into contact with one another.

Since the Vaibhāṣikas believed that the *dravya-paramāṇu* was devoid of parts, any conclusion in respect of this problem should in no way contradict this belief. In fact, the Vaibhāṣikas of Kāśmīr take the *niravayavatva*, partlessness, of the atom as the very premise of the expected conclusion. They grant the possibility of two alternatives, both of which, they say, are inadmissible: (1) if the atoms touch in their totality, then the different atoms will occupy but one locus; (2) if the atoms touch partially, this is to admit that they have parts.[640] Another argument, the one attributed to Ācārya Vasumitra, is based on the theory of momentary being (*kṣaṇikatā*): "if the atoms do touch, that means they exist for two moments."[641] That is to say, an atom should arise first (first moment) in order to touch (second moment)—a view that, if accepted, would go against the doctrine that an element of existence endures but for one moment (*kṣaṇa*). On the strength of these arguments the Vaibhāṣikas conclude that atoms do not come into contact with one another and that between two atoms there is always an intervening space (*antara*). In this intervening space there is no *āloka* (light), and it is so small that another atom cannot occupy it.[642] The presence of *āloka* has to be ruled out because, *āloka* being included in the category of matter, to affirm its existence is to deny the vacuity between the two atoms. To the possible objection that if there is "*antara*" between atoms how is it that the aggregates that are ultimately composed of these atoms do not fall into pieces when struck, the reply is that *vāyu-dhātu*, the air-element, keeps them together.[643]

It is to be expected that the Sautrāntikas should challenge this conclusion, for it is mainly based on the premise that the atom is *niravayavat*—a dogma to which they did not want to subscribe. Hence it is that the author of the Abhidharmakośa, whose sympathies are more with the Sautrāntikas, and his commentator launch severe diatribes against this theory. In their opinion the interpretation given by Bhadanta—namely, that contact is another expression for *nirantaratva*, is the best. They propose to interpret *nirantaratva* in this context as indicating absence of interval.[644] For otherwise, the argument runs, what would prevent the atoms from moving within the interval?[645] In putting forth this objection, they seem to have overlooked the fact that in the case of momentary elements, as reminded by Ācārya Vasumitra, there is no motion: wherever an element arises, there itself it perishes. On the other hand, Ācārya Saṃghabhadra, a celebrity of the Vaibhāṣika School, interprets *nirantaratva* of Bhadanta as lending support to the theory that there is *antara*, interval between atoms.[646] The main objection directed against the Vaibhāṣika theory is that it is absurd to deny contact between the atoms while recognizing contact between the aggregates.[647]

Since the theory of *rūpakalāpas*, as suggested earlier, is modeled on the atomic theories of the schools of Sanskrit Buddhism, it may be interesting to consider what position the Theravādins took up in respect of this problem. According to the Theravādins, since the *kalāpaṅgas* that constitute a *kalāpa* are positionally inseparable, the possibility of their being separated by an interval does not arise. Hence the problem boils down to this: Can two *kalāpas* come into (physical) contact?

The question is not raised, let alone being answered, in the earlier commentaries where we meet with the theory in its rudimentary form. The authors of the later works took up the matter and provided the answer: *rūpakalāpas* do not come into contact; between them there is space.

Every *rūpakalāpa* is delimited (*paricchindate*) by the environing *ākāsa*, space.[648] This *ākāsa* is so small that the fact of delimitation is described as "as if delimiting" (*paricchindantī viya*).[649] However, the *kalāpas* are not touching one another, for each *kalāpa* is qualified as "not touched" (*asamphuṭṭha*) by the other *kalāpas* separated from it.[650] The implication is that the vacuity is a fact, although it is infinitesimally small. Hence the *ākāsa* is said to manifest itself as "untouchedness" (*asamphuṭṭha-paccupaṭṭhāna*).[651]

In maintaining this view the Theravādins were anxious to stress the separateness of each *kalāpa*. Ācariya Sāriputta and Ācariya Sumaṅgala take special care to emphasize the fact that each *kalāpa* is in itself an entity, physically separated from the others. This separation is not possible if there is contact. And it is the *ākāsa*, the so-called *paricchedākāsa*, that is responsible for their being prevented from mixing (*asaṃkara-bhāva*).[652]

The admission, on the part of the Theravādins, of *ākāsa* between *kalāpas* shows that they agree with the Vaibhāṣika position. However, the reasons given are quite different. This is inevitable, because the Vaibhāṣika theory of non-contact between the *dravya-paramāṇus* is mainly based on the denial of their spatial dimensions (and the denial of motion), whereas for the Theravādins the question as to the possibility or otherwise of physical contact is a question relating to the *kalāpas*, the spatial dimensions of which are not denied.

Hence it is that the Siṃhala *sannē* to the Visuddhimagga attempts to show how the non-contact of the *kalāpas* is only a logical corollary arising from the fact that the *kalāpaṅgas* of a *kalāpa* are positionally inseparable (*padesato avinibhoga*). It is argued that if the *kalāpas* are not separated by *ākāsa*, then this leads to the acceptance of one of two alternatives, both of which are not compatible with the above-mentioned principle.

The first alternative is to deny that there is *ākāsa* between two *kalāpas*.[653] The *kalāpaṅgas* of a *kalāpa*, be it repeated here, are positionally inseparable. Now, if there is no actual separation between two *kalāpas*, then the characteristic of positional inseparability, which applies only to the *kalāpaṅgas* of a *kalāpa*, has to be extended to the two *kalāpas* as well.[654] That is to say, the separateness of each of the *kalāpas* vanishes and both combine to form a bigger *kalāpa*. If the principle could be extended to two *kalāpas*, then it could also be extended to three or more, and so the process could be indefinitely extended. If a given piece of stone is composed, let us say hypothetically, of one million *kalāpas*, then those million *kalāpas* would become one big *kalāpa*, precisely as big as the piece of stone. This would undermine the very foundation of the theory of *kalāpas*.

In the first place, it goes against the established thesis that the *kalāpaṅgas* of a *kalāpa* are not separable, one from another. For if the stone in question is a (big) *kalāpa*, then it should be of such a nature that no part of it can be separated. The moment one breaks the stone we are speaking of into pieces, then the theory—namely, that the constituents of a *kalāpa* are not separable, one from another—looses its tenability.[655]

In the second place, it would also go against the view of a pluralityof *kalāpas*. For according to this alternative under consideration, the Mount Himalaya would be one big *kalāpa*. But the Mount Himalaya is not completely separated from the rest of the physical world. If the physical world is characterized by unbroken continuity, in the sense that no part of it is completely separated from the rest, then one will be forced to the conclusion that the whole physical world is one mighty *kalāpa*.

In this connection it is interesting to note that one of the arguments advanced by the Vaibhāṣikas of Kāśmīr to deny physical contact of the atoms is that if two of them touch in their totality, then the atom being non-resisting (*apratigha*) and partless (*niravayavat*), all the atoms would coalesce into one—the whole universe would coalesce into one atom, so small that no spatial dimensions can be predicated of it.[656] The objection of the Theravādins, when its implications are fully developed, is that if *kalāpas* are not separated by *ākāsa*, then the whole physical world would become one enormous *kalāpa*. The Vaibhāṣika objection is that the world will be reduced to a partless atom; the Theravāda objection is that the atom will be inflated to the size of the world—two situations literally with a world of difference.

The other alternative is to affirm that the *kalāpaṅgas*, not the *kalāpas*, are separated by *ākāsa*. This too would lead to many difficulties somewhat similar to the ones that stem from denying the separateness of the *kalāpas*. If it were assumed that in a given *kalāpa* the *kalāpaṅgas* are separated by *ākāsa*, then the separateness and independence of the *kalāpas* would fade away, establishing the separateness and independence of the *kalāpaṅgas*.[657] The ultimate unit of matter, then, would be the constituent (*kalāpaṅga*) and not the aggregate (*kalāpa*). For the reasons we have given above,[658] the Theravādins were not prepared to accept such a conclusion. Although it is logically true that the *kalāpaṅga* should be smaller (subtler) than the *kalāpa*, yet in a given *kalāpa* the *kalāpaṅgas* are not separable, one from another. They arise, exist, and perish as one unit. There is therefore no point in postulating the *kalāpaṅga* as the ultimate unit of matter. The refutation of the second alternative, although it is not explicitly stated, does amount to a criticism of the Vaibhāṣika standpoint.

In all, there are seventeen kinds of *kalāpa*. The smallest is an octad consisting of the four primary elements and four of the secondary–namely, *rūpa* (color), *rasa* (taste), *gandha* (odor), and *āhāra* (nutriment). This collection of eight material elements, called *suddhaṭṭhaka*,[659] the bare octad, corresponds to the smallest *saṃghāta-paramāṇu* of the Vaibhāṣikas, but for two differences.

First, in place of *āhāra* the Vaibhāṣika list contains *spraṣṭavya* (the tangible).[660] The difference is unavoidable. According to the Theravādins, *phoṭṭhabba* (the tangible) includes only the primary elements with the exception of one—that is, *āpodhātu*.[661] Hence from the point of view of the Theravādins, it is not necessary to repeat *phoṭṭhabba* because it is already represented by the enumeration of the primary elements. According to the Vaibhāṣikas, *spraṣṭavya* includes the four primary elements, that is, *bhūta-spraṣṭavya* (the primary tangible) and eleven secondary elements, that is, *bhautika-spraṣṭavya* (the secondary tangible).[662] It is in order to represent the latter, the so-called *bhautika-spraṣṭavya*, that *spraṣṭavya* is repeated, although one aspect of it is represented by the primary elements. A similar situation is responsible for the inclusion of *āhāra* in the Theravāda list. While the Theravādins have postulated *āhāra* as a separate element of matter, the Vaibhāṣikas have conceived it as a combination of *rasa*, *gandha*, and *spraṣṭavya*, which three items occur in their list.[663]

The two lists are thus representative of the same items except for the fact that *bhautika-spraṣṭavya* is not represented in the list of the Theravādins. This is unavoidable because the latter do not admit that any of the secondary elements of matter come under the object of touch.

The other difference is more significant. It is a Vaibhāṣika principle, with which the Sautrāntikas do not seem to have had any sympathy, that each secondary element is dependent on a separate tetrad of the primary elements. Those primary elements that serve as a support (*āśraya*) for a given secondary element, say, color, do not at the same time serve as a support for another, say, smell.[664] Hence, as the Abhidharmakośa rightly points out, the smallest *saṃghāta-paramāṇu* should consist of not eight, but twenty elements, for, since each secondary element is dependent on a separate tetrad of the primary elements, the four secondary elements of the *saṃghāta-paramāṇu* should have, for their support, sixteen separate primary elements.[665] The Vaibhāṣika reply is that the nature of the four elements remains the same and that therefore there is no anomaly in counting the primary elements as four, although there are four of each type.[666] In contrast, the Theravādins believe that the four primary elements of the *suddhaṭṭhaka* are the common support (*ekanissaya*) of the secondary elements.[667]

These, then, are the two significant differences between the *suddhaṭṭhaka* of the Theravādins and the octuple *saṃghāta-paramāṇu* of the Vaibhāṣikas.

The remaining sixteen *kalāpas* are formed according to the same principle as adopted by the Vaibhāṣikas in forming the *saṃghāta-paramāṇus* other than the octad. The (eight) items of the octad are the basic material elements; they are present in every instance of matter. Therefore, in all the *kalāpas* these eight material elements are present as their basis. The other *kalāpas* are formed by adding one or more, as the situation demands, of the remaining material elements (= those other than the eight in question) to the basic octad.

Since we have already examined all the material elements,[668] we shall confine ourselves to the way they enter into the composition of the *kalāpas*.

Next to the basic octad comes *sadda-navaka*, the sound-nonad, which, according to both schools, is formed by adding one element of sound to the basic octad.[669]

As to the formation of the five sense-organ *kalāpas* or *saṃghātas*, the two schools follow two slightly different methods. According to the

Vaibhāṣikas, of the sense-organs, the *kāyendriya* (the organ of touch) consists of the minimum number of *dravya-paramāṇus*. It is a nonad consisting of the basic octad and one *dravya-paramāṇu* of *kāyendriya* added to it. Each of the other four sense-organ *saṃghāta*s is formed by adding one *dravya-paramāṇu* of each of them to the *kāyendriya-nonad*. Thus while the *kāyendriya saṃghāta* is a nonad, the other sense-organ *saṃghāta*s are decads.[670] For the Theravādins every sense-organ *kalāpa* is a decad (dasaka).

First one *kalāpaṅga* of *rūpa-jīvitindriya* (the material faculty of life) is added to the basic octad to make it organic. The resulting nonad is called *jīvita-navaka*, the vital-nonad. The five sense-organ *kalāpas* are then formed by adding each of the sense-organ *kalāpaṅgas* to the *jīvita-navaka*. Thus there are *cakkhu-dasaka* (eye-decad), *sota-dasaka* (ear-decad), *ghāna-dasaka* (nose-decad), *jivhā-dasaka* (tongue-decad), and *kāya-dasaka* (body-decad).[671]

The Vaibhāṣikas add one *dravya-paramāṇu* of *kāyendriya* to the other four sense-organ *saṃghātas*, because the other four sense-organs are said to be associated with *kāyendriya* (*tat-pratibaddha-vṛttitvāt*).[672] They seem to have taken the view that the organs of sight, hearing, taste, and smell are certain modifications of the organ of touch—a view accepted by certain Nyaya-Vaiśeṣikas, too.[673] It is rather strange that the Theravādins do not add one *kalāpaṅga* of *kāyendriya* to the other four sense-organ *kalāpas*. For in the commentaries we are told that the organ of touch is present in every part of the body (*sabba-sarīra-byāpaka*), existing as it were like oil soaked in cotton.[674] Why the Vaibhāṣikas, unlike the Theravādins, do not include *jīvitendriya* in the sense-organ *saṃghātas* is understandable. For, as stated earlier,[675] they have recognized only one variety of *jīvitendriya* that is included in the category of (*rūpa*)-*citta-viprayukta-saṃskāras*.

Since the Theravādins have defined the two faculties of sex as separate elements of matter rather than regarding them as part of the organ of touch,[676] and since they have postulated the heart-basis as the seat of mental activity,[677] these three items, too, are explained by way of *kalāpas*, to which corresponding *saṃghāta-paramāṇus* are not found in Sanskrit Buddhism. The method of their formation is like that of the sense-organs. That is to say, one *kalāpaṅga* of *itthindriya* (faculty of femininity), *purisindriya* (faculty of masculinity), and *hadaya-vatthu* (heart-basis) is added to the *jīvita-navaka*; the resulting three decads are called *itthibhāva-dasaka* (femininity-decad), *pumbhāva-dasaka* (masculinity-decad), and *vatthu-dasaka* (basis-decad), respectively.[678]

The *kalāpaṅgas* or the constituents of the *kalāpas* that we have considered so far are all *nipphanna-rūpa*. Of the ten *anipphanna-rūpas*, only five are recognized as *kalāpaṅgas*.

The five that are not recognized as *kalāpaṅgas* are *ākāsa-dhātu* (space-element), *upacaya* (growth), *santati* (continuity), *jaratā* (decay), and *aniccatā* (impermanence). Why they are excluded needs hardly any explanation. Akāsa-*dhātu*—that is, space delimited by matter—is not something that enters into the composition of the *kalāpas*; it is that which intervenes between the *kalāpas*. That is to say, it sets bounds to, and is itself bounded by, the *kalāpas*. The other four items are merely indicative of certain phases of matter.[679] As such they are not material constituents of the *kalāpas*.[680]

The five *anipphanna-rūpas* that are recognized as *kalāpaṅgas* are the two *viññattis* (intimation) and the triad of *lahutā* (lightness), *mudutā* (plasticity), and *kammaññatā* (wieldiness). We have already shown that, although the *anipphanna-rūpas* are called *rūpa-dhammas*, they do not stand for something distinct from the *nipphanna-rūpas*.[681] Accordingly, although some *anipphanna-rūpas* are recognized as *kalāpaṅgas*, they do not stand for something distinct from the *nipphanna-kalāpaṅgas*. Let us take one example to clarify the situation.

Kāyaviññatti, it may be recalled here, signifies an *ākāra-vikāra* (a particular position or situation) of a set of *cittasamuṭṭhāna-rūpas* that are *nipphanna*.[682] According to the theory under consideration, *kāyaviññatti* signifies an *ākāra-vikāra* of the *cittasamuṭṭhāna-kalāpas* (for the *cittasamuṭṭhāna-rūpas*, too, exist by way of *kalāpas*). Now, each of these *kalāpas*, an *ākāra-vikāra* of which is called *kāyaviññatti*, is indicated by the addition of *kāyaviññatti* as one of its *kalāpaṅgas*. Thus the recognition of *kāyaviññatti* as a *kalāpaṅga* does not carry the implication that it is something distinct from the *nipphanna-kalāpaṅgas*. Its purpose is to indicate the type of *kalāpas*, an *ākāra-vikāra* of which is represented by the *kāyaviññatti*. It is in this manner that we should understand the significance of the five *kalāpaṅgas* that are *anipphanna*.

Let us now consider those *kalāpas*, some of the *kalāpaṅgas* of which are *anipphanna-rūpa*.

The first, called *kāyaviññatti-navaka* (bodily-expression-nonad), is formed by the addition of one *kalāpaṅga* of *kāyavinññatti* to the basic octad. It represents the *cittasamuṭṭhāna-kalāpa*, an *ākāra-vikāra* of which is called *kāyaviññatti*. Next comes *vacīviññatti-dasaka* (vocal-expression-decad), which is formed by the addition of two *kalāpaṅgas* of sound and *vacīviññatti* to the basic octad. This represents the *cittasamuṭṭhāna-kalāpa*, an *ākāra-vikāra* of which is called *vacīviññatti*.[683] The addition of sound is necessary because *vacīviññatti* is intimately connected with vocal sound.[684] Since the Vaibhāṣikas treat *kāyavijñapti* as a part of *rūpāyatana*,[685] they do not recognize a separate *saṃghāta-paramāṇu* corresponding to it. But the same is not true of *vāgvijñapti*. Although it is treated as a part of *śabdāyatana*,[686] its composition as a *saṃghāta* is more complex than that of ordinary sound. For, "the sound that is produced by the great material elements, which form part of the organism (*upātta*), does not exist independently of the organs."[687] Hence in the case of a *saṃghāta-paramāṇu* of *vāgvijñapti* sound, the usual sound-nonad becomes an undecad by the addition of two *dravya-paramāṇus* of *kāyendriya* and *jiḥvendriya*.[688]

The last four *kalāpas*, to which, except perhaps to one, no corresponding *saṃghāta-paramāṇus* can be traced in Sanskrit Buddhism, have as their *kalāpaṅgas* the usual eight inseparables of the basic octad: the triad of *lahutā*, *mudutā*, and *kammaññatā*, and the two *viññattis*.[689]

The first, called *lahutādekādasaka* (undecad of plasticity), consists of the basic octad plus three *kalāpaṅgas* of *lahutā*, *mudutā*, and *kammaññatā*. It may be recalled here that the last three items, which represent the body when it is healthy and efficient, arise always together (*na aññam' aññaṃ vijahanti*).[690] This explains why the three items are included in the same *kalāpa* rather than establishing three separate *kalāpas*.

The second and the third, called *kāyaviññatti-lahutādi-dvādasaka* (dodecad of bodily expression and plasticity, etc.) and *vacīviññatti-sadda-lahutādi-terasaka* (tredecad of vocal expression, sound, plasticity, etc.), are formed by adding *lahutā*, *mudutā*, and *kammaññatā* to the previously mentioned *kāyaviññatti-navaka* and *vacīviññatti-dasaka*, respectively. The occurrence of the two *viññattis* could be accompanied (facilitated) by the triad of *lahutā*, etc.[691] It seems that it is in order to explain such situations that these two *kalāpas* have been postulated.

The last *kalāpa* is *sadda-lahutādi-dvādasaka* (dodecad of sound, plasticity, etc.).

It is the same as the previously mentioned *vacīviññatti-sadda-lahutādi-terasaka* except for the absence of one constituent—namely, *vacīviññatti*. Since the triad of *lahutā*, etc., is included here, it certainly concerns itself with a phenomenon associated with the physical body of a living being.[692] And since *vacīviññatti* is lacking, we may interpret it as representative of vocal sound unaccompanied by *vacīviññatti* as well as sound produced by the other parts of the body. In the Abhidharmakośa there is reference to a *saṃghāta-paramāṇu*, called the sound-decad, which consists of the basic octad and two *dravya-paramāṇus* of sound and the organ of touch. It represents the phenomenon of *upātta-mahā-bhūtika* sound—that is, sound produced, say, by the clapping of hands, etc.[693] Cases like these, it may be observed, are represented by the *kalāpa* in question. The non-inclusion of *kāyendriya* as a constituent of this *kalāpa* is understandable, for we have already seen that, unlike the Vaibhāṣikas, the Theravādins do not add *kāyendriya* either to the *kalāpas* of the first four sense-organs or to the *kalāpa* of *vacīviññatti*-sound.

This brings us to an end of our survey of the seventeen kinds of *kalāpa*. They all are again classified into four groups on the basis of the four generative conditions (*rūpa-samuṭṭhāna-paccaya*) of matter—namely, *kamma*, *citta*, *utu*, and *āhāra*. Since we have discussed them elsewhere,[694] herein we shall confine ourselves to indicating how the *kalāpas* are classified accordingly. It should also be noted here that if a *kalāpa* is conditioned by more than one of the four factors, say, by three (*ti-samuṭṭhāna*), then that particular *kalāpa* is counted thrice. In this way, although there are seventeen distinct *kalāpas*, the number is brought up to twenty-one.

Since the eight *rūpa-indriyas* and the *hadaya-vatthu* are recognized as coming into being through the action of kamma,[695] the five sense-organ *dasakas*, the two sex *dasakas*, the *jīvita-navaka*, and the *vatthu-dasaka* are brought under *kammasamuṭṭhāna*. Since the two *viññattis* represent *ākāra-vikāras* of *cittasamuṭṭhāna-rūpa*,[696] the four *kalāpas*—*kāyaviññatti-navaka, vacīviññatti-dasaka, kāyaviññatti-lahutādi-dvādasaka*, and *vacīviññatti-sadda-lahutādi-terasaka*—are brought under *cittasamuṭṭhāna*. The two *kalāpas*, *sadda-navaka* and *sadda-lahutādi-dvādasaka*, are *utusamuṭṭhāna*. These two *kalāpas* refer to two varieties of sound, the first to sound produced in the body of a living being and the second to sound produced in the insentient (*aviññāṇika*) world. It should be noted here that, although sound arises owing to the concussion (*ghaṭṭana*) of the primary elements, *utu* (the temperature of cold and heat) is considered as a special condition for its continuity.[697]

On the other hand, the two *kalāpas*, *lahutādekādasaka* and *suddhaaṭṭhaka*, are *ti-samuṭṭhāna* in the sense that they are alternatively conditioned by *citta*, *utu*, and *āhāra*.

The first, which refers to the triad of *lahutā*, etc., is *ti-samuṭṭhāna* because bodily efficiency, which is implied by the triad, could be brought about by a wholesome state of mind (*citta*), or by agreeable nutrition (*āhāra*), or by good temperature (*utu*).[698]

When the *suddhaṭṭhaka*, which consists of the four primary elements and the four secondary elements inseparably associated with them, is brought into relation with consciousness, as in the case of bodily movements arising in response to a thought, it is *cittasamuṭṭhāna*. When it arises conditioned by nutrition or by temperature of cold and heat, it is called *āhārasamuṭṭhāna* and *utusamuṭṭhāna*, respectively. All matter, other than that which enters into the composition of living beings, is ultimately constituted of *suddhaṭṭhakas* and *sadda-navakas*, both conditioned only by *utu*.[699] For the temperature of cold and heat, according to the Theravādins, is an essential factor for the arising, continuity, and changes of all such matter.[700]

Why the *suddhaṭṭhaka* is not *kammasamuṭṭhāna* needs explanation. It is true that the (eight) constituents of this octad enter into the composition of all *kalāpas*, including those that are kamma-conditioned. It should, however, be recalled here that, although some material elements come into being, being conditioned by kamma, yet their uninterrupted continuity is said to depend on the *rūpa-jīvitindriya*.[701] Therefore, a *kammasamuṭṭhāna-kalāpa* should at least be a nonad (*navaka*), consisting of the eight inseparables (basic octad) and one *kalāpaṅga* of *rūpa-jīvitindriya*. An octad in itself can never be *kammasamuṭṭhāna*.

Before we conclude this chapter a few comments are called for on the position of *kalāpas* in relation to *Rūpa-loka*, the second plane of existence according to Buddhist cosmology.

The Theravādins and the Vaibhāṣikas share the view that all elements of matter exist in the *Kāma-loka* and none in the *Arūpa-loka*. Therefore the same situation is true of the *kalāpas/saṃghāta-paramāṇus* in relation to these two planes of existence.[702]

That some material elements exist in the *Rūpa-loka* is admitted by both schools, but opinion differs as to what they are.

The Vaibhāṣika view is that *gandha*, *rasa*, and the two faculties of sex that are a part of *kāyendriya* do not obtain in the *Rūpa-loka*.[703] The first two are eliminated because along with *spraṣṭavya* they form what is called *kavaḍikārāhāra*.[704] Since no person who is not free from attachment to this kind of nutriment is born in *Rūpa-loka*, it has to be excluded. But *spraṣṭavya*, which is also a part of *kavaḍīkāra-ahāra*, is retained, partly because in itself it cannot constitute *kavaḍīkārāhāra*, and partly because—this is the more important reason—the four primary elements are included in the *spraṣṭavya*.[705] Since the primary elements are the support (*āśraya*) of the secondary elements (*bhautika*), their presence must be admitted. The reason given for the elimination of the two faculties of sex is that they arise as a result of desire for tactile consciousness associated with sexual union, from which desire the beings who are destined to be born in the *Rūpa-loka* are completely free.[706]

Since the two faculties of sex are conceived not as independent material elements but as a part of the organ of touch, the elimination of the former does not affect the principle of atomic aggregation. On the other hand, since savor (*rasa*) and odor (*gandha*) are conceived, not only as two separate elements of matter but also as two of the constituents of the basic octad, their elimination necessitates the reduction of every *saṃghāta-paramāṇu* of the *Rūpa-loka* by two *dravya-paramāṇus*. Consequently, the smallest *saṃghāta-paramāṇu* of the *Rūpa-loka* becomes an aggregate of six constituents, and this quantitative deficiency is reflected in the composition of the other *saṃghāta-paramāṇus*, too.[707]

The Theravādins agree with the Vaibhāṣikas in eliminating the two faculties of sex,[708] presumably for the same reason. However, they disagree with the latter over the other elements of matter to be eliminated. Instead of savor (*rasa*) and odor (*gandha*) they have excluded the two sense-organs corresponding to them and also the organ of touch. Consequent on this reduction, the two *bhāva-dasakas* (sex-decads), the *jivhā-dasaka*, the *ghāna-dasaka*, and the *kāya-dasaka* get eliminated from the *Rūpa-loka*.[709]

A comparison between the two lists of material elements eliminated by the two schools should show that the differences are of a considerable nature, the Vaibhāṣikas eliminating the sense-objects and the Theravādins the sense-organs. Although it might appear that the two schools have completely parted ways, yet on closer examination it will be seen that they are following two different methods for a common purpose.

Both schools agree on the view that *jivhā-viññāṇa* (gustatory consciousness) and *ghāna-viññāṇa* (olfactory consciousness) are absent in the *Rūpa-loka*; the Theravāda eliminates, in addition, *kāya-viññāṇa* (tactile consciousness).[710] If this latter fact is overlooked for the moment, then there is complete agreement between the two schools. Since consciousness (*viññāṇa*) requires for its arising the conjunction between the sense-organ and the sense-object, its absence can be indicated in one of two ways, either by the exclusion of the sense-organ or by the exclusion of the sense- object. The Theravādins have followed the first alternative, and the Vaibhāṣikas the second.

Although the two methods brought the two schools to a common conclusion, yet they separated them over one vital issue, an issue concerning the composition of the *saṃghātaparamāṇus/kalāpas*. In pursuance of the second alternative, the Vaibhāṣikas had to eliminate *gandha* and *rasa* from each and every *saṃghāta-paramāṇu* of the *Rūpa-loka*. Thereby the theory of *avinirbhāga-rūpa*, according to which the four *mahābhūtas* and *rūpa, rasa, gandha*, and *bhautika-spraṣṭavya* are necessarily coexistent (*niyata-sahotpanna*), could not be retained in the same form both in the *Kāma-loka* and in the *Rūpa-loka*. On the other hand, the adoption, on the part of the Theravādins, of the first alternative did not necessitate such a course. For what required reduction was not the number of constituents of each *kalāpa* but the number of *kalāpas*.

The concern of the Theravādins to retain the theory of *avinibhoga-rūpa* unmodified is also shown by the way they solved the problem of *āhāra-rūpa*. They, too, were of the opinion that the beings in the *Rūpa-loka* were completely detached from *kabaḷiṅkāra-āhāra*. But since *āhāra* is one of the *avinibhoga-rūpas*, it could not be eliminated from the *kalāpas*. The desired effect was realized by eliminating all the *āhāra-samuṭṭhāna-kalāpas* from the *Rūpa-loka*.[711] Thereby they admitted that there was *āhāra-rūpa* in the *Rūpa-loka*, but denied that the beings therein were nourished by it.

Abbreviations

1 = *paṭhavī-dhātu* (earth-element)
2 = *āpo-dhātu* (water-element)
3 = *tejo-dhātu* (fire-element)
4 = *vāyo-dhātu* (air-element)
5 = *rūpa* (color)
6 = *sadda* (sound)
7 = *gandha* (smell)
8 = *rasa* (taste)
9 = *āhāra* (nutriment)
10 = *cakkhu* (organ of sight)
11 = *sota* (organ of hearing)
12 = *ghāna* (organ of smell)
13 = *jivhā* (organ of taste)
14 = *kāya* (organ of touch)
15 = *jīvitindriya* (faculty of life)
16 = *itthindriya* (faculty of femininity)
17 = *purisindriya* (faculty of masculinity)
18 = *hadaya-vatthu* (heart-basis)
19 = *kāyaviññatti* (bodily expression)
20 = *vacīviññatti* (vocal expression)
21 = *rūpassa lahutā* (lightness of matter)
22 = *rūpassa mudutā* (pliancy of matter)
23 = *rūpassa kammaññatā* (wieldiness of matter)

Composition of the *Rūpakalāpas*

Rūpakalāpas	Kalāpaṅgas
(a) *suddhaṭṭhaka* (basic octad)	1+2+3+4+5+7+8+9
(b) *sadda-navaka* (sound-nonad)	(a) + 6
(c) *jīvita-navaka* (vital-nonad)	(a) + 15
(d) *cakkhu-dasaka* (eye-decad)	(c) + 10
(e) *sota-dasaka* (ear-decad)	(c) + 11
(f) *ghāna-dasaka* (nose-decad)	(c) + 12
(g) *jivhā-dasaka* (tongue-decad)	(c) + 13

(h) *kāya-dasaka* (body-decad)	(c) + 14
(i) *itthibhāva-dasaka* (decad of femininity)	(c) + 16
(j) *pumbhāva-dasaka* (decad of masculinity)	(c) + 17
(k) *vatthu-dasaka* (decad of heart-basis)	(c) + 18
(l) *kāyaviññatti-navaka* (nonad of bodily expression)	(a) + 19
(m) *vacīviññatti-dasaka* (decad of vocal expression)	(b) + 20
(n) *lahut'ād'ekādasaka* (undecad of plasticity)	(a) + 21 + 22 + 23
(o) *kāyaviññatti-lahut'ādi-dvādasaka* (dodecad of bodily expression and plasticity)	(a) + 19 + 21 + 22 + 23
(p) *vacīviññatti-sadda-lahut'ādi-terasaka* (tredecad of vocal expression, sound, and plasticity)	(b) + 20 + 21 + 22 + 23
(q) *sadda-lahut'ādi-dvādasaka* (dodecad of sound and plasticity)	(b) + 21 + 22 + 23

9

TIME AND TEMPORALITY

WE HAVE HAD the occasion to discuss the concept of space as understood in Buddhism in two previous chapters. It was observed that unlike in many systems of Indian Philosophy, in Buddhism space is not elevated to the level of an elemental substance (*mahābhūta*). Rather, it was brought down to the level of a concept (*paññatti*), a mental construct with no corresponding objective reality.

The same situation is true of time as well. The very fact that time is not postulated as a dhamma, conditioned or unconditioned, obviously means that time too is a mental construct with no corresponding objective reality. There is, however, reference to one Buddhist school that took up the opposite position. It maintained that like all other dhammas, time, moment, or "any stroke of time" is something positively produced (*parinipphanna*).[712] Positive production, according to Theravāda, is true only of conditioned dhammas because, unlike mental constructs, they are produced by causes and conditions.

The overall Buddhist theory of time is in sharp contrast to that of the substantialist schools of Indian philosophy, where we find time recognized as an eternal, all-pervading substance; its existence is said to be inferred from facts of consecution and simultaneity between phenomena. An extreme position on the nature of time was maintained by the eternalist school of Kālavādins. They insisted that absolute time is the primordial cause of everything, an all-mighty force that brings under its inexorable sway all that exists. We find their theory summarized in a Pāli sub-commentary:

It's Time that creates all living beings;
it's Time that destroys them all.
It's Time that's awake while the world is asleep;
irreversible indeed is the flow of Time.[713]

A direct Buddhist response to this we find in the Mūlapariyāya Jātaka:

Time all consumes, even time itself as well.
He who isn't (consumed by time), consumes the
all-consumer.[714]

It is the arahant, the one who has attained *nibbāna*, who has consumed the all-consuming time. Hence the arahant is also called "the one who has gone beyond time (*gataddha*), the one who has transcended saṃsāric time (*saṃsāraddham atikkanta*)."[715]

In the Abhidhamma there are at least five technical terms signifying time. These are *kāla* (time, season), *addhan* (length of time, duration), *samaya* ("coming together" = occasion), *santati* (series, continuum), and *khaṇa* (moment). What is interesting to note here is that *kāla* is the term most often used when the objective reality of time is denied. The reason for this could be Kālavāda, the time-doctrine, which, as noted above, asserted the absolute reality of time. *Addhan* is used to mean "stretch, length," not only of time but of space as well.[716] In the sense of time, it means a lifetime or long period like the beginningless cycle of births and deaths (*saṃsāraddhāna*). This explains why *nibbāna* is described as free from *addhan*.[717] As we shall see, *santati* as series or continuum means perceptible time, the actual experience of a "now." This is in contrast to momentary time, which is not perceptible. *Khaṇa* is used in a general sense to mean a small fraction of time, and also in a technical sense to mean the briefest temporal unit. It is also used to mean the right occasion, the opportune time (*khaṇoti okāso*).[718]

Samaya is the term that Buddhism prefers most. In its technical sense it means "the confluence of conditions" (*paccaya-sāmaggi*) or "the coming together of the appropriate causes" (*karaṇa-samavāya*). This is another way of referring to a particular occurrence.[719] Every occurrence is, for the Abhidhamma, a concurrence, in view of its causal principle that a multiplicity of conditions gives rise to a multiplicity of effects. To clarify where *samaya* differs from *kāla*, a Pāli sub-commentary cites this sentence: "Perhaps tomorrow we might go there, considering both *kāla* and *samaya*." Here *kāla* means the due time for arriving (*yutta-kāla*), whereas *samaya* means the confluence of conditions (*paccaya-sāmaggi*) necessary for the arrival.[720] "Arrival" is not something distinct from "the confluence of conditions." The confluence of conditions is itself the arrival.[721]

There is another important difference to be noted between *kāla* and *samaya*. It is *kāla* in the sense of objective time that the Abhidhamma denies. Samaya in the sense of time is in fact not denied, because what it really means is "the coming together of conditions" (*sameti samavetī ti samayo*).[722] In fact, *samaya* is the Abhidhamma's answer to what the substantialist schools call *kāla*, in the sense of absolute time.

An interesting commentarial observation on *samaya* concerns why it is used in three different cases in the Sutta-, Vinaya-, and Abhidhamma Piṭaka. A sutta begins with *ekaṃ samayaṃ*, "at one time." Here *samaya* is used in the accusative case (*upayoga-vacana*). *Vinaya* begins with *tena samayena*, "at that time." Here *samaya* is used in the instrumental case (*karaṇa-vacana*). Abhidhamma begins with *yasmiṃ samaye*, "at which time." Here *samaya* is used in the locative case (*bhumma-vacana*). The use of the term in three different cases, it is claimed, is not accidental but purposefully done. If the suttas use the accusative case, this is to show that the time intended here is non-specific, non-definite (*aniyamita*). If Vinaya uses the instrumental case, this is to focus on the factors that are instrumental (*hetubhūtena karaṇabhūtena*) for the promulgation of ecclesiastical rules. If the Abhidhamma uses the locative case, this is to show how time serves as a location, a sort of receptacle for the coming together of consciousness and its concomitants.[723]

There are in all six kinds of concept-as-name (*nāma-paññatti*). The term "time" comes under one of them as an *avijjamāna-paññatti*—that is, a term that refers to a thing that does not exist in a real sense. The notion of "time" is based on the continuous flow of the dhammas. It is the dhammas, which arise and perish in continual succession, that serve as a base for our construction of the notion of "time." What is denied is not succession, but a distinct entity called "time" apart from the dhammas succeeding one another. Only the dhammas are real (*paramattha, saccikaṭṭha*); time is a conceptual construct, a product of interpretative function of our mind (*kappanā siddha*). Unlike the dhammas, time has no own-nature (*sabhāvato avijjamāna*).[724]

That time is determined by events is aptly summarized by the following statement: "Chronological time denoted by reference to this or that event is only a conventional expression" (*taṃ taṃ upādāya paññatto kālo vohāra-mattako*).[725] Temporal sequence is based on eventuation, but there is no time distinct from events (*dhammas*). Different "times" means not different parts of one and same time, but "times" determined by different events:

> Time is only a concept derived from this or that phenomenon, such as (a) states expressed in such phrases as "temporal (aspect) of mind," "temporal (aspect) of matter"; (b) the phenomenal occurrence expressed by such phrases as "the past" and "the future"; (c) the phenomenal succession in an organism expressed by "the time of seed germination" and "the time of sprouting"; (d) the characteristic marks of phenomena expressed by "the time of genesis" and "the time of decay"; (e) the functions of phenomena expressed by "the time of feeling," "the time of cognizing"; (f) functions of living beings expressed by "the time of bathing" and "the time of drinking"; (g) the modes of posture expressed by "the time of going" and "the time of stopping"; (h) the revolution of the moon, sun, etc., expressed by "morning," "evening," "day," and "night"; or (i) grouping of days and nights, etc., into periods expressed by "half-month," "month."[726]

Accordingly, the Pāli commentaries speak of a "plurality of times" (*samaya-nānatta*), and in the same context, of a plurality of causal confluences as well.[727] A causal confluence is the completeness of conditions (*paccaya-sāmaggi*) necessary for the occurrence of an event. All causal confluences, in the final analysis, are causal confluences of mental and physical dhammas. Apart from the dhammas, there is no discrete entity called "time" (*na hi tabbinimmutto añño koci kālo nāma atthi*).[728]

The question is raised whether any reference to temporal distinctions of past, present, and future implies the recognition of time as a real existent (*addhā nāmāyaṃ dhammo eva āpannoti*?).[729] The answer given is that there is no such dhamma called "time" because all temporal distinctions are, in the final analysis, distinctions pertaining to dhammas themselves (*dhammassa pana avatthābhedo*). Although time does not exist in its own-nature (*sabhāvena avijjamāno'pi*), yet it is possible to speak of things as belonging to the three divisions of time by considering time as a receptacle (*adhikaraṇa*) and as a support (*ādhāra*) for their serial occurrence.[730]

All conceptual constructs, according to the Buddhist commentarial exegesis, are time-free (*kāla-vimutta*). If time is a conceptual construct, how are we to understand time as time-free? What we need to remember here is that time divisions are not divisions of an absolute time. They refer to the dhammas that arise, exist, and dissolve. In other words, time does not exist in time. If time exists in time, then this (second) time will require a third time to exist. And the third a fourth, and thus it will involve what Buddhist exegesis calls a process of interminability (*anupaccheda*) or infinite regress (*anavaṭṭhāna*).

Dhammas become past, present, and future in three different ways: by way of moments, series, and lifespan. According to moments, past means the dhammas that have ceased after going through the three moments of arising, presence, and dissolution (*tayo khaṇe patvā niruddha)*; future means the dhammas that have not yet arrived at the three moments (*tayo khaṇe asampatta*); and present means the dhammas that pass through the three moments (*tayo khaṇe sampatta, khaṇattaya-pariyāpanna*).[731] In like manner, we need to understand the other two, by way of series and by way of lifespan.

Strictly speaking, "present" means the momentary present (*khaṇa-paccuppanna*) consisting of the three moments of arising, presence, and dissolution. Obviously this kind of time is not actually perceptible. Serial present (*santati-paccuppanna*) is the answer for perceptible time. As to its definition, we find two different opinions. In illustrating it, those who recite the Majjhimanikāya give the following examples: when a person, after having sat in darkness, goes to the light, material objects do not become manifest to him all at once. The time that required for the material objects to become manifest is equal to one or two continua. Similarly when a person, after having walked in the night, enters a room, the time that takes place until the objects become manifest should be understood as one or two continua. When a person standing afar sees the bodily movements of people washing clothes or beating drums and ringing bells, he does not hear at once the sound they make. The time that passes until he hears the sound is equal to one or two continua.[732]

On the other hand, Saṃyuttabhāṇakas, or those who recite the Saṃyuttanikāya, recognize two kinds of continua: one material (*rūpa-santati*) and the other mental (*arūpa-santati*). "The material continuity is when the ripples of the water stepped into by one crossing to the bank have not settled down; or when, after a journey, the heat of the body has not subsided; or when, to one coming into a room out of the glare, the gloom is not yet dispelled; or when, after being occupied indoors with religious exercise, one looks out of the window during the day and the quivering of the eyes has not subsided. A mental continuum is equal to two or three cognitive processes (*javana-vithi*), each lasting seventeen mind-moments.[733]

Two or three cognitive processes, as Venerable Nyanaponika Thera observes, appears too brief a time-interval to "ascribe actual perceptibility," while "the earlier examples imply a duration too long to convey the idea of "present." However, as he further observes, "still we must suppose that the second division, the 'serial present,' is intended to refer to the actual experience of a now."[734]

The third way of defining the present is with reference to the present life-term (*addhā-paccuppanna*). This is according to the teaching of the suttas. It is an exposition of relative validity. The other two ways of defining the present, by way of series and moment, are according to the Abhidhamma. It is an exposition of absolute validity.[735]

On the mutual relationship between time and consciousness, a Pāli commentary says:

> *Samaye niddisi cittaṃ cittena samayaṃ muṇi*
> *Niyametvāna dīpetuṃ dhamme tattha pabhedato.*[736]

As translated by Venerable Nyanaponika Thera:

> By time the Sage described the mind
> and by the mind described the time,
> in order to show, by such definition,
> the phenomena there arranged in classes.[737]

We need to understand this in the light of the Abhidhamma's description of the arising of consciousness and its mental factors, as described in the Dhammasaṅganī. The first part of the description begins with "in which time" (*yasmiṃ samaye*), and the second with "at that time" (*tasmiṃ samaye*). "In which time," as the Pāli commentary says, "is an indefinite locative," "an indefinitely marked time" Its purpose is to identify the time during which consciousness and its mental factors arise (*samaya-niddesa*). On the other hand, "at that time" refers to the time during which all the mental states (both consciousness and mental factors) arise together as a single cognitive act (*dhamma-uddesa*). Now, *samaya* in the phrase *yasmiṃ samaye* is said to occur in the sense of occasion or time, and here time is defined to mean "support" (*ādhāra*) or "locus" (*adhikaraṇa*). It is true that time does not exist in a real and ultimate sense. However, for the purpose of description, here it is considered as a support (*ādhārabhāvena paññatto*). On the other hand, *samaya* in the phrase *tasmiṃ samaye* is used not in the sense of time (support), but in the sense of "aggregation" or "coming together," not one after another, but all together. Here the reference is to the causally connected occurrence of consciousness and its mental factors.[738]

It is with reference to *samaya* in the sense of "time" that *samaya* in the sense of "coming together" gets delimited. A Pāli commentary illustrates this situation as follows: "The man who went out when the cows are being milked returned when the cows have been milked." Here it is the time of milking the cows (*dohana-kiriyā*) that delimits the time of the man's movement (*gamana-kiriyā*). In the same way, "at which time" delimits the time of the arising of consciousness and such mental factors as sensory contact.[739]

The Pāli commentators interpret "at which time" of the Dhammasaṅganī as "in which moment," and "at that time" as "at that moment." Here the term "moment" (*khaṇa*) is used in its technical sense to mean the briefest temporal unit.[740] In the context of this commentarial interpretation, the moment as the briefest temporal unit becomes definable as equal to the duration of consciousness and its mental factors. Thus while a consciousness and its mental factors (a cognitive act) determine the measure of the moment as the briefest temporal unit, the moment in turn determines the time during which a consciousness and its mental factors arise.

In concluding this section, it is necessary to refer here to another meaning "time" has assumed in Buddhism. Because "past," "present," and "future" are not entities distinct from the dhammas, therefore, as an extension of its meaning time came to be reckoned as another expression for the cycle of births and deaths (*saṃsāraddha*).[741] When King Milinda asked Sage Nāgasena "What is time?" the latter explains it as the process of dhammas and *saṅkhāras* (that constitute saṃsāra).[742] If the formula of dependent arising with its twelve factors involves three periods, each period is not distinct from the factors that belong to the particular period. Time comes to an end with the realization of nibbāna. Therefore, nibbāna is the transcendence of time through full understanding (*addhāna-pariññā*). Since the three temporal divisions are predicable of the dhammas, in the sense that we have examined above, the dhammas came to be described as "belonging to the three times" (*tekālika*). On the other hand, nibbāna is "free from time" (*kāla-vimutta*).[743] As mentioned above, one who has attained nibbāna "has gone beyond time" (*gataddha*), "has transcended the cycle of time" (*saṃsāraddhānam atikkanta*), and "has consumed (the all-consuming) time" (*kālaghaso*). We find this same idea in a pre-Abhidhamma work where the arahant is described as one who has transcended time (*kappātīta*).[744]

The Abhidhamma theory of time requires that we make a clear distinction between the types of entities that exist in a real and ultimate sense (*dhammas*) and the types of entities that exist only as conceptual constructs (*paññatti*). The former refer to those entities that truly exist independently of the cognitive act, and the latter to those entities that owe their being to the act of cognition itself. It is in this context that we need to understand the place Abhidhamma assigns to time and space.

10

THE ETHICO-PHILOSOPHICAL BASIS OF THE BUDDHIST ANALYSIS OF MATTER

THE EXACT NATURE of the earliest form of Buddhism is, for some scholars, still a matter of controversy.[745] However, on the basis of the Pāli Nikāyas as they exist in their present form, we can certainly conclude that Buddhism is, in the main, a doctrine of emancipation. Deliverance from the saṃsāric plane of existence—in other words, the realization of nibbāna—is its final goal. The Buddha himself says that as a religious teacher he teaches only two things: suffering and its cessation.[746] Buddhism's analysis of the world of experience is undertaken not for its own sake, but for evolving a rationale for its doctrine and discipline. Attention is not concentrated on the empirical world in and for itself. The Buddhist inquiry into the nature and constitution of matter and its relevance for Buddhism cannot be properly understood if the subject is divorced from this religious context.

The close connection between the Buddhist analysis of matter and Buddhist ethics is indicated by the oft-recurring statement *rūpaṃ saññojaṇīyo dhammo*[747]—that is, matter is something that is favorable to, or productive of, fetters (*saññojana*), the fetters that bind the living being to saṃsāric existence. The description of *rūpa* as *saññojanīya*, conducive to the creation of fetters, does not mean that it is a fetter in itself. It is the *upādāna*, "the laying hold of"—that is, the craving for or attachment to *rūpa*—that constitutes the *saññojana*. One is said to be bound by Māra when one grasps *rūpa*—*Rūpaṃ upādiyamāno baddho*

Mārassa.[748] Since *rūpa* is favorable or leading to *upādāna*, it is called *upādānīya*;[749] since *upādāna* is a *gantha*, a tie, fetter, it is also called *ganthanīya*;[750] and since *gantha* nourishes and prolongs *ogha*, the flood (of saṃsāric existence), it is also called *oghanīya.*[751]

That *rūpa* in itself is neither a *saṃyojana* nor a *gantha* is very well illustrated by a conversation between Venerable Sāriputta and Venerable Mahākoṭṭhita.[752] When the latter asks whether the eye (*cakkhu*) is a bond in relation to the visible (*rūpa*), or vice versa, the former denies both alternatives and goes on to say that what constitutes the bond is the *chanda-rāga*—any desire or passion that might arise as a result of their contact. If two oxen, one white and another black, are tied by a yoke or a yoke-tie, it is not correct to say that the black ox is a bond for the white ox or vice versa. It is the yoke or the yoke-tie that constitutes the bond; it is that which unites them both. So it is in the case of the eye and the visible. The *saṃyojana* lies in the *chanda-rāga*. This situation is true between the whole cognitive apparatus on the one hand and the external sense-objects on the other. If it were otherwise, then one had to rule out the very basis of the practice of higher life (*brahmacariyavāsa*), which has as its goal the elimination of all suffering (*sammā-dukkhakkhaya*).[753]

More or less the same idea is reflected in the *Indriyabhāvanā Sutta*,[754] where the Buddha questions a disciple of Pārāsariya how his master teaches the culture of the senses. In reply the latter says that the senses are to be trained to the extent when they fail to fulfill their respective functions: the eye does not see forms; the ear does not hear sounds. The Buddha rejoins that this kind of sense-culture would lead to the conclusion that the blind and the deaf have their senses best cultivated. The implication is that mental culture is not to be associated with the suppression of the senses; they should be cultivated to see the truth, to see things as they really are (*yathābhūtaṃ*).

Because *rūpa* in itself is not a *saṃyojana*, therefore freedom from *rūpa* (*rūpassa nissaraṇa*) means not the abandonment and elimination of *rūpa*, but the abandonment and elimination of *chanda-rāga* toward *rūpa.*[755] One is said to be freed from the Evil One when one ceases to grasp at *rūpa—rūpaṃ anupādiyamāno mutto pāpimato.*[756] It is with the complete waning away (*khayā*), cessation (*nirodhā*), letting go (*cāgā*), or abandonment (*paṭinissaggā*) of whatever desire (*chanda*), passion (*rāga*), attachment (*nandi*), craving (*taṇhā*), grasping (*upādāna*), and all kinds of mental prejudices and biases (*cetaso adhiṭṭhānābhinivesānusaya*) toward (in relationto) *rūpa* that the mind is said to be *suvimutta*, well-freed, from *rūpa.*[757] Hence it is that the monks are constantly advised to eschew all kinds of desire and passion in respect of *rūpa—yo bhikkhave rūpasmiṃ chandarāgo taṃ pajahatha.*[758]

But this *chanda-rāga* cannot be properly disciplined or eliminated without a proper knowledge about the nature of *rūpa*. In other words, because *rūpa* is *saṃyojanīya*—therefore it should be *pariññeyya* (understood, comprehended).[759] Ignorance breeds attachment, which in turn impedes spiritual progress. For it is by not knowing, not seeing things as they truly are, that one gets attached to them—*ajānaṃ, apassaṃ, sārajjati.*[760] Hence if one wants to free oneself from *rūpa*—that is, to free from the attachment to *rūpa*, one should know its true nature. One who is wanting in such knowledge cannot be expected to make an end of suffering (*dukkha*)—*Rūpaṃ bhikkhave anabhijānaṃ aparijānaṃ . . . abhabbo dukkhakkhayāya.*[761] Hence it is that the monks are advised to be *rūpaññū*, "knowers of matter." One who is not *rūpaññū* cannot be expected to reach the higher stages of spiritual progress (*vuddhi, virūḷhi*).[762] Here then is the relevance of the analysis of matter to the practical doctrine and discipline of Buddhism. Buddhism recognizes that *rūpa* is *saṃyojanīya* and concludes that it should (therefore) be *pariññeyya*. The analysis of matter is thus necessitated by an ethical need and is therefore elaborated mainly in the interests of ethics. This is also true of the Buddhist analysis of mind (*nāma*). Both mind (*nāma*) and matter (*rūpa*) are analyzed and described with a practical end in view.

In the earlier texts where *rūpa* is explained in simple and general terms the ethical approach to the subject is much more pronounced. That *rūpa* is impermanent and that therefore it cannot be made the basis of true happiness is the main theme that runs throughout all such discussions.

Whatever form it assumes *rūpa* is certainly not permanent (*nicca, dhuva*).[763] Its origination is manifested (*uppādo paññāyati*), so is its dissolution (*vayo'pi paññāyati*).[764] It arises owing to a complex of causes (*paṭicca-samuppanna*), is conditioned (*saṅkhata*), is subject to becoming otherwise or to change (*aññathābhāvī*), to waning away (*khayadhamma*), to passing away (*vayadhamma*), to cessation (*nirodhadhamma*).[765] This is true of all *rūpa*, whether it exists as a part of the complex that makes the living being (*ajjhattaṃ ajjhattika*) or whether it exists externally (*bahiddhā, bāhira*). "There comes a time when the external water-element is angry and the external earth-element disappears before it. Then will this external earth-element, ancient though it be, reveal how transient is its nature, how subject to dissolution and decay, how mutable. And what of this short-lived body bred of cravings?"[766] Since all *rūpa* in which one participates is characterized by impermanence, it cannot be made the basis of true happiness. It may give rise to some kind of pleasure—for otherwise the living beings would not get attached to it[767]—but certainly not permanent happiness. The things one gets attached to are constantly changing. Hence attachment to them would inevitably lead to unrest and sorrow.[768] One who follows them with avid greed and passion will have his mind scattered and dissipated (*vikkhitta, visaṭa*).[769]

Rūpa give rise to ideas of attachment and repugnance, and hence to a desire to satisfy the feelings so excited. Accordingly *rūpa* is often described in such a way as to bring into relief the dangers (*ādinava*) that arise from attachment to it and the happiness that results from detachment from it. Hence it is that *rūpa* is often described as, or compared to, Māra, a slayer (*māretā*), a disease (*roga*), a pestering wound (*gaṇḍa*), an arrow (*salla*), pain (*agha*), a slaughterer (*vadhaka*), or fire (*āditta*).[770] These are descriptions made for the purpose of religious edification, and as such should be understood in a profoundly religious context. They testify not only to the reality of *rūpa* but also to its provocative influence.

With this same purpose in view, sometimes *rūpa* is sought to be described in quite a different way—in a way that seems to suggest its unreality. *Rūpa*, it is said, should be approached as *suñña* (void), *tuccha* (false), *ritta* (empty), and *asāra* (essenceless).[771] Similar statements are extended to the other four *khandhas*, too. In the Saṃyuttanikāya, for instance, *rūpa* is compared to a drop of froth (*phenapiṇḍa*), *vedanā* to a bubble of water (*bubbula*), *saññā* to a mirage (*marici*), *saṅkhāra* to a plantain-trunk (*kadali*), and *viññāṇa* to an illusion (*māyā*).[772] In the Suttanipāta, Mogharāja is bidden to consider the world as *suñña*—*suññato lokaṃ avekkhassu*.[773] Then we have: "*Ajjhattañ ca bahiddhā ca natthi kiñciti passato*" (There is nothing internal or external to one who thinks, "Is there anything?");[774] "*Natthīti nissāya tarassu oghaṃ*" (Cross the flood based on the thought, "There is nothing.").[775]

Statements such as these seem to give the impression that Buddhism (as represented in the Nikāyas) does not believe in the reality of *rūpa* or any other *khandhas*, and that it is, or at least tends to be, nihilistic. In fact, Professor Kern, who agrees with Professor Waddell's suggestion—namely, that early Buddhism is an "idealistic nihilism[776]—refers to the last two statements as an instance where "nihilism is tersely expressed."[777] These statements, it seems to us, are made in a profoundly religious context. And once they are understood in this context, they do not lend themselves to such an interpretation.

Suññatā, as explained in the Nikāyas, does not really mean void (although we have translated it so), but devoid—devoid of *atta* (self, substance) or of anything pertaining to *atta* (*attaniyena*).[778] *Ritta*, *tuccha*, and *asāra* carry more or less the same meaning. To deny a persistent or ever-perduring substance, mental or material, does not mean that the world of experience is unreal. It only amounts to a different interpretation of the world. The Nikāyas make it abundantly clear that the cosmos or the world (*loka*) is lacking (*ūṇa*) in any persistent and permanent substance and that consequently it cannot be held to be permanent (*dhuva*). In view of this fact, it is not possible to regard it as one's own (*saka*) or as a haven of security (*tāna*).[779] Hence the description of the world as *suñña*, *tucha*, and *ritta* is not without significance even within a realistic context.

Stated otherwise, those statements that seem to suggest a nihilistic metaphysic are really indicative of the fact of dukkha, which characterizes all forms of saṃsāric existence. The term *dukkha*, as pointed out by Professor Stcherbatsky,[780] should not always be translated as "pain," "misery," or "suffering." As a philosophical term it means much more, in the sense that it includes such ideas as "imperfection," "absence of an abiding substance," "conflict," and "unrest." This explains why the characterization *dukkha* is extended even to matter. It also explains why the states of *jhāna*, resulting from the practice of higher meditation, and which are free from suffering as ordinarily understood, are also included in *dukkha*. For, they, too, are conditioned and subject to change. The Buddhist discourses recognize the wider implications of the term when they explain it as threefold—namely, *dukkha-dukkha* (*dukkha* as suffering), *vipariṇāma-dukkha* (*dukkha* as change), and *saṅkhāra-dukkha* (*dukkka* as conditioned state).[781]

It is, in fact, these wider implications of the term *dukkha* that are brought into relief in the few quotations we have cited above. Moreover, if the texts sometimes describe saṃsāric existence in such a way as to suggest its unreality, this is understandable, particularly in a religious context. That is to say, for the purpose of religious edification it was necessary to show what a worthless thing saṃsāric existence is when compared to the eternal bliss of nibbāna. What is involved here is a question of valuation. Since nibbāna represents the highest goal, from the point of view of nibbāna, saṃsāra is, in a way, a "non-entity," for it does not afford a permanent basis on which permanent happiness can be established. In this sense it is unreal. This seems to be the reason why the Suttanipāta says that one should cross the "flood" thinking that there is nothing here.

Statements that, at first sight, seem to countenance an idealistic interpretation of the world are also not wanting: "The world is led by the mind and is activated by the mind."[782] "Verily I declare to you, my friend, that within this very body, mortal as it is and only a fathom high, but conscious and endowed with mind, is the world and the waxing thereof and the waning thereof and the way that leads to the passing away thereof."[783]

Here, too, we should guard ourselves against relying on isolated passages, and those, too, taken out of their context. For on the basis of such statements as these one may be tempted to conclude that Buddhism as revealed from the earlier texts is, or at least tends to be, idealistic. The presence of such statements should become clear if we constantly keep in mind the obvious fact that Buddhism is a religion and that mental culture plays an important part in it.

Since the whole Buddhist practical doctrine and discipline, which has the attainment of nibbāna as its final goal, is based on a course of mental culture, it is but natural if Buddhism gives a preeminent position to mind. But from this circumstance the conclusion does not necessarily follow that matter exists by virtue of mind. *Rūpa* is not *manomaya*, mind-made, but *manorāma*,[784] pleasing the mind, provoking the mind. Consciousness (*viññāṇa*) is said to be "externally agitated and dissipated" (*bahiddhā vikkhittaṃ, visaṭaṃ*) when one with avid greed and passion follows the sense-objects.[785] To one who is not free from passion, craving, desire, and thirst toward *rūpa*, with the change and dissolution of *rūpa* there arise all kinds of frustration.[786] But when one knows things as they truly are—that is, as impermanent (*anicca*), as suffering (*dukkha*), and as non-self (*anatta*)—one ceases to get agitated by them, one ceases to seek refuge in them.[787] On one's understanding of things depends one's reaction to them. Just as attachment to things is to get fettered by them, even so detachment from them is to get freed from them. Thus both the malady and the remedy lie within. In this context we could conveniently understand the significance of those statements that give a prominent place to mind.

The latter quotation, as pointed out by Professor Keith,[788] need not be understood as a metaphysical deliverance. It points to the fact that emancipation is within oneself and that therefore one must work out one's own salvation—a theme on which the Nikāyas constantly dwell on.[789] It is more in the nature of a counsel on self-reliance, and it is scarcely possible to draw any idealistic implications from it.

A somewhat similar idea seems to be reflected in another oft-recurrent statement—namely, "Where there is eye, where there is visible (*rūpa*), where there is visual consciousness . . . , there lies the world." The same formula is extended to the other sense-organs and the corresponding sense-objects.[790] This has sometimes been understood as countenancing a phenomenalistic interpretation of the external world: the external world has no independent reality but is dependent on the activities of the senses.[791] Taken in itself the quotation does point to such a conclusion. However, it seems doubtful whether it was meant to be an exhaustive definition on the nature of the external world. It seems more proper if we understand it as an attempt, made in the interests of the Buddhist practical doctrine and discipline, to show what "world" (*loka*) means for each individual. As far as each individual is concerned, his knowledge of things, mental as well as material, is gained through the activities of his six sense-spheres (*saḷ-āyatana*).[792] And all his ideas of attachment and repugnance and the desire to satisfy the feelings so excited function within this (his) "world." Since the Buddhist practical doctrine and discipline advocates the elimination of all ideas of attachment and repugnance, it is understandable if the texts say that, as far as each individual is concerned, the world is synonymous with the activities of his six sense-spheres. This, it seems to us, is the context in which the above and similar statements should be understood. The severely practical approach of Buddhism seems to be responsible for their presence. It is also not without significance that the above-mentioned definition of the world is often accompanied by the words *ariyassa vinaye*[793]—that is, in (according to) the noble discipline. That it was made in a truly Buddhistic sense is therefore fairly obvious.

If we base ourselves on the Pāli Nikāyas, then we should be compelled to conclude that Buddhism is realistic. There is no explicit denial anywhere of the external world. Nor is there any positive evidence to show that the world is mind-made or simply a projection of subjective thoughts. That Buddhism recognizes the extra-mental existence of matter and the external world is clearly suggested by the texts. Throughout the discourses it is the language of realism that one encounters.[794] The whole Buddhist practical doctrine and discipline, which has the attainment of nibbāna as its final goal, is based on the recognition of the material world and the conscious living beings living therein.

As soon as an individual is born, the outside world plays upon that individual. Sensations are stirred up within. Sensations give rise to ideas of attachment and repugnance. There arises desire to satisfy the excited feelings. This is the problem in which Buddhism is mainly interested. What matters is the given. It is seen that the individual is constantly played upon by the outside world. It is also seen that it is this contact between within and without that signifies the beginning of all kinds of unrest and attendant miseries.[795] It is this situation that Buddhism seeks to explain, not for its own sake, but for making an end of all suffering. As a philosophy Buddhism begins where necessity sets in.

The *Siṃsapā Sutta*,[796] as Professor Oldenberg observes, states briefly what Buddhism is and what it is not. "It does not purport to be a philosophy which inquires into the ultimate ground of things, unfold to thought the breadths and depths of the universe."[797] For it is little interested in metaphysical questions and in constructive speculations of the universe, which have no immediate relevance and reference to the problem of salvation. Hence questions concerning the first and final causes or the original germ of all things are set aside. Speculative questions on the infinity and duration of the world are among those brought under the heading *avyākata*[798] (not answered). The reason for this attitude is that knowledge of such questions—whether they can be known or not is another question—is not essential for one to work out one's own salvation.

It is in the problem of dukkha and its elimination that Buddhism is primarily interested. "As the vast ocean, O disciples, is impregnated with one taste, the taste of salt, even so this doctrine and discipline is impregnated with one taste, the taste of deliverance."[799] But in order to fashion out a way of deliverance from saṃsāra, it was necessary to study the nature of saṃsāric existence. The individual should be shown exactly where he stands in relation to the universe around and within her, the obstacles with which she is besotted, and the potentialities with which she is endowed. It is for this reason that Buddhism seeks to explain the empiric individuality in relation to the external world.

The earlier attempts to explain this situation are represented by the analyses into aggregates (*khandha*), sense-spheres (*āyatana*), and sense-elements (*dhātu*). They are the component factors into which existence is analyzed. They purport to show that there does not exist a "unity," "substance," "*atta*," or "*jīva*." Unity is really a complex of factors; "one" is really "many." This applies to both mind (*nāma*) and matter (*rūpa*). Both exist as complexes. In the case of living beings there is no self (*atta*) that is immortal, while in the case of things in general there is no essence that is ever-perduring. That existence does not consist of a primary substance, mental or material, but is composed of a variety of factors is the conclusion that could be drawn from the analyses into *khandha*, *āyatana*, and *dhātu*. "The Tathāgata sees in its true perspective the world that consists of a plurality of elements, a variety of elements" (*Tathāgato . . . aneka-dhātu-nānā-dhātu-lokaṃ yathābhūtaṃ pajānāti*).[800] Since existence, both mental and material, is sought to be explained with reference to a plurality of basic factors, we may, following Professor Stcherbatsky,[801] call Buddhism (as represented in the Nikāyas) pluralistic.

Professor Murti is inclined to believe that the doctrine of elements (*khandha-dhātu-āyatana*) was not meant to be taken as an ultimate standpoint: "On our interpretation the doctrine of elements was necessary as a preliminary step. If there had been only the substance view (*ātmavāda*) in the field, the Buddha could not have been led to the dialectical consciousness. A modal view too was necessary. A thesis had to be opposed by a counterthesis before there could emerge the dialectical consciousness. Then alone could there be a Conflict in Reason and the attempt to transcend it. As a matter of dialectical necessity then did the Buddha formulate, or at least suggest, a theory of elements."[802]

There are certain trends in the canonical works that seem to support such a conclusion.[803] However, if we take into consideration the immense emphasis with which Buddhism advocates the eradication of all kinds of attachment to, or craving for, any kind of thing, mental or material, we could understand them in a different way. Here we may do well to draw a sharp distinction between the Buddhist analysis of existence and the Buddhist practical doctrine and discipline. Although existence is reduced to a multiplicity of basic factors, this certainly does not mean that one should lean on them, that one should have any attachment to them. They are as impermanent as the compounds they produce. They too belong to the level of saṃsāric existence. Hence they too should be transcended in the sense that one should free oneself from any kind of desire toward them. *Dhātu-kusalatā*,[804] the ability in the analysis of existence into different elements, is in itself not sufficient. In the context of the practical doctrine and discipline, it is only a preliminary step to *manasikāra-kusalatā*,[805] the ability to reflect on their true nature—that is, as impermanent (*anicca*), as devoid of any persistent substance (*anatta*), and as characterized by unrest or as a source of suffering (*dukkha*). It is only then that the yogin begins to turn away from them and ceases to have any kind of attachment to them.[806] Thus within the context of the Buddhist ethical discipline, *dhātu-kusalatā* is only a preliminary step to *manasikāra-kusalatā*, and *manasikāra-kusalatā* is only a preliminary step to the elimination of all desires, which in turn has the realization of nibbāna as its goal. But the advocacy of non-attachment (even) to the basic factors does not necessarily mean that they are considered as ultimately unreal. It seems that it is the immense emphasis with which Buddhism advocates its doctrine of non-attachment (*virāga*) that is responsible for the presence, in the texts, of certain trends that seem to suggest that the doctrine of elements (*khandha-dhātu-āyatana*) is not meant as an ultimate standpoint.

The fundamental character of Buddhist philosophy (as represented in the Nikāyas) is well illustrated by the Buddhist refutation of the four theses—namely, *sabbaṃ atthi*, *sabbaṃ natthi*, *sabbaṃ ekattaṃ*, and *sabbaṃ puthuttaṃ*.[807]

Avoiding the two extremes (*anta*) of *sabbaṃ atthi* (everything is) and *sabbaṃ natthi* (everything is not), it steers a middle course: "This world, O Kaccāna, generally proceeds on a duality, of the 'it is' and the 'it is not.' But, O Kaccāna, whoever perceives in truth and wisdom how things originate in the world, in his eyes there is no 'it is not' in this world. Whoever, Kaccāna, perceives in truth and wisdom how things pass away in this world, in his eyes there is no 'it is' in this world."[808] Thus neither being nor non-being is the truth. There is only becoming, happening by way of cause, continuity without identity, persistence without a persisting substance. "He who discerns origin by way of cause, he discerns the Dhamma; he who discerns the Dhamma, he discerns origin by way of cause."[809] No permanence is associated with the basic factors of existence or the compounds they produce. They are conditioned (*saṅkhata*), brought about by certain causes (*paticcasamuppanna*), and are subject to dissolution (*nirodha-dhamma*). *Anicca* (impermanence), *aññathatta* (becoming otherwise), *vipariṇāma* (fluctuation), *khaya* (waning away), *vaya* (passing away), *udayabbaya* (rise and fall): these words, more or less synonymous, and occurring in the texts with more or less equal frequency, indicate the great emphasis with which Buddhism advocated its doctrine of change.[810]

Buddhism also steers a middle course between *sabbaṃ ekattaṃ* and *sabbaṃ puthuttaṃ*.[811] *Ekattaṃ* implies a unity, a whole with fractions. The component parts of the universe, according to the Buddhist analysis, are not fractions of a whole indicating an absolute unity (*ekatta*), but a number of coordinate basic factors. This seems to be the reason why Buddhism refuses to subscribe to the view of existence implied by the thesis, *sabbaṃ ekattaṃ*. *Puthutta*, on the other hand, implies a theory of "absolute separateness" and suggests that the world is a concatenation of separate and discrete factors with no interconnection, with no interdependence. A theory of this kind is, in fact, advocated by one of the six *paribbājakas* mentioned in the *Sāmaññaphala Sutta*.[812] The Buddhist view of existence does not amount to such an extreme (*anta*). For according to Buddhism, the factors of existence are interconnected by laws of causality. Although the factors are not the fractions of a whole, yet they are interconnected and interdependent. Thus causality emphasizes some kind of unity, but not an extreme form of unity as implied by *sabbaṃ ekattaṃ*.

In the works of the Abhidhamma Piṭaka and its exegesis the realistic and pluralistic view of existence is retained and is developed further. That existence does not consist of a primary substance is the main theme that is sought to be explained here. Although the analyses into *khandha*, *āyatana*, and *dhātu* are retained, the general pattern of the analysis has undergone some notable change. *Nāma* (mind, the mental) is divided into two broad groups as *citta* (consciousness) and *cetasika* (consciousness-concomitants). *Rūpa* (matter) is divided (analyzed) into twenty-eight items. These mental and material factors of existence are introduced by the technical term *dhammā*.

The definition of these mental and material dhammas and the explanation of their interconnection form the primary function of the works of the Abhidhamma Piṭaka. One cardinal principle that is implicitly accepted is that to understand properly any given item is to know it in all relations, under all the aspects recognized in the philosophy and the practical doctrine and discipline of Buddhism. Therefore the same material is sought to be classified in different ways and from different points of view. This explains why in the Dhammasaṅganī and other Abhidhamma Pakaraṇas, one encounters interminable lists of classifications. Although they may appear as repetitive and therefore monotonous, yet they serve a useful purpose. For they bring into relief not only the individual characteristics of each dhamma, but also its position in relation to other dhammas.

In the list of rūpa-dhammas given in the works of the Abhidhamma Piṭaka, some of the items—particularly those that in the post-canonical Abhidhammic works are brought under the heading *anipphanna*—may appear as artificial constructions. However, if we try to understand the list in the context of the Buddhist (Theravāda) philosophy and its practical doctrine and discipline, the selection of the items becomes meaningful.

Of the twenty-eight rūpa-dhammas, the four *mahābhūtas* and *rūpa*, *gandha*, *rasa*, and *āhāra* explain the constitution of matter in general. For they are the basic elements (the *avinibhoga-rūpa* of the commentators) present in all instances of matter, whether they exist as a part of the complex that makes the living being or otherwise. *Sadda* stands for sound, and *ākāsa-dhātu* for delimited space, the space delimited by matter. All the remaining seventeen items pertain exclusively to the body of a living being. This fact, at least indirectly, suggests that it was the physical aspects of a personality more than matter in general that drew the special attention of the Ābhidhammikas. When we remember the nature and the scope of the Buddhist analysis of existence, such a situation becomes quite understandable. Of the seventeen items in question, five—namely, *cakkhu*, *sota*, *ghāna*, *jivhā*, and *kaya*—are the first five sense-organs, the physical bases of the five kinds of consciousness named after them, or the material constituents of the cognitive apparatus. *Itthindriya* and *purisindriya* signify the sex distinctions, and *rūpa-jīvitindriya* accounts for the life principle of kamma-caused matter. The two *viññattis*—namely, *kāyaviññatti* and *vacīviññatti*—explain how a personality expresses itself. They are really connected with the Buddhist theory of kamma. For they represent the physical manifestation of karmically qualifiable thoughts. The triad of *lahutā*, *mudutā*, and *kammaññatā* shows the special importance attached to bodily health or efficiency (which is necessary for mental culture). The last four items—namely, *upacaya*, *santati*, *jaratā*, and *aniccatā*—represent four phases of the history of the body, from the moment of conception to the moment of death. It will thus be seen that the list of rūpa-dhammas is an attempt to explain and account for all the physical aspects—as well as certain facts connected with these physical aspects—of a personality and its physical environment.

ABBREVIATIONS

A.	Aṅguttaranikāya
AA.	Aṅguttaranikāya Aṭṭhakathā
Abhd.	Abhidharmadīpa (with Vibhāṣāprabhāvṛtti)
Abhmṛ.	Abhidharmāmṛta
AbhMṬ.	AbhidhammaMūlaṬīkā
Abhvk.	Abhidhammatthavikāsiṇī
Abhs.	Abhidharmasamuccaya
Abhvt.	Abhidhammāvatāra
ABORI.	Annals of the Bhandarkar Oriental Research Institute, Poona
ADS.	Abhidhammatthasaṅgaha
ADSS.	Abhidharmārthasaṃgrahasannaya
ADSVṬ.	AbhidhammatthasaṅgahaVibhāvinī Ṭīkā
AK.	L'Abhidharmakośa de Vasubandhu
AKvy.	(Sphuṭārthā) Abhidharmakośavyākhyā
AM.	Asia Major, Leipzig
AMG.	Annales du Musée Guimet, Paris
AO.	ArchivOrientální, Journal of the Czechoslovak Oriental Intitute, Prague
Asl.	Atthasālinī (Dhammasaṅganī Aṭṭhakathā)
BB.	Bibliotheca Buddhica, St. Petersburg

BEFEO.	Bulletin de l'École Française d'Extrême-Orient, Hanoi
BJS.	Buddha Jayanti Series, Colombo
BL.	Buddhist Logic
BP.	Buddhist Philosophy in India and Ceylon
BPE.	Buddhist Psychological Ethics
BPP.	Buddhist Psychology of Perception
BSOAS.	Bulletin of the School of Oriental and African Studies, London
CCB.	Central Conception of Buddhism
CJS.	Ceylon Journal of Science, Colombo
CMA.	Comprehensive Manual of Abhidhamma
CPB.	Central Philosophy of Buddhism
Cpd.	Compendium of Philosophy
CP. Mdhy. Vṛt.	Candrakīrti Prasanapadā Mādhyamakavṛtti
D.	Dīghanikāya
DA.	Dīghanikāya Aṭṭhakathā
DṬ.	DīghanikāyaṬīkā
Dhp.	Dhammapada
Dhs.	Dhammasaṅganī
DhsA.	Dhammasaṅganī Aṭṭhakathā
Divy.	Divyāvadāna
Dkp.	Dukapaṭṭhāna
ERE.	Encyclopaedia of Religion and Ethics, 13 vols., ed. J. Hastings
HIP	History of Indian Philosophy
HJAS.	Harvard Journal of Asiatic Studies, Cambridge, Massachusetts.
IC.	Indian Culture, Calcutta
IHQ.	Indian Historical Quarterly
IP.	Indian Psychology
Iti.	Itivuttaka
JA.	Journal Asiatique, Paris
JOIB.	Journal of the Oriental Institute, Baroda

JPTS.	Journal of the Pali Text Society, London, Oxford
JRAS.	Journal of the Royal Asiatic Society
KSP.	Le traité de la demonstration de l'act (Karmasiddhiprakaraṇa)
Kvu.	Kathāvatthu
KvuA.	Kathāvatthuppakaraṇa Aṭṭhakathā
La Siddhi	La Siddhi de Hiuan Tsang
M.	Majjhimanikāya
MA.	Majjhimanikāya Aṭṭhakathā
MBP.	Manual of Buddhist Philosophy
MCB.	Mélanges Chinois et Bouddhiques, l'Institut Belge des Hautes ÉtudesChinoises, Brussels
Mdhy. Vṛt.	Mādhyamakavṛtti
MhNd.	Mahāniddesa
MhNdA.	Mahāniddesa Aṭṭhakathā
Mil.	Milindapañha
MV	Mahāvastu
Mvn.	Mohavicchedanī
NRP.	Nāmarūpapariccheda
NRS.	Nāmarūpasamāsa
PBO.	Polski Biuletyn Orientalistyczny, Polish Bulletin of Oriental Studies
Peṭ.	Peṭakopadesa
PIPC.	Proceedings of the Indian Philosophical Congress
Psm.	Paṭisambhidāmagga
PsmA.	Paṭisambhidāmagga Aṭṭhakathā
PTS.	Pali Text Society, London, Oxford
PTSD.	Pali-English Dictionary of the Pali Text Society
PugA.	Puggalapaññatti Aṭṭhakathā
S.	Saṃyuttanikāya
SA.	Saṃyuttanikāya Aṭṭhakathā
SBB.	Sacred Books of the Buddhists
SBH.	Sacred Books of the Hindus
SBJ.	Sacred Books of the Jainas

Sn.	Suttanipāta
SnA.	Suttanipāta Aṭṭhakathā
ThīgA.	Therīgāthā Aṭṭhakathā
Tkp.	Tikapaṭṭhāna (with commentary)
Triṃś.	Triṃśikā (Vijñaptimātratāsiddhi)
UCR.	University of Ceylon Review, Colombo
Ud.	Udāna
UdA.	Udāna Aṭṭhakathā
Vbh.	Vibhaṅga
VbhA.	Vibhaṅga Aṭṭhakathā
VBQ.	Visva-Bharati Quarterly, Calcutta
VG.	Verspreide Geschriftenonderzijn Toezicht Verzameld, 15 vols., ed. H. Kern
Viṃś.	Viṃśatikā (Vijñaptimātratāsiddhi)
Vin.	Vinaya
Vsm.	Visuddhimagga
VsmS.	Viśuddhimārgasannaya
VsmṬ.	Visuddhimagga Ṭīkā
VS.	Vaiśeṣika Sūtras of Kanāda
Yam.	Yamaka
YamA.	Yamaka Aṭṭhakathā

NOTES

1. AA. I, 21, and ThīgA. 98; see also *Abhidhānappadīpikā-sūci*, 304ff.
2. See, e.g., S. II, 252; III, 68, 80.
3. See below, 9ff.
4. See, e.g., M. I, 259.
5. Asl. 317.
6. Dhs. 139.
7. Asl. 317.
8. Stcherbatsky, *Central Conception of Buddhism*, 11.
9. See below, 43ff.
10. Vsm. 180ff.
11. A. I, 83.
12. AA. I, 21, II, 154.
13. A. I, 82–83.
14. *Nidānaṃ hetu saṃkhāro paccayo rūpan ti sabbāni pi hi etāni kāraṇaveva-canān'eva.* AA. II, 154.
15. AA. II, 154.
16. AA. II, 154, n. 1.
17. ThīgA. 98.
18. Yam. I, 16ff.
19. Cpd. (Appendix), 273.
20. Yam. I, Introduction, ix.
21. HIP. I, 94.
22. See, e.g., S. II, 108–9; Iti. 114; Psm. I, 40.
23. Vbh. 101ff.
24. Ven. Nyanatiloka, *Guide through the Abhidhamma Piṭaka*, 33.
25. Yam. I, 54; also 167.
26. Yam. I, 54; also 168. See, e.g., S. II, 108; Psm. I, 40.

27. Ven. Nyanatiloka, *Guide through the Abhidhamma Piṭaka*, 31.
28. See, e.g., S. II, 108; Psm. I, 40.
29. YamA. 59.
30. S. III, 86.
31. Abhvk. 45; VsmS. 51: *Mihi ruppana nam kimayat? Sītādi virodhapratyaya sanniddhiyayehi visadosotpatti yayi.*
32. Abhvk. 245: *Ruppatīti sītunhādīhi vikāraṃ āpajjati, āpādiyatī ti attho. Vikāruppatti ca sītādi-virodha-paccaya-sannidhāne visaduppatti yeva. Na hi yathāsakaṃ paccayehi uppajjitvā ṭhita-dhammānaṃ aññena kena ci vikāruppādanaṃ sakkā kātuṃ; tasmā purima-samuppannarūpasantati viya ahutvā pacchā uppajjamānānaṃ visabhāga-paccaya-samavāyena visaduppatti yeva idha ruppanan ti daṭṭhabbaṃ.*
33. Abhvk. 245.
34. DhsA. 328; Vsm. 449.
35. AKvy. I, 26.
36. Dhs. 147; DhsA. 264.
37. Cf. VsmṬ. 459–66.
38. S. IV, 382; see also S. III, 47; M. III, 16.
39. DhsA. 337; Abhvk. 294.
40. Cf. Abhvk. 294.
41. AKvy. I, 43.
42. Vbh. 2–3.
43. See above, 9–10.
44. AbhMṬ. 121: *Dhammoti sabhāvo*; Mvn. 6: *paccayehi dhāriyantīti dhammā.*
45. ADSVṬ. 112.
46. ADSVṬ. 112.
47. Cf. VsmṬ. 559–60: *Svāyaṃ rūpasaddo rūḷhiyā ataṃsabhāve'pi pavattitī ti aparena rūpasaddena visesetvā vuttaṃ rūpa-rūpan ti*; see also ADSVṬ. 113.
48. Seal, *Positive Sciences of the Hindus*, chap. 1.
49. Bhaduri, *Studies in Nyāya-Vaisesika Metaphysics*, chap. 3.
50. Pañcastikāyasāra, 79 ff.
51. BPE. 86.
52. Cf., e.g., D. III, 274; M. I, 431ff.
53. Cf., e.g., M. III, 31; A. I, 176.
54. See below, 83 ff.
55. M. I, 421ff.
56. Cf. D. I, 215ff.; D. III, 87; S. I, 15.
57. Dhs. 177; Vbh. 82.
58. Vsm. 286: *Tattha paṭhamaṃ lakkhana-vacanaṃ, dutiyaṃ ākāra-vacanaṃ.*
59. VsmṬ. 362–63: *Nanu ca kakkhalattam'eva paṭhavī-dhātū ti? Saccam'etaṃ. Tathā'pi viññātāviññāta-saddatthatā-vasena abhinne'pi dhamme kappanāsiddhena bhedena evaṃ niddeso kato. Evaṃ hi atthavisesāvabodho hotī ti.*

60. MV. I, 339: *Yato ca bhiksavas te satvā taṃ prthivī-rasam ālopakārakam āhāram āhārensuh atha tesam kāye gurutvam ca kharatvam ca kakkatatvam ca upanīpate.*
61. AK. I, 22; Akvy. I, 57, 66.
62. Abh. 3.
63. Vsm. 287; Abhvt. 64.
64. Cpd. 155, n. 1.
65. Vsm. 289; see also Asl. 332; Mvn. 58.
66. Vsm. 289; see also Asl. 332; Mvn. 58; Abhvk. 249.
67. AKvy. I, 33.
68. ADSVT. 110: *Tarupabbatādīnaṃ pakatipaṭhavī viya sahajātarupānaṃ patiṭṭhānabhāvena pakkhāyati, upaṭṭhātī ti vuttaṃ hoti.*
69. Dhs. 177; Vbh. 83.
70. Asl. 335: *Ayapinḍi-ādīni hi āpo-dhātu ābandhitvā thaddhāni karoti, tāya ābaddhattā tāni thaddhāni nāma honti. Pāsāna-pabbata-tālaṭthi-hatthi-danta-gosingādisu'pi eseva nayo. Sabbāni h'etāni āpo-dhātu eva ābandhitvā thaddhāni karoti, āpo-dhātuyā ābaddhattā va thaddhāni honti* (in *The Expositor*).
71. Vsm. 289; Asl. 336; Abhvk. 250; Mvn. 58.
72. AK. I, 23, n. 3.
73. VS. 56.
74. Bhaduri, *Studies in Nyāya-Vaisesika Metaphysics*, 126.
75. AKvy. I, 33.
76. Asl. 332; Abhvt. 65; Abhvk. 250.
77. Dhs. 177; Vbh. 83.
78. VS. 59.
79. Bhaduri, *Studies in Nyāya-Vaisesika Metaphysics*, 129.
80. AKvy. I, 33.
81. AK. II, 146.
82. *Kiñcā'pi hi sītatā phsitvā gayhati, sā pana tejo yeva. Mande hi unhatte sītabuddhi, sītatā-sankhātassa kassa ci gunassa abhāvato. . . . Tathā hi ghammakāle ātāpe thatvā chāyaṃ pavitthānam sītabuddhi hoti; tattheva cirakālam thitānam unhabuddhi.* ADSVT. 111. See also VsmT. 459; VsmS. V, 75ff.
83. *Tejeti paripāceti niseti vā tikkhabhāvena sesabhūtattayam usmāpetī ti tejo*: ADSVT. 110.
84. Dhs. 177; Abhvk. 251; AK. I, 23; see also Vbh. 84.
85. Asl. 332; Abhvk. 251.
86. AK. I, 23 n. 2; AKvy. I, 33.
87. AK. I, 23.
88. See, e.g., ADSVT. 110.
89. See chapter 5, "Secondary Elements: Group B."
90. AK. IV, 4–5.

91. AK. I, 22–23.
92. AKvy. I, 33; see also KSP: MCB. IV, 268.
93. AKvy. I, 33.
94. Stcherbatsky, *Buddhist Logic*, vol. 1, 99.
95. VsmT. 359; ADSVT. 110; Abhvk. 249, 251.
96. VsmT. 359.
97. See chapter 5, the section "Phases of Matter."
98. Vsm. 346: . . . *sabbāsam'pi dhātūnaṃ salakkhānadito nānattam. Aññāni eva hi pathavīdhātuyā lakkhana-rasa-paccupatthānāni, aññāni eva hi āpo-dhātu-ādīnam.*
99. Asl. 336.
100. Vsm. 289.
101. Bhaduri, *Studies in Nyāya-Vaisesika Metaphysics*, 125.
102. Tkp. 3, 14, 36; AK. II, 248.
103. See chapter 5, the section "The Phases of Matter."
104. Tkp. 3, 14.
105. Tkp. 3, 14.
106. *Path of Purification*, 405 (Vsm. 391).
107. Vsm. 381.
108. *Path of Purification*, 401 (Vsṃ. 387): *Yathā ca yakkhādīni mahābhūtāni yam ganhanti n'eva nesam tassa anto na bahi ṭhanaṃ upalabhanti, na ca tam nissāya na titthanti, evam eva etāni'pi n'eva aññam aññassa anto na bahi thitāni hutvā upalbbhanti. Na ca aññam aññam nissāya na titthantī ti.*
109. *Yadi hi imā dhātuyo aññam'aññassa anto thita na sakiccakarā siyum. . . . Atha bahitthā vinibbhuttā siyum. Tathā sati avinibbhuttavādo hāyeyya. Tasmā na niddisitabbatthānā.* VsmT. 364. See also Abhvk. 248.
110. *Path of Purification*, 403 (Vsm. 452).
111. AKvy. I, 33.
112. Seal, *Positive Sciences of the Ancient Hindus*, chap. 1 (Note: "mono-bhautic" = based on one mahābhūta; "tetra-bhautic" = based on four mahābhūtas; "penta-bhautic" = based on five mahābhūtas.)
113. Seal, *Positive Sciences of the Ancient Hindus*, chap. 1.
114. Bhaduri, *Studies in Nyāya-Vaisesika Metaphysics*, 152.
115. *Kāranagunapūrvakah kāryaguno drstah.* VS. 63.
116. Bhaduri, *Studies in Nyāya-Vaisesika Metaphysics*, 151–52.
117. Vsm. 444: *Te vattabbā, iccheyyāma yadi āpādhikassa āsavassa gandhato pthavī-adhike kappāse gandho adhikataro siyā, tejādhikassa ca unhodakassa vannato sītūdakassa vanno parihāyetha. Yasmā pan'etam ubhayam'pi natthi, tasmā pahāyeth'etam p'etesam nissaya-bhūtānam visesa-kappanam.*
118. Vsm. 444: *Avinbbhoga-vuttīsu hi bhūtesu, ayam imassa guno ayam imassa guno ti na labbhā vattun ti.*
119. Bhaduri, *Studies in Nyāya-Vaisesika Metaphysics*, chap. 4.
120. VsmT. 450–51; Abhvk. 273–74.

121. VsmT. 451: *Aññathā hi avinibbhogavuttitā na yujjeyya*; see also Abhvk. 273–74.
122. AKvy. I, 124.
123. Asl. 333; AK. I, 18–19.
124. VsmT. 451; Abhvk. 273.
125. Asl.: *Kim pana etāni tīni mahābhūtāni ekappahāren'eva āpātham āgacchanti udāhu no ti? Agacchanti. Evam āgatāni kāyappasādam ghattentī ti? Ghattenti. Ekappahāren'eva tāni ārammanam katvā kāya-viññānam uppajjati n'uppajjatī ti? N'ūpajjati. Kasmā? Abhunjita-vasena vā hi usada-vasena vā ārammana-karanam hoti.*
126. *Expositor*, vol. 2, 434 (Asl. 333–34).
127. *Expositor*, vol. 2, 434 (translation slightly changed).
128. AK. II, 147.
129. AK. II, 148.
130. VsmT. 451.
131. AK. II, 146.
132. AK. II, 147.
133. Vsm. 357; Abhvk. 274.
134. AK. I, 23.
135. Kv. 331; KvuA. 93.
136. AK. I, 18–20.
137. AK. I, 18–19.
138. ADSVT. 111; VsmS. V, 233.
139. Cpd. 155, n. 6.
140. Dhs. 179.
141. Seal, *Positive Sciences of the Ancient Hindus*, chap. 1.
142. Seal, *Positive Sciences of the Ancient Hindus*, chap. 1.
143. Pañcastikāyasāra, 28: *Adesamattamutto dhādu-catukkassa kāranam jo du— so neo paramāno parināmaguno sayamasaddo.*
144. Bhaduri, *Studies in Nyāya-Vaisesika Metaphysics*, chap. 3.
145. See chapter 8, "Atomic Clusters."
146. Vsm. 422.
147. See, e.g., M. I, 111–12, 259–60, 190; S. IV, 39–40, 67ff.
148. See, e.g., S. IV, 225; M. I, 92ff., II, 92ff., II, 220, III, 62ff.
149. Dhs. 134ff.
150. BPE 159, n. 2.
151. Cf., e.g., AK. I, 15; AKvy. I, 24.
152. Dhs. 178.
153. AK. I, 15; AKvy. I, 24. Here *indriya* is used with reference to the first five sense-organs only.
154. AKvy. I, 24.
155. *Na hīndriyāṇi dvi-dhā bhavanti chinnasyāṃgasya kāyād apagatasya nirindriyatvāt. idam api kathaṃ gamyate. nirindriyaṃ tad aṃgaṃ yac chinnaṃ kāyād*

apagatam iti. yasmāt tat pratītya spraṣṭavy'ādikaṃ ca kāy'ādi-vijñānānupapattiḥ. AKvy. I, 68.

156. *Kathaṃ tarhi chinnena punar lagnena nāsikāgrena kāya-vijñānotpattiḥ. nāsikā-mūla-saṃbandhena punaḥ kāyendriyotpatteḥ adoṣaḥ. katham iha gṛhagodhik'ādīnāṃ pucchāni chinnāni spandante yadi tatra kāyendriyaṃ nāsti. vāyu-dhātor eṣa vikāro.* AKvy. I, 113. See also Stcherbatsky, *Central Conception of Buddhism*, 12.
157. AK I, 56, 65; also AKvy. I, 24.
158. Asl. 306–7.
159. Translation mainly based on Ñānamoli's *Path of Purification* (Vsm. 445–46; Asl. 307ff.).
160. Asl. 312; Vsm. 444.
161. Stcherbatsky, *Central Conception of Buddhism*, 12.
162. Sinha, *Indian Psychology*, vol. I, chap. 1.
163. *Cātummahābhūtiko ayaṃ puriso, yadā kālaṃ karoti paṭhavī paṭhavī-kāyaṃ anupeti anupagacchati, āpo āpa-kāyaṃ anupeti anupagacchati, tejo teja-kāyaṃ anupeti anupagacchati, vāyo vāya-kāyaṃ anupeti anupagacchati, ākāsaṃ indriyāni saṃkamanti.* D. I, 55.
164. Bhaduri, *Studies in Nyāya-Vaiśeṣika Metaphysics*, 152ff.
165. *Keci pana tejādhikānaṃ bhūtānaṃ pasādo cakkhu, vāyu-paṭhavī-āpādhikānaṃ bhūtānaṃ pasādo sota-ghāna-jivhā, kāyo sabbesan ti vadanti. Apare tejādhikānaṃ pasādo cakkhu, vivara-vāyu-āpa-paṭhavādhikānaṃ sota-ghāna-jivhā-kāyā ti vadanti.* Vsm. 376. See also Asl. 312–13. Our interpretation of "*bhūtānaṃ*" as "among the supporting primary elements" is supported by the rest of the passage in Vsm. and by VsmS. V, 56–57.
166. Vsm. 444; see also Asl. 312.
167. Vsm. 431.
168. VsmS. V, 57.
169. Ñānamoli, *Path of Purification*, 491–92 (Vsm. 444–45); also Asl. 312–13.
170. See below, 105ff.
171. Vsm. 445; also Asl. 313.
172. BPP. 40.
173. Vsm. 491ff.
174. Vsm. 493.
175. Vsm. 493; see AK. II, 107–8, and AKvy. I, 96, where a similar explanation is given.
176. See, e.g., D. I, 233; M. I, 503, III, 143, 233; S. I, 144, III, 107, 139.
177. Dhs. 139
178. See below, 59ff.
179. AK. I, 16; AKvy. I, 25–26.
180. AK. I, 16–17, IV, 8ff; KSP: MCB. IV, 209 ff. See also Stcherbatsky, *Central Conception of Buddhism*, 11. Cf. Yaśomitra's comment: *na hi cākṣusam etat saṃsthāna-grahaṇaṃ. mānasaṃ tv etat parikalpitaṃ. varṇa-saṃniveśa-viśeṣa*

eva hi saṃsthānaṃ. na saṃsthānaṃ nāma dravyaṃ kiṃcid asti. varṇāgrahaṇe saṃsthāna-grahaṇābhāvāt. AKvy. I, 26.

181. See chapter 8 of this volume.
182. AK. IV, 8–12; AKvy. II, 348ff.; KSP: MCB. IV, 209ff.
183. See below, 59ff.
184. See above, 13ff.
185. See above, 43.
186. *Dīghādīni hi aññam'aññaṃ upanidhāya siddhāni, vaṭṭādīni sannivesena. Tattha rassaṃ upanidhāya tato uccataraṃ dīghaṃ taṃ upanidhāya tato nīcataraṃ rassaṃ thūlam upanidhāya tato khuddakataraṃ anukaṃ taṃ upanidhāya tato mahantataraṃ thūlaṃ*. Asl. 317.
187. *Tattha yasmā dīghādīni phusitvā pi sakkā jānituṃ, nīlādīni pan'eva na sakkā tasmā na nippariyāyena dīghaṃ rūpāyatanaṃ; tathā rassādīni*. Asl. 317.
188. Asl. 317.
189. Murti, *Central Philosophy of Buddhism*, 81ff.
190. See below, 59ff.
191. AbhMT. passim.
192. Dhs. 140.
193. Asl. 313.
194. *Dūre rukkhaṃ chindantānam pi rajakānañ ca vatthaṃ dhovantānaṃ dūrato va kāyavikāro paññāyati. Saddo pana dhātuparamparāya sotaṃ ghaṭṭetvā saṇikaṃ vavatthānaṃ gacchatī ti vuttaṃ*. Asl. 313.
195. BPP. 34.
196. Sinha, *Indian Psychology*, 22.
197. *Saddo pi sace saṇikaṃ āgaccheyya dūre uppanno cirena sūyeyya paramparāghaṭṭanāya ca āgantvā sotaṃ ghaṭṭento asukadisāya nāmā ti na paññāyeyya*. Asl. 314.
198. Asl. 314.
199. VsmṬ. 446–47.
200. ADSVṬ. 114.
201. AK. I, 67; AKvy. I, 69. The rejection, on the part of the Pāli commentators, of the earlier view is necessitated by the introduction of a new theory concerning the position of the sense-organs in relation to their respective objects. According to the (*Sīhala*) Aṭṭhakathā (see Asl. 313) the sense-organs are "*sampatta-gocara*," i.e., they apprehend their objects when the latter come into actual contact with them. Buddhaghosa and his successors modified this to the effect that in the case of *cakkhu* and *sota*, they are not *sampatta-gocara*, i.e., they apprehend their objects at a distance; see Vsm. 445; Asl. 313; ADS. 76; Abhvt. 67; Abhvk. 262. The same idea is expressed in AK. I, 87ff. and AKvy. I, 83. Consult BPP. 32ff. and Cpd. 160, n. 2, for details. Although Asl. denies that *cakkhu* and *sota* are *sampatta-gocara*, sometimes it uses the term *sampatta* in respect of the corresponding objects, e.g., *vaṇṇo . . . cakkhusampatto* (314). It seems that *sampatta* is used not only as referring to the

physical contact between the organ and the object, but sometimes as referring to the apprehension of the object by the sense-organ. See AK. I, 87, n. 1, where Poussin cites a Vibhāṣā passage according to which *prāpta*, which in this context, corresponds to Pāli *sampatta*, occurs in the same two senses.

202. See chapter 8.
203. See below, 142ff.
204. VsmT. 452.
205. See above, 26–27.
206. Dhs. 141.
207. AK. I, 18.
208. AKvy. I, 27.
209. Dhs. 142.
210. AKvy. I, 27.
211. Dhs. 142; see also Vbh. 122–23.
212. A. IV, 57.
213. ... *itthiliṅgādi pana na itthindriyaṃ, ... yathā bīje sati bījaṃ paṭicca rukkho vaḍḍhitvā sākhā-viṭapasampanno ākāsaṃ pūretvā tiṭṭhati. Evam eva itthibhāvasaṅkhāte itthindriye sati itthiliṅgādīni honti. Bījaṃ viya hi itthindriyaṃ*. Asl. 321.
214. Asl. 321 (... *yanti kāraṇavacanaṃ. Yena kāraṇena* ...).
215. Dhs. 143.
216. AK. II, 104, 108; AKvy. II, 94, 97.
217. Vsm. 378; Abhvk. 269; ADSVṬ. 111.
218. *Na ca kāyappasādena ṭhitokāse ṭhitanti vā aṭṭhitokāse ṭhitanti vā vattabbaṃ*. Vsm. 378.
219. VsmṬ. 448. Cf. *Na ca tassa kāyappasādena saṅkaro lakkhaṇabhedato nissayabhedato vā*. Abhvk. 269.
220. AK. II, 108; see also AKvy. I, 97.
221. See above, 17.
222. VsmṬ. 448.
223. See above, 15ff.
224. AK. II, 104; AKvy. I, 94.
225. Cf. ... *itthindriyañ ca purisindriyañ ca sattapaññāya padaṭṭhānaṃ*. Peṭ. 101.
226. Translated from *Expositor(Atthasālinī)*, vol. 2, 419ff.; arrangement is changed (Asl. 321–22).
227. See below, 128ff.
228. See above, 49.
229. According to the Vibhāṣā, an *ācārya* named Saṅghavasu contended that only the first five sense-organs and the faculty of life (see 161ff.) were *indriyas* in the real sense of the term. AK. XLIII (Introduction). In the opinion of some *ācāryas*, only the six sense-organs (the 6th is *manas*= the mental organ) form what is called "*mūlasattvadravya*," i.e., the fundamental constituents of a living being. AK. II, 111, nn. 1 and 2; AKvy. I, 98. As far as the position of the

two *indriyas* in question is concerned, both these traditions accord well with the above situation that obtains in the Abhidhamma Piṭaka.

230. VsmṬ. 448; VsmS. V62. Cf. *Kiñcāpi itthiliṅgādīni yathāsakaṃ kammādinā paccayena samuṭṭhahanti yebhuyyena pana itthindriyasahite yeva santāne taṃ-tadākārā hutvā sambhavanti, itarattha na bhavantī ti tesaṃ tabbhāv-abhāvitaṃ upādāya indriyaṃ paṭicca jāyantī ti vuttāni*. Abhvk. 266.
231. Dhs. 24, 34.
232. Asl. 123–24; Vsm. 464, 493; Abhvk. 120.
233. ADS. 6.
234. In Vsm. 378 the *kamma-samuṭṭhāna-rūpa* is referred to as that *rūpa* that is "*sahaja*" with *jīvitindriya*, because they come into being simultaneously. See also Abhvk. 270; ADSVṬ. 112.
235. That is, *hadaya-vatthu*, the latest addition; see below, 62ff.
236. Discussed in 96 ff.; *rūpa-jīvitindriya*, too, is *kammasamuṭṭhāna*; see below, 71.
237. See below, 147–48.
238. AK. II, 178–79, 214ff.
239. Kvu. 394ff.
240. AK. II, 211ff.
241. See., e.g., D. III, 228, 276; M. I, 48; S. II, 11, 98.
242. Dhs. 144.
243. Asl. 330.
244. Dhs. 340.
245. Cf. *Kavaḍīkārāhāraṣya trīṣu gandharasaspraṣṭavyāyataneṣu saṃgrahaḥ. Kasmād rūpāyatane na saṃgrahaḥ. Yasmāc cakṣurdarśanāhārena sattvan-ikāyaṣya mahābhūtānāṃ nopacayas tasmāt*. Abhmṛ. 40. See also AK. III, 120ff.
246. See below, 155.
247. See below, 56–57.
248. Dhs. 125, 149.
249. Dhs. 126, 149ff.
250. Dhs. 178.
251. VsmṬ. 449–50; see also Abhvk. 271; ADSS. 154–55; VsmS. VI, 64–65, where the same explanation is given.
252. Cpd. 277–78.
253. Tkp. 4.
254. "What is associated therewith" means those *cetasikas* that arise along with *mano-viññāṇa*.
255. Mrs. Rhys Davids, *Buddhist Psychology*, 71.
256. VsmṬ. 449; VsmS. V, 64–65; Abhvk. 270–71; ADSS. 154–55.
257. . . . *aṭṭhikatvā manasikatvā sabbaṃ cetasā samannāharitvā kiñci cintentassa hadayappadesassa khijjanato tatthedaṃ tiṭṭhatī ti viññāyati*. Abhvk. 271.
258. VsmṬ. 449.
259. See above, 49.

260. VsmṬ. 450; Abhvk. 271.
261. Dasgupta, *A History of Indian Philosophy*, vol. 1, 292.
262. Sinha, *Indian Psychology*, vol. 1, 1.
263. BP. 34.
264. Vbh. 87–88, 144.
265. BPE. 186.
266. Dhs. 143.
267. Dhs. 147.
268. Dhs. 143.
269. KSP: MCB. IV, 212–13; see also 212, n. 21. In the AK. IV, 4, the theory that *kāyavijñapti* = movement is attributed to the Vātsīputrīyas, whereas in *La Siddhi*, 48, it is attributed to the Sāṃmitīyas.
270. KSP: MCB. IV, 214, n. 22.
271. See below, 75–76.
272. *Yatraivotpattiḥ tatraiva vināśaḥ*. AKvy. I, 33.
273. AK. IV, 4–8.
274. AK. IV, 4–12; KSP: MCB. IV, 207–9.
275. AKvy. I, 26.
276. Dhs. 179.
277. *La Siddhi*, 48.
278. KSP: MCB. IV, 219ff.
279. AK. IV, 4.
280. AK. IV, 3, n. 2.
281. KSP: MCB. IV, 219–20.
282. Dhs. 177.
283. Dhs. 147.
284. Asl. 83, 343; Vsm. 448; Abhvk. 273ff.
285. See above, 29.
286. Cf. the theory of *avinibhoga-rūpa*; see above, 36.
287. VsmṬ. 450; Abhvk. 273–74.
288. *. . . mahantaṃ pāsānaṃ ukkhipantassa sabbatthāmena gahanakāle sarīrassa ussahanavikāro viya . . . labbhamāno eko ākāravikāro kāyaviññatti nāmāti vuttaṃ hoti*. Abhvk. 274–75, repeated in ADSVṬ. 13.
289. *. . . ñāpetabbaṃ . . . anumānato siddhaṃ*. Abhvk. 275.
290. Abhvk. 273–75; VsmṬ. 451; ADSVṬ. 113–14.
291. In the previous chapters we took notice of the fact that in the comparatively late works (the *ṭīkās*) of the Theravādins, too, motion was interpreted as *desantaruppatti*—that is, appearance of momentary elements in adjacent locations. From their point of view, therefore, all references to bodily movements should be understood accordingly—a fact explicitly stated in ADSVṬ. 114.
292. Abhvk. 275; Mvn. 65.
293. Dhs. 148.
294. See below, 73–74, 122–23.

295. See Tkp. 3, where *citta* and *cetasikas* are postulated as a condition by way of co-nascence (*sahajāta-paccaya*) in relation to *cittasamuṭṭhāna-rūpa*.
296. Dhs. 147.
297. Asl. 337.
298. AK. IV, 14; KSP: MCB. IV, 156, 260; Mdhy. Vṛt. 307; AKvy. II, 351.
299. Dhs. 143–44.
300. Dhs. 148.
301. Vsm. 379.
302. Vsm. 379.
303. VsmṬ. 452.
304. Abhvk. 277; see also Mvn. 65.
305. Dhs. 144.
306. Abhvk. 281.
307. Cf., e.g., D. I, 67; M. II, 187.
308. Cf. the description of the eight *kusīta-vatthus*, bases of indolence in A. IV, 332ff.
309. Thag. 15.
310. Asl. 326–27; Vsm. 448–49.
311. *Dhātukkhobho: vāta-pitta-semhappakopo; rasādidhātūnaṃ vā vikārāvatthā.* VsmṬ. 453.
312. *Dvidhā vutto pi atthato paṭhavīādidhātūnaṃ yeva vikāro daṭṭhabo.* VsmṬ. 453.
313. Abhvk. 280ff.
314. Dhs. 153.
315. Cf. *Tattha paṭisandhito paṭṭhāya yāva cakkhādidasakānaṃ uppatti, etthantare rūpuppādo upacayo nāma.* ADSVṬ. 114.
316. This is not to suggest that the sense-organs could arise independently of other rūpa-dhammas because they are a variety of *upādā-rūpa*.
317. That is, according to KvuA. 148.
318. Kvu. 493ff.
319. Vsm. 380; Asl. 327.
320. See above, 19–20.
321. See above, 51–52.
322. To this group the later works add *hadaya-vatthu* and the faculty of sex, both of which are said to arise together with (*manāyatana*) and *kāyāyatana*. See VbhA. 22; ADS. 30; ADSS. 199. The addition of the former is necessitated by its being recognized as the physical basis of mind. Cf. Tkp. 3, where it is stated that at the moment of conception the relation between mind and matter is one of reciprocal co-nascence (*aññam' añña sahajāta*). The addition of the latter is necessitated by the new interpretation given to it; see above, 55ff.
323. Dhs. 144; this same description occurs as a stock formula in D. II, 305; M. I, 49; S. II, 2.
324. Dhs. 144.

325. This should be the moment when the *rūpa-jīvitindriya* ceases to function. Cf. KvuA. 113, where it is said that, at the moment of death, both *rūpa-jīvitindriya* and a*rūpa-jīvitindriya* cease to function simultaneously (*Cutikkhaṇasmiṃ dve pi jīvitāni sah'eva bhijjanti*).

326. A. 152.

327. BP. 14.

328. S. II, 94 (translation from BKS 13–14, with minor edits for clarity). Cf. also *N'āhaṃ bhikkhave aññaṃ ekadhammam pi samanupassāmi evaṃ lahuparivattaṃ yathāyidaṃ bhikkhave cittaṃ*. A. I, 10.

329. Kvu. 204–8, 458–59, 620–21.

330. According to KvuA. 196.

331. Kvu. 620ff.

332. *Documents d'Abhidharma*: MCB. V, 136; "Origin and Doctrines of Early Indian Buddhist Schools," 34, n. 12; Bareau, "Les sectes bouddhiques du Petit Véhicule," 73–74.

333. Cf. *Yo py āha nikāyāṃtarīya iti ārya-Sāṃmitīyāḥ. Sa ghaṭ' āder mudgar' ādi-kṛto vināśa iti manyate kālāṃtarāvasthāyī hi taṣya rūpaṃ. Citta-caittānāṃ tu kṣaṇikatvaṃ*. AKvy. 179.

334. "Origin and Doctrines of Early Indian Buddhist Schools," 54.

335. "Origin and Doctrines of Early Indian Buddhist Schools," 54 n. 2; Bareau, *Les sectes bouddhiques du Petit Véhicule*, 103, 105, 144, 186; see *Documents d'Abhidharma*, 137–40, where Ācārya Saṃghabhadra criticizes the view that matter is not of momentary duration. For a compact but comprehensive discussion on this subject, consult Silburn, *Instant et cause*, 227–74.

336. D. I, 54.

337. According to some *ācāryas* both *sthiti* and *jaratā* are represented by *sthityanyathātva*; see AK. II, 93.

338. See below, 85.

339. Jaini, "Origin and Development of the Theory of Viprayuktasaṃskāras," part 3, 531–47.

340. This brief sketch is based on Jaini, "Origin and Development of the Theory of Viprayuktasaṃskāras"; *Documents d'Abhidharma*, 134ff.; Stcherbatsky, *Central Conception of Buddhism*, 39ff.; Stcherbatsky, *Buddhist Logic*, vol. 1, 79–118; and Silburn, *Instant et cause*, 254–62. See also AK. II, 222–38; AKvy. I, 174ff.; CP. Mdhy. Vṛt. 108ff.; *La Siddhi*, 198.

341. See below, 122.

342. VbhA. 7–8, 25–29; Vsm. 291–92, 613–14. The *ṭhitikkhaṇa* of *rūpa* is of longer duration than that of the mental elements; see below, 132–33. On how the theory of perception is explained on the basis of the theory of moments, see Sarathchandra, *Buddhist Psychology of Perception*, 42ff.

343. See below, 79.

344. AA. II, 252.

345. Vsm. 449; Abhvt. 71.

346. Stcherbatsky, *Buddhist Logic*, vol. 1, 96ff.
347. AK. II, 233.
348. It is very likely that they were inspired by the arguments of the AK. The Theravādins of Ceylon show much acquaintance with this (and other notable works of Sanskrit Buddhism). Cf., e.g., VsmS. V, 51ff., where quotations from it are cited, not, as might be expected, with a view to refuting them, but in support of its own statements. On the Theravādins' acquaintance with Sanskrit Buddhist works, see Godakumbura, *Sinhalese Literature*, 41–46; Godakumbura, "References to Sanskrit Buddhist writers in Sinhalese literature," 86–93; and Paranavitana, "Mahāyānism in Ceylon," 35–71.
349. Cf. *Ṭhitikkhaṇe hi jarā nāma; na ca tadā dhammo sabhāvaṃ vijahati. Navabhāvo uppādāvatthā, tassā apagamabhāvena gayhatī ti āha navabhāvāpagamapaccupaṭṭhānā ti*. Abhvk. 284.
350. Abhvk. 305: ADSVṬ. 112.
351. See above, 77.
352. *Vīhipurānabhāvo tāva rasādiṃ apaneti, ayam pana kevalaṃ uppādāvattham-eva apaneti*. Abhvk. 284.
353. See above, 77.
354. We mean the question: *Kasmā pāḷiyaṃ ṭhitikkhaṇo na vutto ti?* (Abhvk. 30). This shows that *ṭhitikkhaṇa* is not taken as representing *ṭhitassa aññathatta*, for the latter is referred to in the *pāḷi*, i.e., the canon (see A. I, 152). We are told that it is because of a purely practical reason—that is, in the interests of the instructed (*vineyyajjhāsayānurodhena*, cf. *upāya-kauśalya* of Mahāyāna)—that the *ṭhitikkhaṇa* is not referred to in the canon. Perhaps this may mean the same as what certain Vaibhāṣikas say: With a view to creating complete detachment in the minds of the disciples from *saṃskṛta-dharmas* it was deemed proper that the static phase (*sthiti*) of the *saṃskṛta dharmas* should be overlooked. See AK. II, 223.
355. See above, 76.
356. Abhvk. 304–5; see also ADSVṬ. 110. The argument attributed to Ānanda—*Api ca yathābhūto dhammo uppajjati, kiṃ-tathābhūto va bhijjati, udāhu aññathābhūto? Yadi tathābhūto va bhijjati na jaratāya sambhavo; aññathābhūto añño eva so ti sabbathā pi ṭhitikkhaṇassa abhāvo yeva* (Abhvk. 305)—is reminiscent of: *yadi sa eva nāsāv athānyathā na sa eva hi-tasmād ekaṣya dharmaṣya nānyathātvaṃ prasidhyate*. AK. II, 233, n. 1.
357. *Ubhayam p'etaṃ jātirūpass' evādhivacanaṃ*. Vsm. 380. See also Asl. 326.
358. See chapter 8.
359. What has been stated so far is based on the accounts given in the commentaries as well as in the *ṭīkās*; cf. Vsm. 449–50; Asl. 327ff.; VsmṬ. 454ff.; Abhvk. 282–84, 287–89; ADSVṬ. 114ff.
360. See above, 72–73.
361. Asl. 328; Vsm. 449.
362. That is, *ṭhitikkhaṇa*; see above, 87: according to Buddhaghosa and others,

jaratā implies some kind of change; according to Sumaṅgala and others, it is only a figurative expression.

363. Asl. 328; Vsm. 449; Abhvk. 283.
364. Abhvk. 283.
365. Momentary means having three momentary phases; see above, 85–86.
366. See above, 80.
367. See above, 77.
368. *Na hi jāti jāyati, jarā jīrati, maraṇaṃ mīyatīti voharituṃ yuttaṃ, anavaṭṭhānato.* Mvn. 67–68. See also Abhvk. 288; AK. II, 238; AKvy. I, 211; CP. Mdhy. Vṛt. 110, n. 126–27, 273.
369. See above, 21.
370. Dhs. 144; Vbh. 84.
371. BP. 189.
372. . . . *yena ca asitapītakhāyitaṃ ajjhoharati, yattha ca asitapītakhāyitaṃ santiṭṭati, yena ca asitapītakhāyitaṃ adhobhāgā nikkhamati* (= *ākāsa-dhātu*). Vbh. 84.
373. AK. I, 7–8 and 49–50; AKvy. I, 15, 57.
374. MBP. I, 110–11.
375. AK. I, 49 n. 4.
376. See below, 87ff.
377. AK. I, 49.
378. Vbh. 72.
379. Vbh. 84–85.
380. McGovern, *A Manual of Buddhist Philosophy*, 111.
381. Vsm. 451.
382. *Rūpāni paricchindati, sayaṃ vā tehi paricchijjati.* Abhvk. 279.
383. Vsm. 448.
384. AKvy. I, 57.
385. AK. I, 49–50; AKvy. I, 57.
386. Kvu. 330–31; and KvuA. 93.
387. See above, 75.
388. AK. I, 8; AKvy. I, 15.
389. Mil. 387–88.
390. Mil. 268.
391. BP. 169.
392. Kvu. 330.
393. Further confirmed by: *Yathā mahārāja ākāso na jāyati na mīyati na cavati na uppajjati, evam' eva kho mahārāja Nibbānaṃ na jāyati na mīyati na cavati na uppajjati.* Mil. 320–21.
394. Kvu. 328ff.
395. KvuA. 92.
396. See above, 37, 59–60.
397. Mil. 270.

398. Kvu. 328 (translated from *Points of Controversy*).
399. Kvu. 330.
400. See, e.g., Mishra, *History of Indian* Philosophy, 403.
401. Jhaveri, "Concept of *Kāla* and *Ākāśa* in the Sāṃkhya-Yoga System," 417–30, where attention is drawn to the fact that in the Sāṃkhya-Yoga works earlier than Vijñānabhikṣu's, only derivative *ākāśa* is mentioned. Also Seal, *Positive Sciences of the Hindus*, 27–28.
402. See Davvasaṅgaha 56–57; Pañcāstikāya Samayasāra, 99, Niyamasāra, 16ff.
403. See, e.g., M. I, 231; II, 47.
404. D. II, 107.
405. M. I, 424.
406. Mil. 388.
407. AKvy. I, 15, (sūtra) passage: *Prthivī bho Gautama kutra pratisṭhitā. Pṛthivī brāhmaṇa ap-manḍale pratisṭhitā. Ap-maṇḍalaṃ bho Gautama kva pratisṭhitaṃ. Vāyau pratisṭhitaṃ. Vāyur bho Gautama kva pratiṣṭhitaḥ. Ākāśe pratiṣṭhitaḥ. Ākāśaṃ bho Gautama kutra pratiṣthitaṃ. Atisarasi mahābrāhmaṇātisarasi mahābrāhmaṇa. Ākāśaṃ brāhmaṇāpratisṭhitaṃ anālambaṇaṃ.*
408. KvuA. 92–93; Abhvk. 279.
409. KvuA. 92.
410. KvuA. 92.
411. See above, 85.
412. Abhvk. 70.
413. 28 = 4 *mahābhūtas* + 14 *nipphanna-upādā* + 10 *anipphanna-upādā*.
414. That is, the section (8th *Bhānavara*) where the subject of *rūpa* is explained. As far as the Pāli canon is concerned, it is the most exhaustive.
415. Our reckoning as first, second, etc., starts from the second section of the Dhs., from where onward we get the classifications. In its first section "all *rūpa*" is considered under single uncorrelated characteristics. See BPE. 154.
416. We use the term "classification" to mean every arrangement of the rūpa-dhammas under two or more headings. Very often only one item falls under one of the two or more headings; in such cases the purpose is to show how a given rūpa-dhamma can be distinguished from the rest.
417. *Atthi rūpaṃ cakkhuviññāṇassa vatthu, atthi rupaṃ cakkhuviññāṇassa na vatthu*. Dhs. 125.
418. See below, 118–19, 122.
419. *Atthi rūpaṃ kabaḷinkāro āhāro, atthi rūpaṃ na kabaḷiṅkāro āhāro*. Dhs. 127.
420. Three *mahābhūtas* are collectively referred to by the fifth objective field; *hadaya-vatthu* is not known to Dhs.; hence in all, twenty-seven items are involved here.
421. See above, 19–20.
422. See above, 10–12.
423. See above, 2.
424. See above, 12ff.

425. See below, 128.
426. See above, 65–67.
427. See above, 65–67.
428. See below, 166.
429. See below, 98–99.
430. See above, 43ff.
431. See above, 12ff.
432. The appended charts will help to understand the relative positions of the various groups involved in the classifications (see below, 109ff.).
433. See above, 92.
434. AK. I, 63, n. 1.
435. AK. I, 63; cf. also *La Siddhi*, 193ff.
436. AK. I, 63.
437. "Les sept *dhātu* de pensée, le *dharmadhātu* et l'audible (*śabdadhātu*) ne sont jamais approppries." AK. I, 62.
438. Dhs. 146.
439. AK. I, 68–70.
440. *Sāsavā kusalākusalānaṃ vipākā kāmāvacarā rūpāvacarā arūpāvacarā vedanakkhandho saññakkhandho sankhārakkhandho viññānakkhandho yañ ca rūpaṃ kammassa kaṭattā, ime dhammā upādinnā.*
441. See, e.g., M. I, 185ff.; 421ff.
442. M. I, 185.
443. M. I, 185.
444. Vsm. 349.
445. *Upādiṇṇanti na kammasamuṭṭhānam eva, avisesena pana sarīraṭṭhakassa etaṃ gahaṇaṃ. Sarīraṭṭhakaṃ hi upādiṇṇaṃ vā hotu anupādiṇṇaṃ vā ādinna-gahita-parāmaṭṭhavasena sabbaṃ upādiṇṇam eva nāma.* MA. II, 222.
446. See, e.g., M. I, 185ff., 421 ff.
447. Dhs. 146; also see below, 112–13.
448. AK. I, 63.
449. That is, from the point of view of the Kośa definition.
450. AK. I, 63, n. 1.
451. Vbh. 2, 6.
452. *Aṣṭādaśasu katyupattāḥ kati niranupattāḥ. Nava upāttānupāttabhedena dvividhāḥ. Indriyena saha pratyutpannā upāttāḥ. Cittacaitasikadharmānāṃ sahabhāvāt.* Abhmṛ. 58.
453. Asl. 336–37; ADS. 28; ADSS. 12l.
454. Vsm. 451.
455. Dhs. 108.
456. Cpd. 159, n. 6.
457. Dhs. 146.
458. See below, 137.
459. See above, 125–26.

460. See above, 62ff.
461. Kvu. 460–62; 353–55.
462. That is, according to KvuA. 136.
463. *Points of Controversy*, 267 (Kvu. 467ff.).
464. *Rūpadhammesu panāyaṃ vohāro vā natthī ti dassetuṃ pucchā sakavādissa.* KvuA. 136.
465. Kvu. 467ff.
466. See above, 97.
467. See, e.g., Tkp. 5; Dkp. 16–17.
468. Mil. 65.
469. Vsm. 445.
470. *Ekam pi kammaṃ pañcāyatanikāttabhāva-bhavapatthanā nipphannaṃ cakkhādivisese hetu tāya aññamaññassa asādhāranan ti ca kammaviseso ti ca vuttan ti daṭṭhabbaṃ.* VsmṬ. 444.
471. *Na hi taṃ yena visesena cakkhussa paccayo teneva sotassa paccayo hoti, indriyantarābhāvappattito.* VsmṬ. 444.
472. *Kiṃ pana taṃ yam aññamaññassa asādhāranaṃ, kammam eva nesaṃ visesakāraṇaṃ, tasmā kammavisesato etesaṃ viseso na bhūtavisesato.* Vsm. 445.
473. See above, 41.
474. That is, according to the commentaries; see above, 65.
475. BPE. 188, n. 3.
476. See above, 59ff.
477. Tkp. 3; see below, 131.
478. Dhs. 147–48.
479. See above, 59ff.
480. See above, 59ff.
481. See above, 83.
482. Vsm. 366, 451–52; Asl. 340ff.
483. ADS. 29; NRP. 39.
484. See above, 93–94.
485. Dhs. 148.
486. Vsm. 450 and ADSVṬ. 115.
487. See above, 100–101.
488. *Kāmaṃ aññe pi hi ajjhattasambhūtā atthi, rūḷhīvasena pana cakkhādikaṃ yeva ajjhattikaṃ.* ADSVṬ. 115.
489. *Athavā yadi mayaṃ na homa tvaṃ kaṭṭhaliṅgarūpam abhavissasīti vadantā viya attabhāvassa sātisayaṃ upakārattā cakkhādineva visesato ajjhattikāni nāma.* ADSVṬ. 115.
490. AK. I, 74. Cf. *Ātmānāṃ vā cittaṃ adhikṛtya ye dharmāḥ pratyāsanna-bhūtvā āśraya-bhāvena vartante, te ādhyātmikāḥ.* AKvy. I, 74.
491. Cf. *Arūpino hi khandhā cakkhādīnaṃ vatthūnaṃ abbhantarato nikkhantā viya uppajjanti.* Tkp. 53–54.
492. See above, 93ff.

493. *Sthavira āha. Pāryāyikaṃ eṣāṃ ādhyātmika-bāḥyataṃ. Vijñānaṃ āśrayās te cakṣu ādaya ity ādhyātmikāḥ. Mano-vijñāna-viṣayatvāt tu bāḥyā iti.* AKvy. I, 40.
494. AK. I, 73, n. 1.
495. Vbh. 1ff.; Dhs. 187–88.
496. Vbh. 1ff.; Dhs. 187–88.
497. D. I, 28; Ud. 69.
498. DhsA. 60; AbhMṬ. 46 says that here the term *ekakāraṇavāda* refers either to Sāṃkhya philosophy or the theory of divine creation: *ekakāraṇavādo ti pakatikāraṇavādo issarakāraṇavādo vā.*
499. DhsA. 79.
500. *A Comprehensive Manual of Abhidhamma*, 77.
501. *A Comprehensive Manual of Abhidhamma*, 253ff.
502. *A Comprehensive Manual of Abhidhamma*, 61.
503. PsmA. 140; VsmṬ. 546.
504. Tkp. 11.
505. Tkp. 1.
506. AK. II, 245 and 299ff.
507. *Hetūnāṃ-pratyayānāṃ ca kaḥ prativiśeṣaḥ. Na kaścid ity āha ... hetuḥ pratyayo nidānaṃ kāraṇaṃ nimittaṃ liṅgam upaniṣad iti paryāyāḥ.* AKvy. I, 188.
508. AKvy. I, 188.
509. See e.g., D. III, 284; S. II, 224, IV, 68, 151; A. I66.
510. Tkp, 12.
511. For more details on the subject, see Mrs. Rhys Davids' article "Relations (Buddhist)"; Ledi Sadaw, *Paṭṭhānuddesa Dīpanī (Buddhist Philosophy of Relations)*; Ven. Nyanatiloka, *Guide through the Abhidhamma Piṭaka*, 58ff.; Tatia, "Paṭiccasamupāda"; and Karunaratne, *Development of the Theory of Causality in Early Theravāda Buddhism.*
512. ADS. 39.
513. AK. II, 299, n. 1.
514. See *Comprehensive Manual of Abhidhamma*, 317.
515. Tkp. 12, 23.
516. Dhs. 124–25.
517. Tkp. 2, 12ff.
518. See chapter 4.
519. Tkp. 13, 31.
520. Tkp. 13, 31ff.
521. *Na ekakkhaṇe bahū jeṭṭhakā nāma honti.* Tkp. 31.
522. Tkp. 2.
523. AK. II, 307.
524. AK. II, 248; see also AKvy. I, 189ff.
525. Sogen, *Systems of Buddhist Thought*, 86.
526. AK. II, 308.
527. Cf. *Jeṭṭhakaṭṭhena upakārako dhammo adhipatipaccayo.* Tkp. 13.

528. Tkp. 14, 36.
529. Tkp. 14, 36.
530. *Iminā va etesaṃ dhammānaṃ ekakkhaṇe paccayabhāvañ c'eva paccayuppannabhāvañ ca dīpeti*. Tkp. 36.
531. AK. II, 248ff.; AKvy. 191ff.
532. AK. II, 253ff.
533. AK. II, 253ff.
534. AK. II, 254. See also Tkp. 14.
535. AK. II, 255.
536. AK. I.
537. See chapter 3.
538. Tkp. 3, 14, 37ff.
539. Tkp. 3, 14.
540. Tkp. 4.
541. Tkp. 3–4.
542. Tkp. 17, 42ff.
543. Tkp. 17, 42ff.
544. Kvu. 620.
545. See the section on "phases of matter" in chapter 5 of this volume.
546. VbhA. 25ff.; Vsm. 613.
547. Tkp. 42.
548. Tkp. 43.
549. See above,119.
550. Tkp. 5, 43ff.
551. Based on the implications of the relation between *citta* and *cetasikas* and the definition of *samanantara-paccaya*; see below, 139ff.
552. Tkp. 45ff.
553. ADS. 6.
554. Tkp. 45ff.
555. *Kusalākusalaṃ hi kammaṃ attano pavattikkhaṇe phalaṃ na deti. Yadi dadeyya, yaṃ manusso devalokūpagakusalakammaṃ karoti, tass'ānubhāvena tasmiṃ yeva khaṇe devo bhaveyya*. Tkp. 46.
556. AK. II, 275.
557. See above, 103, 128.
558. See above, 101.
559. Tkp. 18.
560. Tkp. 47–48.
561. Tkp. 47–48.
562. AKvy. I, 112.
563. Tkp. 48ff.
564. ADS. 6.
565. Tkp. 3, 14.
566. Tkp. 48.

567. Tkp. 5, 15.
568. Tkp. 18.
569. Tkp. 6, 19.
570. Tkp. 6, 9.
571. Cf. *indriya-paccaya.*
572. See above, 103, 128.
573. Tkp. 50.
574. See above, 49ff.
575. Tkp. 53.
576. AKvy. I, 128.
577. Tkp. 12, 23ff.
578. Tkp. I, 23ff.
579. Cf. *rūpaṃ avyākataṃ*. Dhs. 125. See also Vbh. 12; Kvu. 532ff.
580. Tkp. 12.
581. Tkp. 55ff.
582. Cf. *atthi-paccya.*
583. See above, 120, 130.
584. *Buddhist Philosophy of Relations (Paṭṭhānuddesa Dīpanī)*, 12. Cf. *Āsevanaṭṭhena anantarānaṃ guṇabalavabhāvāya upakārako dhammo āsevana-paccayo ganthādīsu purima·purimābhiyogo viya*. Tkp. 17.
585. Tkp. 17–18, 44ff.
586. Cf. implications of *hetu-paccaya.*
587. ADS. 6.
588. See above, 123.
589. Tkp. 53.
590. Tkp. 53.
591. Tkp. 53–54.
592. Cf. *Citta·viprayuktā iti citta-grahaṇaṃ citta-samāna·jātīya-pradarśanārthaṃ. Cittam iva cittena ca viprayuktā ity arthaḥ*. AKvy. I, 142.
593. Tkp. 13–14, 33ff.
594. AK. II, 300ff.; AKvy. I, 232ff.
595. Tkp. 13.
596. Tkp. 59.
597. Tkp. 7.
598. *L'Abhidharmakośa de Vasubandhu* (AK. II, 143ff.); *La Siddhi*, 39 ff.; Sogen, *Systems of Buddhistic Thought*, 121ff.; McGovern, *A Manual of Buddhist Philosophy*, 125ff.; Levi, *Materiaux pour l'étude du système Vijñaptimātra*, 51ff.; Stcherbatsky, *Central Conception of Buddhism*, 200ff.; Murti, *Central Philosophy of Buddhism*, 200ff.; and Rosenberg, *Probleme der buddhistischen Philosophie*, 158ff.
599. AK. I, 90, n. 1; MBP. I, 126ff.
600. AK. I, 89 ff.; AKvy. I, 85.
601. On the various theories of Indian atomism and on the question of its ori-

gin and development, see Jacobi, "Atomic Theory (Indian)"; Keith, *Indian Logic and Atomism*; Basham, *History and Doctrines of the Ājīvikas*, 262ff.; and Bhaduri, *Studies in Nyāya-Vaiśeṣika Metaphysics*, 54ff.

602. AK. II, 144; and AKvy. I, 34, 123. Cf. *Sarvasūkṣmāḥ khalu rūpasaṃskāropadāna-saṃcaya-bheda-paryantaḥ paramāṇuriti prajñapyate*. Abhd. 65.

603. Cf. *Tad etad dig-bhāga-bhedattvaṃ necchanti Vaibhāṣikāḥ. Dig-bhāga-bhedo hi saṃghāta-rūpānam eva kalpayate.* AKvy. I, 85. See also *La Siddhi*, 39ff.; Viṃś. 7.

604. AK, II, 144, n. 3.

605. AK. II, 144ff.; and AKvy. I, 123ff. (*na vai paramāṇu-rūpam ekaṃ pṛthagbhūtam asti.* —AKvy. I, 34.)

606. AK. II, 144ff.; and AKvy. I, 123ff. Cf. *Sarvasūkṣmaḥ khalu rūpa-saṃskāropadāna-saṃcaya-bheda-paryantaḥ paramāṇur iti prajñapyate. Sa tu saptadravyāvinirbhāgī catubhir bhūtais tribhiś copādāya rūpais tribhis tribhir vā bhūtaiś caturbhiś copādāya rūpair avinirbhāgavarty asāv aṣṭama iti*. Abhd. 65.

607. *Kalāpato ti yā ayaṃ kesā lomā ti ādinā nayena vīsatiyā ākārehi paṭhavīdhātu, pittaṃ semhan ti ādinā nayena dvādasākārehi āpodhātu niddiṭṭhā. Tattha yasmā: Vaṇṇo gandho raso ojā catasso cāpi dhātuyo/aṭṭhadhammasamodhānā hoti kesā ti sammuti / tesaṃ yeva vinibbhogā natthi kesā ti sammutī // Tasmā kesā pi aṭṭhadhammakalāpamattam eva*; ... Vsm. 364.

608. *Imasmiṃ hi sarīre majjhimena pamāṇena parigayhamānā paramāṇubhedasañcuṇṇā sukhumarajabhūtā paṭhavīdhātu doṇamattā siyā, sā tato upaḍḍhappamānāya āpodhātuyā saṅgahitā*. Vsm. 365.

609. Cf., e.g., ADS. 29; ADSS. 156; ADSVṬ. 58; SS. 4; NRS. 19.

610. This conclusion is also confirmed by VsmS. IV, 136, where it is said that *aṭṭha-dhamma-kalāpa* refers to the eight kinds of *rūpa*, which in their combination make up what is called "head hair": (*aṭṭhadhammakalāpamattam eva*) *yanudu keśa prajñaptiyata kāraṇa vū varṇādīn ekatvayen gena kīha. ovun aṣṭadharmamātra noveyi data yutu.*

611. See above, 137, 155.

612. See above, 137, 155.

613. See above, 33–35, 136–37.

614. Vsm. 365.

615. See above, 137, 155.

616. See above, 137, 155.

617. *Ekuppādā ekanirodhā ... rūpakalāpa nāma*. ADS. 29.

618. ADS. 28; ADSS. 166.

619. See above, 137, 155.

620. ADSS. 166. Cf. ... *etāni rūpāni kammādito uppajjamānāni pi ekekaṃ va na samuṭṭhahanti, atha kho piṇḍato va samuṭṭhahanti*. ADSVṬ. 58.

621. ADS. 29; NRP. 51.

622. See above, 139.

623. Asl. 311.
624. AK. II, 89 ff.; AKvy. I, 85.
625. AKvy. I, 34, II, 355.
626. AK. I, 25.
627. AK. II, 143; AKvy. I, 34ff.
628. Cf. *Naiva hi paramāṇavaḥ saṃyujyante niravayavatvāt. Mā bhūd eṣa doṣaprasaṅghaḥ saṃhatās tu parasparaṃ saṃyujyanta iti kāśmīravaibhāṣikāsta idaṃ praṣṭavyaḥ. yaḥ paramāṇūnāṃ saṃghāto na sa tebhyo' rthāntaram iti.* Viṃś. 7. See also *La Siddhi*, 39ff.
629. *La Siddhi*, 40. Cf. also: *Chāyāvatī kathaṃ vā yady ekaikasya paramāṇor digbhāgabhedo na syād ādityodaye katham anyatra chāyā bhavaty anyatrātapaḥ. Na hi tasyānyaḥ pradeso'sti yatrātapo na syāt. Āvaraṇaṃ ca kathaṃ bhavati paramānoh paramānvantarena yadi digbhāgabhedo neṣyata. Na hi kaścid api paramāṇoḥ parabhāgo'sti yatrāgamanād anyenānyasya pratighātāḥ syāt.* Viṃś. 7.
630. Cf. *Ṣaṭkena yugapadyogāt paramāṇoḥ ṣaḍaṃśatā, ṣaḍbhyo digbhyaḥ ṣaḍbhiḥ paramāṇubhir yugapadyoge sati paramāṇoḥ ṣaḍaṃśatāṃ prāpnoti. Ekasya yo deśas tatrānyasyasaṃbhavāt. Saṇṇāṃ samānadeśatvāt piṇḍaḥ syād aṇumātrakaḥ. Atha ya evaikasya paramāṇor deśah sa eva ṣaṇṇāṃ. Tena sarveṣāṃ samānadeśatvāt sarvaḥ piṇḍaḥ paramāṇumātraḥ syāt.* Viṃś. 7.
631. *La Siddhi*, 40–41.
632. *Ākāsadhātu . . . mē uḍaya mē yaṭa yayi kalāpayange paryantaya pahaḷa kirīma kṛtya koṭa ettīyi.* VsmS. V, 68.
633. VbhA. 343; S. 66; also *Abhidhānappadīpikā-sūci*, 138ff.
634. Seal, *Positive Sciences of the Ancient Hindus*, 82ff.; Ray, *History of Chemistry in Ancient and Medieval India*, 248ff.
635. Sogen, *Systems of Buddhist Thought*, 122.
636. Takakusu, *Essentials of Buddhist Philosophy*, 64.
637. *Tattha paramāṇu nāma ākāsakoṭṭhāsiko* . . . VbhA. 343.
638. . . . *maṃsacakkhussa āpāthaṃ n'āgacchati, dibbacakkhuss'eva āgacchati.* VsmṬ. 286.
639. See, e.g., *Pañcāstikāyasāra*, 84.
640. AK. I, 89.
641. AK. I, 91.
642. AK. I, 89ff.; AKvy. I, 85: *Yan madhye nāst ikiṃcid iti bruvānā Vaibhāṣikā madhye ālok'ādi necchanti. Anya-paramāṇu-praveśanāvakāśaṃ tu na bruvate.*
643. AK. I, 89ff.; AKvy. I, 84ff.
644. AK. I, 89ff.; AKvy. I, 84ff. Cf. *Nirantare tu spṛṣṭa-saṃjñe ti Bhadantaḥ. Bhadanta-mataṃ caiṣṭavyam iti. Vaibhāṣika-mataṃ kasmān naiṣṭavyaṃ. Nanu Vaibhāṣikair apy evam uktaṃ. Tad evaiṣāṃ nirantaratvaṃ yan madhye nāsti kiṃcid iti. Asty evaṃ. Sāvakāśaṃ tu tad vacanaṃ.* AKvy. I, 85.
645. *Anyathā hi sāntarāṇām paramāṇūnāṃ śūnyesv antaresu gatiḥ kena pratibadhyeta gatimata iti vākya-śeṣaḥ.* AKvy. I, 85.

646. AK. I, 91, n. 3.
647. AK. I, 92; Viṃś. 7. Cf. *Na ca paramāṇubhyo'nye saṃghātaḥ yathā Vaibhāṣikā kalpayanti. Ta eva te saṃghātāḥ. Paramāṇavaḥ spṛṣyante yathā rūpyanta iti.* AKvy. I, 85.
648. VsmṬ. 453; ADSVṬ. 98; Abhvk. 279; VsmS. V, 67. Cf. (*ākāsa-dhātu*), *karmādi eki ekī pratyayen samurthita vū cakṣurdaśakādi kalāpayan kalāpantaraya hā saṃkara novana heyin pirisindinā svabhāva vū ākāśadhātu tomo; (pariccheda-rūpaṃ nāma) paricchedarūpa nam vē.* ADSS. 156.
649. VsmṬ. 453.
650. VsmṬ. 453.
651. (*Rūpa-mariyāda-paccupaṭṭhānā*) *ti yasmiṃ kalāpe bhūtānaṃ paricchedo teh'eva asamphuṭṭhabhāva-paccupaṭṭhānā.* VsmṬ. 453.
652. Abhvk. 279; ADSS. 156: . . . *ekeka-kalāpa-gata-rūpānaṃ, kalāpantarehi asaṃkiṇṇabhāvāpādana-vasena paricchedakaṃ rūpaṃ, pariccheda-rūpaṃ. Ācariya Dhammapāla takes the fact of separateness as synonymous with untouchedness—abyāpitā hi asamphuṭṭhatā.* VsmṬ. 453.
653. Cf. . . . *paricchedākāśaya teme rū pirisinda rūpakalāpa hema ekkoṭa pirisindiyeti yi.* VsmS. V, 68.
654. Cf. *Esē hot nan kalabūyehi rū da ekakalabuyehi rū seyin ma avinirbhoga-bavaṭa peminena heyin hē no meneva.* VsmS. V, 68.
655. Ledi Sadaw, the Burmese *thera*, argues that it is solely because there is *ākāsa* around *kalāpas* that "lumps of stones and iron can be broken up, or cut into pieces, or pounded into dust, or melted." See [no title], *Buddhism in England*, no. 4 (1930).
656. AK. I, 89.
657. Cf. *Ekkalāpayakama rū ven ven koṭa pirisindiyen. Mē esē vuvahot ek kalabuyehi rū da nānā kalāpayehi rū seyin ma vinirbhogabavaṭa peminena bevin hē da no menava.* VsmS. V, 68.
658. See above, 146–47.
659. ADS. 29; SS. 5; NRP. 39.
660. AK. II, 145.
661. See above, 144.
662. AK. I, 18ff.
663. See above, 135, 137.
664. Cf. *Yad bhūta-catuṣkam āśraya ekasyopādāya rūpasya nīlasya pītasya vā. na tad evānyasyopā dāyarūpasya gandhasya rasasya v'āśrayaḥ. kiṃ tarhi. Anyad eva bhūta-catuṣkaṃ tasyāśraya iti. Vaibhāṣika-siddhāntaḥ.* AKvy. I, 123.
665. AK. II, 148.
666. AK. II, 149.
667. ADSS. 166. Cf. *Suddhaṭṭhakan ti cattāri mahābhūtāni tannissitā vaṇṇa-gandha-rasa-ojā ti idaṃ.* Abhvk. 297.
668. See chapters 2–4.
669. AK. II, 144; AKvy. I, 123; ADS. 29; SS. 5.

670. Cf. *Kāmeṣṭadravyakośabdaḥ, paramāṇur anindriyaḥ. Kāyendriyo navadravyo daśadravyo' parendriyaḥ.* AK. II, 22.
671. ADS. 29; SS. 4; NRP. 38.
672. Cf. *Yatra hi cakṣuḥ, śrotr' ādi vā tatra kāyendriyena bhavitavyaṃ tat-pratibad-dha-vṛttitvāc cakṣur' ādīnāṃ.* AKvy. I, 123.
673. Bhaduri, *Studies in Nyāya-Vaiśeṣika Metaphysics*, chap. 3.
674. Asl. 311, Vsm. 432; see above, 131–32.
675. See above, 185–86.
676. See above, 153, 155.
677. See above, 149, 155.
678. ADS. 29.
679. See above, 179–80.
680. *Kalāpānaṃ pariccheda-lakkhaṇattā vicakkhanā/ na kalāpaṅgam icc'āhu ākāsaṃ lakkhaṇāni ca//.* ADS. 29.
681. See chapter 2.
682. See above, 150–52.
683. See above, 150–52.
684. See above, 66–67.
685. See above, 43, 60.
686. See above, 43, 60.
687. AK. II, 145.
688. AK. II, 145.
689. ADS. 29ff.
690. See above, 149.
691. See above, 150ff.
692. See above, 149–52.
693. AK. II, 145 and I, 17.
694. See above, 155.
695. See above, 103, 128.
696. See above, 127–28.
697. Cf. ADSS. 167–68.
698. Cf. *Lagutādi-traya; (utucittāhārehi) satprāya ṛtuya prasanna cittaya satprāya āhāraya yana meyin (sambhoti) vannēyi.* ADSS. 165.
699. Cf. *Tattha suddhaṭṭhakaṃ, saddanavakañ ceti dve utusamuṭṭhānakalāpā bahiddhā pi labbhanti avasesā pana sabbe pi ajjhattam evā ti.* ADS. 29.
700. Asl. 342ff.
701. See above, 186, 189.
702. ADSS. 172; NRP. 40.
703. AK. I, 55 ff. Cf. *na sto rūpa-dhātau gandha-rasau niḥprayojanatvāt. strī-pu-ruṣendriya-viṣayavad iti.* AKvy. I, 61.
704. See above, 54.
705. See above, 146–47.

706. AK. I, 55. Cf. *Maithuna-sparśa-vītarāgaś ca rūpāvacarāḥ sattvāḥ. Tasmāt tatra na tṛṣṇā pūrvakaṃ karma bhavati. tasmād ahetukatvāt.* AKvy. I, 63.

707. AK. II, 147ff. Cf. *Ya ihāṣṭa-dravyaka ukto nirindriyo' śabdaḥ. Sa tatra ṣaddravyakaḥ. Yo nava-dravyakaḥ kāyendriyah. Sa sapta-dravyakaḥ. yo daśadravyako'parendriyaḥ. So'ṣṭa-dravyakaḥ. Sa-śabdakāḥ punar ete saptāṣṭa-nava-dravyakā ity avagantavyaṃ.* AKvy. I, 125.

708. ADS. 30.

709. ADS. 30.

710. ADS. 30.

711. ADS. 30.

712. Kvu. 51ff.

713. VsmṬ. 543: *Kālo karoti bhūtāni kālo saṃharati pajā, kālo suttesu jāgarati kālo hi duratikkamo ti kālavādino.*

714. Jātaka II, 181; Jātakapāli II, 260.

715. MA. I, 29: *Yo ca kālaghaso bhūto ti ettha khīṇāsave bhūtasaddo.* See also MhNdA. 85.

716. VsmṬ. 259: *ayaṃ hi addhāna-saddo kālassa desassa ca vācako.*

717. SA. III, 119; MhNdA. 59.

718. DṬ. 32: *Kālañ ca samayañ ca upādāyā ti ettha kālo nāma upasankamanassa yutta-payutta-kālo. Samayo nāma tass'eva paccaya-sāmaggi.*

719. AbhMṬ. 47.

720. DhsA. 57–58; AbhMṬ. 47: *Appeva nāma sve'va upasaṅkameyyāma kālañ ca samayañ ca upādāyā ti ettha kālo nāma upasaṅkamanassa yutta-payutta-kālo. Samayo nāma tass'eva paccaya-sāmaggi.*

721. DhsA. 57–58; AbhMṬ. 47. A free translation of: *sace amhākaṃ sve'va gamanassa yuttakālo bhavissati kāye balamattā c'eva . . . gamanapaccayā ca añño aphāsuvihāro na bhavissati, athetaṃ kālañ ca gamana-k āraṇa-samavāya-sankhātaṃ samayañ ca upadhāretvā api eva nāma sve āgaccheyyamā ti.*

722. DṬ. 32.

723. UdA. 30ff.

724. DhsA. 59.

725. DhsA. 59.

726. *Expositor (Atthasālinī)*, vol. 1, 78 (DhsA. 59).

727. DhsA. 76 (BJS, vol. 42).

728. Abhvk. 407.

729. DṬ. 679.

730. AbhMṬ. 47: *Kālo'pi hi citta-paricchinno sabhāvato avijjamāno'pi ādhārabhāvn'eva saññato adhikaraṇan ti vutto.* DT. 32: *Dhammappavattimattatāya atthato abhūto'pi hi kālo dhammappavattiyā adhikaraṇaṃ viya kappanā-matta-siddhena rūpena vohāriyati ti.*

731. VbhA. 12; PsmA. 20, 28–29, 361–62; Vsm. 496.

732. DhsA. 420ff.

733. DhsA. 420ff. The translation has been lightly edited for clarity.
734. Ven. Nyanaponika Thera, *Abhidhamma Studies*, 106–7.
735. VbhA. 10–11; VsmS. 233ff.
736. DhsA. 78 (BJS, vol. 42).
737. Ven. NyanaponikaThera, *Abhidhamma Studies*, 93.
738. UdA. 31.
739. UdA. 31; *yathā hi gāvisu duyhamānāsu gato, duddhasu āgato ti, ettha gāvīnaṃ dohana-kiriyāya gamana-kiriyā lakkhīyati.*
740. DhsA. 161.
741. SA. III, 156–57; MhNdA. 122.
742. Mil. 49–50.
743. SA. III, 155.
744. Sn. v. 373
745. On various theories on the nature of the earliest form of Buddhism and the connected problems, see specially Keith, *Buddhist Philosophy in India and Ceylon*, 74; Keith, "The Doctrine of the Buddha," 393–404; Keith, "Pre-Canonical Buddhism," 1–20; Kern, *Manual of Indian Buddhism*, 46ff.; Falk, *Nāmarūpa and Dharmarūpa*; Murti, *Central Philosophy of Buddhism*, 14ff.; Przyluski, "Origin and Development of Buddhism," 307–35; Radhakrishnan, *Indian Philosophy*, 341–476, 676–94; C. A. F. Rhys Davids, *Sakya or Buddhist Origins*; Rosenberg, *Die Probleme der buddhistischen Philosophie*, 47ff.; Schayer, "Precanonical Buddhism," 121–32, Schayer, "New Contributions to the Problem of Pre-Hinayānistic Buddhism," 8–17; Stcherbatsky, *Buddhist Logic*, vol. 1, 3–7; Stcherbatsky, "The Doctrine of the Buddha," 867–96; Stcherbatsky, "The 'Dharmas' of the Buddhists and the 'Guṇas' of the Sāṃkhyas," 737–60; Sarathchandra, *Buddhist Psychology of Perception*, 1–22, 97–105; L. A. Waddell, *Buddhism of Tibet*, 76–122; Warder, "On the Relationships between Early Buddhism and Other Contemporary Systems," 43–63; Buddhadatta and Warder, "Mātikā," in *Mohavicchedanī*, xixff.; and Winternitz, "Problems of Buddhism," 41–56. Further references can be obtained from the works cited here.
746. M. II, 171; Sn. v. 895.
747. See, e.g., S. III, 166, IV, 57.
748. S. III, 74.
749. S. III, 167; also Dhs. 125, 133.
750. Dhs. 125, 133.
751. Dhs. 125, 133.
752. S. IV, 162–65.
753. *Cakkhu vā āvuso rūpānaṃ saṃyojanaṃ abhavissa rūpā vā cakkhussa saṃyojanaṃ, na yidaṃ brahmacariyavāso paññāyetha sammā-dukkhakkhayāya.* S. IV, 163.
754. M. III, 29ff.

755. Cf. *Yo bhikkhave rūpesu chandarāgavinayo chandarāgappahānaṃ, idaṃ, rūpassa nissaranaṃ*. S. IV, 99.
756. S. III, 74.
757. S. II, 66.
758. S. III, 159.
759. Cf. *Rūpaṃ bhikkhave pariññeyyo dhammo....* S. II, 159.
760. M. III, 287.
761. S. III, 27; see especially S. III, 260–63.
762. M. I, 220–23.
763. S. III, 139.
764. M. III, 282.
765. S. III, 24, 43, 125.
766. SBB. V, 134 (M. I, 185).
767. *No cedaṃ bhikkhave rūpānaṃ assādo abhavissa na yidaṃ sattā rūpesu sārajjeyyuṃ. Yasmā ca kho bhikkave atthi rūpānaṃ assādo tasmā sattā rūpesu sārajjanti*. S. IV, 43.
768. Cf. S. III, 107.
769. M. III, 225.
770. S. III, 32, 33, 114; IV, 189; cf. MhNd. II, 277, where forty-three ways of approaching *rūpa* are given.
771. MhNd. II, 277.
772. *Pheṇapiṇḍūpamaṃ rūpaṃ vedanā bubbulūpamā/ marīcikūpamā saññā saṅkhārā kadalūpamā / māyūpamañ ca viññāṇaṃ dīpitādiccabandhunā//*. S. III, 142.
773. Sn. v. 1119.
774. Sn. v. 1113.
775. Sn. v. 1070.
776. Waddell, *Buddhism of Tibet*, 121; Waddell, "Buddha's Secret from a Sixth-Century Pictorial Commentary and Tibetan Tradition," 367ff.
777. Kern, *Manual of Indian Buddhism*, 50, n. 6.
778. Cf. *Suñño loko suñño loko ti bhante vuccati. Kittāvatā nu kho bhante suñño loko ti vuccati? Yasmā ca kho Ānanda suññaṃ attena vā attaniyena vā tasmā suñño loko ti vuccati*. S. IV, 54; see also Coomaraswamy, "Some Pāli Words," 358–401.
779. See, e.g., M. II, 68ff.
780. Stcherbatsky, *Conception of Buddhist Nirvāna*, 54ff.; see also Rahula, "The Beginnings of Buddhism," 249 ff.
781. Vsm. 499.
782. *Cittena niyyatī loko cittena parikissati*. S. I, 39.
783. *Api khvāhaṃ āvuso imasmiṃ yeva vyāmamatte kaḷevare saññimhi samanake lokañ ca paññāpemi lokasamudayañ ca lokanirodhañ ca lokanirodhagāminiṃ paṭipadañ ca*. S. I, 62. See also A. II, 48, translated from *Dialogues of the Buddha (Dīghanikāya)*, vol. 1, 273.

784. M. II, 56.
785. Cf. *Kathaṃ c'āvuso bahiddhā viññānaṃ vikkhittaṃ visaṭan ti vuccati? Idh'āvuso bhikkhuno cakkhunā rūpaṃ disvā rūpanimittānusāriṃ viññāṇaṃ hoti rūpanimittassādagathitaṃ rūpanimittassādavinibaddhaṃ*... (applied to the other sense-organs, too). M. III, 225.
786. Cf. . . . *rūpe avigatarāgassa avigatachandassa avigatapemassa avigatapipāsassa avigatataṇhassa tassa rūpassa vipariṇāmaññathābhāvā uppajjanti soka-parideva-dukkha-domanassupāyāsā*. S. III, 123.
787. D. I, 239; S. III, 123.
788. BP. 56.
789. Cf. *Attā hi attano nātho*. Dhp. 24. *Attadīpā bhikkhave viharatha*. D. II, 187.
790. *Yattha . . . atthi cakkhuṃ, atthi rūpā atthi cakkhuviññāṇaṃ, . . . atthi tattha loko*. S. IV, 39.
791. Sarathchandra, *Buddhist Psychology of Perception*, 11.
792. S. IV, 87, 96.
793. S. IV, 95; A. IV, 430.
794. Keith, *Buddhist Philosophy in India and Ceylon*, chap. 3.
795. Cf. *Cakkhuñ ca paṭicca rūpe ca uppajjati cakkhuviññāṇaṃ tiṇṇaṃ saṅgati phasso phassapaccayā vedanā vedanāpaccayā taṇhā taṇhāpaccayā upādānaṃ upādānapaccayā bhavo bhavapaccayā jāti jātipaccayā jarāmaraṇaṃ soka-parideva-dukkha-domanassupāyāsā sambhavanti* (applied to the other sense-organs and the sense-objects). S. I, 73.
796. S. V, 437–38.
797. Oldenberg, *Buddha*, 205.
798. M. I, 426 ff.; S. V, 438.
799. *Seyyathā'pi bhikkhave mahāsamuddo ekaraso loṇaraso, evam eva kho bhikkhave ayaṃ dhamma-vinayo ekaraso vimuttiraso*. Vin. II, 239.
800. M. I, 70.
801. BL. I, 3–7.
802. CPB. 54.
803. Cf., for instance, the *Mūlapariyāya Sutta* in M. I, 1ff.; see also Warder, "On the Relationships between Early Buddhism and Other Contemporary Systems," 50.
804. A. I, 83.
805. A. I, 83.
806. Cf. *Puna ca paraṃ āvuso bhikkhuno rūpaṃ manasikaroto rūpesu cittaṃ na pakkhandati nappasīdati na santiṭṭhati*. . . . D. I, 239.
807. S. II, 77.
808. *Dvayānissito khvāyaṃ, Kaccāyana, loko yebhuyyena atthitañ ca natthitañ ca. Lokasamudayaṃ kho, Kaccāyana, yathābhūtaṃ sammappaññāya passato yā loke natthitā sā na hoti. Lokanirodhaṃ kho, Kaccāyana, yathābhūtaṃ sammappaññāya passato yā loke atthitā sā na hoti*. S. II, 17.

809. A. I, 78.
810. In the earlier texts "change" is not explained on the basis of a formulated theory of moments. See above, 73ff.
811. S. II, 77.
812. Cf. the doctrine attributed to Pakudha Kaccāyana in D. I, 56.

BIBLIOGRAPHY

Primary Sources: Pāli, Sanskrit, Prakrit, and Siṃhala Works

Abhidhammatthavikāsinī. Edited by A. P. Buddhadatta. Colombo, 1961.

Abhidhammatthasaṅgaha. In *Journal of the Pali Text Society*, 1–48. Edited by T. W. Rhys Davids. London, 1884.

Abhidhammatthasaṅgaha-Vibhāvinī-Ṭīkā. Edited by D. Paññānanda. Colombo, 1889.

Abhidhammāvatāra. Edited by A. P. Buddhadatta. Buddhadatta's Manuals 1: 1–142. PTS, 1915.

Abhidhānappadipikā-sūci (Dictionary of the Pali Language by Moggāllana). Edited by W. Subhuti. Colombo, 1865, 1938. (English and Sinhalese interpretations by W. Subhuti. Pāli terms in Sinhala script.)

Abhidharmakośavyākhyā (*Sphuṭarthā*), vols. 1–2. Edited by U. Wogihara. Tokyo, 1932–36.

Abhidharmadīpa (with *Vibhāṣāprabhāvṛtti*). Edited by P. S. Jaini. Tibetan Sanskrit Works Series 4. Patna, 1959.

Abhidharmasamuccaya. Edited by P. Pradhan. Visva-Bharati Studies 12. Santiniketana, 1950

Abhidharmāmṛta. Restored from the Chinese into Sanskrit by Santi Bhiksu. Santiniketana, 1953.

Abhidharmārthasaṃgrahasannaya, included in *Abhidhammatthasaṅgaha*. Edited by Paññāmoli Tissa. Ambalangoda, 1926.

Aṅguttaranikāya, vols. 1–6. Edited by R. Morris, E. Hardy, and C. A. F. Rhys Davids. PTS, 1885–1910.

Aṅguttaranikāya Aṭṭhakathā (*Manorathapūraṇī*), vols. 1–5. Edited by M. Walleser and H. Kopp. PTS, 1924–56.

Davvasangaha (with a commentary by Brahmadeva). Edited and translated by S. C. Ghoshal. Sacred Books of the Jainas 1. Allahabad, 1917.

Divyāvadāna. Edited by E. B. Cowell and R. A. Neil. Cambridge, 1886.

Dīghanikāya, vols. 1–3. Edited by T. W. Rhys Davids and J. E. Carpenter. PTS, 1890–1911.

Dīghanikāya Aṭṭhakathā (*Sumaṅgalavilāsinī*), vols. 1–3. Edited by T. W. Rhys Davids, J. E. Carpenter, and W. Stede. PTS, 1886–1932.

Dukapaṭṭhāna. Edited by Mrs. Rhys Davids. PTS, 1906.

Dhammapada. Edited by S. Sumaṅgala. PTS, 1914.

Dhammasaṅganī. Edited by E. Muller. PTS, 1885.

Dhammasaṅganī Aṭṭhakathā (*Atthasālinī*). Edited by E. Muller. PTS, 1897.

Dharmapada, Gāndhārī. Edited by J. Brough. London, 1962.

Itivuttaka. Edited by E. Windisch. PTS, 1889

Kathāvatthu, vols. 1–2. Edited by A. C. Taylor. PTS, 1894–97.

Kathāvatthuppakaraṇa Aṭṭhakathā. In *Journal of the Pali Text Society*, 1–222. Edited by J. Minayef. London, 1889.

Khuddakapāṭha. Edited by H. Smith. PTS, 1915.

Mādhyamakavrtti. Edited by Louis de la Vallee Poussin. Bibliotheca Buddhica 4. St. Petersburg, 1903–13

Majjhimanikāya, vols. 1–4. Edited by V. Trenckner, R. Chalmers, and Mrs. Rhys Davids. PTS, 1888–1925.

Majjhimanikāya Aṭṭhakathā (*Papañcasūdanī*), vols. 1–4. Edited by J. H. Woods, D. Kosambi, and I. B. Horner. PTS, 1922–38.

Mahāniddesa, vols. 1–2. Edited by Louis de la Vallée Poussin and E. J. Thomas. PTS, 1928–31.

Mahāniddesa Aṭṭhakathā (*Niddesavaṇṇanā = Saddhammappajjotikā*), vols. 1–3. Edited by A. P. Buddhadatta. PTS, 1931–41.

Mādhyamakavṛtti. Edited by Louis de la Vallée Poussin. Bibliotheca Buddhica 4. St. Petersburg, 1903–13.

Milindapañha. Edited by V. Trenckner. London, 1880.

Mūla-Ṭīkā. Edited by D. Paññāsāra and P. Vimaladhamma. Colombo, 1939.

Mohavicchedanī. Edited by A. P. Buddhadatta and A. K. Warder. PTS, 1961.

Nāmarūpapariccheda. In *Journal of the Pali Text Society*, 1–114. Edited by A. P. Buddhadatta. London, 1914.

Nāmarūpasamāsa. In *Journal of the Pali Text Society*, 1–19. Edited by P. Dhammārāma. London, 1916.

Niyamsara. Edited and translated U. Sain. Sacred Books of the Jainas 9. Lucknow, 1931.

Pañcastikāyasāra. Edited and translated by A. Chakravartinayanar. Sacred Books of the Jainas 3. Allahabad, 1920.

Paṭisambhidāmagga, vols. 1–2. Edited by A. C. Taylor. PTS, 1905–7.

Paṭisambhidāmagga Aṭṭhakathā (*Saddhammappakāsinī*), vols. 1–3. Edited by C. V. Joshi. PTS, 1933–47.

Puggalapaññatti Aṭṭhakathā. In *Journal of the Pali Text Society*, 170–254. Edited by Landsberg and Mrs. Rhys Davids. London, 1914.

Peṭakopadesa. Edited by A. Barua. PTS, 1949.

Rūpārūpavibhāga. Edited by A. P. Buddhadatta. Buddhadatta's Manuals 1: 149–59. PTS, 1915.

Saccasaṃkhepa. In *Journal of the Pali Text Society*, 1–25. Edited by P. Dhammarama. London, 1917–19.

Samayasara. Edited and translated by J. I. Jaini. Sacred Books of the Jainas 8. Lucknow, 1930.

Saṃyuttanikāya, vols. 1–6. Edited by L. Feer and Mrs. Rhys Davids. PTS, 1884–1904.

Saṃyuttanikāya Aṭṭhakathā (*Sāratthappakāsinī*), vols. 1–3. Edited by F. L. Woodward. PTS, 1929–37.

Suttanipāta. Edited by D. Anderson and H. Smith. PTS, 1913.

Suttanipāta Aṭṭhakathā (*Paramatthajotikā*, I–III). Edited by H. Smith. PTS, 1916–18.

Tikapaṭṭhāna (with commentary), vols. 1–2. Edited by Mrs. Rhys Davids. PTS, 1921–23.

Triṃśikā (*Vijñaptimātratāsiddhi*), with the commentary of Sthiramati. Edited by S. Levi. Paris, 1925.

Theragāthā. Edited by H. Oldenberg. PTS, 1883.

Therīgāthā Aṭṭhakathā (*Paramatthadīpanī*). Edited by E. Muller. PTS, 1893.

Udāna Aṭṭhakathā (*Paramatthadīpanī*). Edited by F. L. Woodward. PTS, 1926.

Vibhaṅga. Edited by Mrs. Rhys Davids. PTS, 1904.

Vibhaṅga Aṭṭhakathā (*Sammohavinodanī*). Edited by A. P. Buddhadatta. PTS, 1923.

Visuddhamagga, vols. 1–2. Edited by C. A. F. Rhys Davids. PTS, 1920–21.

Visuddhimagga Ṭīkā (*Paramatthamañjūsā*). Edited by M. Dhammananda. Colombo, 1928.

Viśuddhimārgasannaya, vols. 1–6. Edited by M. Dharmaratne. Colombo, 1890–1917.

Viṃśatikā (*Vjñaptimātratāsiddhi*). Edited by S. Levi. Paris, 1925.

Vaiśeṣika Sūtras of Kanāda. Edited and translated by N. Sinha. Sacred Books of the Hindus 6. Allahabad, 1911.

Yamaka, vols. 1–2. Edited by C. A. F . Rhys Davids. PTS, 1911–13.

Yamakappakaraṇa Aṭṭhakathā. In *Journal of the Pali Text Society*, 51–107. Edited by C. A. F . Rhys Davids. London, 1910–12.

Primary Sources Translated into Modern Languages

L'Abhidharmakośa de Vasubandhu, vols. 1–4. Translated by Louis de la Vallée Poussin. Paris: Société Belge d'Etudes Orientales, 1923–31.

Buddhist Manual of Psychological Ethics (Dhammasaṅganī). Translated by Mrs. Rhys Davids. Oriental Translation Fund, New Series 12. London, 1923.

Budddhist Philosophy of Relations (Paṭṭhānuddesa Dīpanī). Translated by Ven. Ledi Sadaw. Reprint. Kandy: BPS, 1986.

Candrakīrti Prasannapadā Mādhyamakavṛtti: Douze chapitres, traduits de Sanscrit et du Tibétain . . . Translated by J. May. Paris, 1959.

Compendium of Philosophy (Abhidhammatthasaṅgaha). Translated by S. Z. Aung. Revised and edited by Mrs. Rhys Davids. London: H. Frowde for the Pali Text Society, 1910.

A Comprehensive Manual of Abhidhamma: The Abhidhammattha Sangaha of Acariya Anuruddha. Translated by Bhikkhu Bodhi. Buddhist Publication Society, 1993

Dhammasaṅganī. Translated into French by A. Bareau. Paris, 1951.

Dialogues of the Buddha (Dīghanikāya). In *Sacred Books of the Buddhists*, vols. 2–4. Translated by T. W. Rhys Davids. London, 1899–1912.

Discourse on Elements (Dhātukathā). Translated by U. Narada (assisted by T. Nyuan). London: PTS, 1962.

Documents d'Abhidharma. Translated by Louis de la Vallée Poussin. *Mélanges Chinois et Bouddhiques* 5 (1937): 7–187.

The Expositor (Atthasālinī), vols. 1–2. Translated by Maung Tin. Revised and edited by Mrs. Rhys Davids. London: PTS, 1920–21.

Further Dialogues of the Buddha (Majjhimanikāya). In *Sacred Books of the Buddhists*, vols. 5–6. Translated by Lord Chalmers. London: H. Frowde, 1895.

The Jātaka: Stories of the Buddha's Former Births, vol. 2. Translated by W. H. D. Rouse. Edited by E. B. Cowell. Cambridge: The University Press, 1895. http://www.sacred-texts.com/bud/j2/index.htm.

"Origin and Doctrines of Early Indian Buddhist Schools" (Hsuan Chwang version of Vasumitra's Treatise). Translated by J. Masuda. *Asia Minor* 2 (1925): 1–78.

"L'origine des sectes bouddhiques d'apres Paramārtha." Translated by P. Demieville. *Mélanges Chinois et Bouddhiques, l'Institut Belges des Hautes Etudes Chinoises*. Brussels, 1932.

The Path of Purification (Visuddhimagga). Translated by Bhikkhu Ñānamoli. Colombo, 1956.

Points of Controversy (Kathāvatthu). Translated by S. Z. Aung and Mrs. Rhys Davids. London: PTS, 1915.

Sacred Books of the Buddhists. 40 vols. Edited by F. M. Müller. Translated by various scholars. London: H. Frowde, 1895.

La Siddhi de Hiuan Tsang. Translated by Louis de la Vallée Poussin. Paris, 1928–29.

"Le traité de la demonstration de l'acte (Karmasiddhiprakaraṇa)." Translated by E. Lamotte. *Mélanges Chinois et Bouddhiques* 4 (1936): 151–228.

"Trois traités sur le sectes bouddhiques attribute a Vasumitra, Bhavya et Vinītadeva." Translated by A. Bareau. *Journal Asiatique* 242 (1954): 229–66.

"Les versions chinoises du Milindapañha." Translated by P. Demieville. *Bulletin de l'École Française d'Extrême-Orient* 24 (1924): 1–264.

Secondary Sources

Aneski, M., and J. Takakusu. "Dhyāna." In Hastings, *Encyclopaedia of Religion and Ethics*, vol. 4, 702–4.

Aung, S. Z. "Abhidhamma Literature in Burma." *Journal of the Pali Text Society* (1910–12): 112–32.

Bareau A. *L'absolu en philosophie bouddhique: Evolution de la notion d'asaṃskṛta*. Paris 1951.

———. "Les origines du Śāriputrābhidharmaśāstra." *MUSEON* 63 (1950): 69–95.

———. "Les sectes bouddhiques du Petit Véhicule et leurs Abidharmapiṭaka." *Bulletin de l'École Française d'Extrême-Orient* 44, fasc. 1, 1951: 1–11.

Basham, A. L. *History and Doctrines of the Ājīvikas*. London, 1951.

Bhaduri, S. *Studies in Nyāya-Vaiśeṣika Metaphysics*. Poona, 1947.

Bhattacharya, V. *The Basic Conception of Buddhism*. Calcutta, 1930.

Buddhadatta, A. P., and A. K. Warder. "Mātikā." Introductory essay to Buddhadatta and Warder, *Mohavicchedanī*, xix–xxx.

———, eds. *Mohavicchedanī: Abhidhammamātikatthavaṇṇanā by Kassapatthera of Cola*. London: Luzac and Co. for the Pali Text Society, 1961.

Chatterji, D. "The Problem of Knowledge and the Four Schools of Later Buddhism." *Annals of the Bhandarkar Oriental Research Institute* 12 (1931): 205–15.

Coomaraswamy, A. K. "Some Pāli Words." *Harvard Journal of Asiatic Studies* 4 (1939): 358–401.

Dasgupta, S. *A History of Indian Philosophy*, vol. 1. Cambridge, 1922.

Divanji, P. C. "Naturalism in Greek and Indian Philosophies." *Journal of the Oriental Institute* 4 (1954–55): 85-97.

Dutt, N. "The Dhammasaṅgaṇī." *Indian Historical Quarterly* 15 (1939): 345–72.

———. *Early History of the Spread of Buddhism and the Buddhist Schools*. London, 1925.

Falk, Maryla. *Nāmarūpa and Dharmarūpa: Origin and Aspects of an Ancient Indian Conception*. Calcutta, 1943.

Filliozart, J. "The Psychological Discoveries of Buddhism." *University of Ceylon Review* 13 (1959): 69–82.

Foley, C. A. "The *Vedalla Sutta* as Illustrating the Psychological Basis of Buddhist Ethics." *Journal of the Royal Asiatic Society* (1894): 321–33.

Godakumbura, C. E. "References to Buddhist Sanskrit Writers in Sinhalese Literature." *University of Ceylon Review* 1 (1943): 86–93.

———. *Sinhalese Literature*. Colombo, 1955.

Guenther, H. *Philosophy and Psychology in the Abhidharma*. Lucknow,1957.

Hastings, J., ed. *Encyclopaedia of Religion and Ethics*. 13 vols. Edinburgh, 1908–26.

Heimann, B. *Significance of Prefixes in Sanskrit Philosophical Terminology*. Royal Asiatic Monographs 25. London, 1961.

Hiriyana, M. *Outlines of Indian Philosophy*. London, 1932.

Horner, I. B. "Abhidhamma Abhivinaya." *Indian Historical Quarterly* 17 (1941): 548–60.

———. "Foundations of Theravāda." *Middle Way* 24 (1950): 115–19; 25: 19–22.

Jacobi, H. "Atomic Theory (Indian)." In Hastings, *Encyclopaedia of Religion and Ethics*, vol. 2, 199–202.

Jaini, P. S. "Buddha's Prolongation of Life." *Bulletin of the School of Oriental and African Studies* 21 (1958): 546–52.

———. "Origin and Development of the Theory of Viprayuktasaṃskāras." *Bulletin of the School of Oriental and African Studies* 22 (1959): 531–47.

Jayatilleke, K. N. *Early Buddhist Theory of Knowledge*. London, 1964.

———. "Some Problems of Translation and Interpretation." Part 1, *University of Ceylon Review* 7 (1959): 212–23; Part 2, *University of Ceylon Review* 8 (1960): 45–55.

Jhaveri, I. H. "Concept of *Kāla* and *Ākāśa* in the Sāṃkhya-Yoga System." *Journal of the Oriental Institute* 5 (1956): 300–307.

Karunaratne, W. S. *The Development of the Theory of Causality in Early Theravāda Buddhism*. PhD thesis, SOAS University of London, 1956.

Kasyap, J. *The Abhidhamma Philosophy*, vols. 1–2. Benares, 1943.

Keith, A. B. *Buddhist Philosophy in India and Ceylon*. Oxford, 1923.

———. "The Doctrine of the Buddha." *Bulletin of the School of Oriental and African Studies* 6 (1930–32): 393–404.

———. *Indian Logic and Atomism*. Oxford, 1921.

———. "Pre-Canonical Buddhism." *Indian Historical Quarterly* 12 (1936): 1–20.

———. "Some Problems of Indian Philosophy." *Indian Historical Quarterly* 8 (1932): 425–41.

Kern, J. C. H. *Manual of Indian Buddhism*. Strassburg, 1896.

———. "*Ruppati, ruppana*." In *Verspreide Geschriftenonderzijn Toezicht Verzameld*, vol. 2, 261–62. The Hague, 1913–36.

La Vallée Poussin, Louis. "Agnosticism." In Hastings, *Encyclopaedia of Religion and Ethics*, vol. 1, 220–25.

———. "Cosmogony and Cosmology (Buddhist)." In Hastings, *Encyclopaedia of Religion and Ethics*, vol. 4, 128–38.

———. *The Way to Nirvana*. London,1925.

Law, B. C. "Non-Canonical Pāli Literature." *Annals of the Bhandarkar Oriental Research Institute* 13 (1932–33): 115–63.

Ledi Sadaw. "On the Philosophy of Relations." *Journal of the Pali Text Society* (1915–16): 21–53.

———. "Some Points in Buddhist Doctrine." *Journal of the Pali Text Society* (1913–14): 115–63.

Levi, S. *Materiaux pour l'étude du systèmeVijñaptimātra*. Paris, 1932.

Malkani, G. R. "The Conception of Reality as Dynamic." *Proceedings of the Indian Philosophical Congress* (1953): 179–87.

Masson-Oursel, P. *Esquisse d'une histoire de la philosphie indienne*. Paris, 1923.

McGovern, W. M. *A Manual of Buddhist Philosophy*, vol. 1. London, 1923.
Mishra, U. *History of Indian Philosphy*. Allahabad, 1957.
———. *Physical Theory of Sound and Its Origin in Indian Thought*. Allahabad University Studies 2. Allahabad, 1926.
Mookerji, S. *Buddhist Philosophy of Universal Flux*. Calcutta, 1936.
Murti, T. R. V. *The Central Philosophy of Buddhism*. London, 1955.
Nyanaponika Thera. *Abhidhamma Studies: Researches in Buddhist Psychology*. Island Hermitage Publication, no. 2. Colombo, 1949.
Nyanatiloka Mahāthera. *Buddhist Dictionary*. Island Hermitage Publication, no. 1. Colombo, 1956.
———. *Guide through the Abhidhamma Piṭaka*. Colombo, 1949.
Oldenberg, H. *Buddha:His Life, His Doctrine, His Order*. London, 1882.
Oltramare, P. *L'histoire des idees theosophiques dans l'Inde: La theosophie bouddhique. Annales du Musée Guimet* 31. Paris, 1923.
Paranavitana, S. "Mahayanism in Ceylon." *Ceylon Journal of Science* 2 (1928): 35–71.
Przyluski, J. "Dārsṭāntika, Sautrāntika and Sarvāstivāda." *Indian Historical Quarterly* 16 (1940): 246–54.
———. "Origin and Development of Buddhism." *Journal of Theological Studies* 35 (1934): 307–35.
Radhakrishnan, S. *Indian Philosophy*, vol. 1. London, 1948.
Rahula, W. "The Beginning of Buddhism." *Indian Historical Quarterly* 32 (1956): 249ff.
Raju, P. T. *Idealistic Thought of India*. London, 1953.
Ray, P. C. *History of Chemistry in Ancient and Medieval India (incorporating History of Hindu Chemistry)*. Edited by P. Ray. Calcutta, 1956.
Rhys Davids, C. A. F. "Buddhism and the Negative." *Journal of the Pali Text Society* (1924–27): 237–50.
———. *Buddhist Psychology*. London, 1914.
———. "Dhyāna in Early Buddhism."*Indian Historical Quarterly* 3 (1927): 689–715.
———. "Relations (Buddhist)." In Hastings, *Encyclopaedia of Religion and Ethics*, vol. 10, 648–49.
———. *Sakya or Buddhist Origins*. New York: Routledge Revival, 2018 [1928].
Rhys Davids, T. W. "The Sects of the Buddhists." *Journal of the Royal Asiatic Society* (1891): 409–22.
Rhys Davds, T. W., and W. Stede. *Pali-English Dictionary*. PTS, 1925.
Rosenberg, O. K. J. *Die Probleme der buddhistischen Philosophie*. Heidelberg, 1924.
Sarathchandra, E. R. *Buddhist Psychology of Perception*. Colombo, 1958.
Schayer, S. "New Contributions to the Problem of Pre-Hinayānistic Buddhism." *Polski Biuletyn Orientalistyczny* 1 (1937): 8–17.
———. "Precanonical Buddhism."*Archiv Orientální, Journal of the Czechoslovak Oriental Institute* 7 (1935): 121–32.

Seal, B. N. *Positive Sciences of the Ancient Hindus*. Delhi, 1925.
Silburn, L. *Instant et cause: Le discontinue dans la pensée philosophique de l'Inde*. Paris, 1955.
Sinha, T. N. *Indian Psychology: Perception*. London, 1934.
———. *Indian Realism*. London, 1938.
Sogen, Y. *Systems of Buddhist Thought*. Calcutta, 1934.
Stcherbatsky, Th. *Buddhist Logic*. 2 vols. Bibliotheca Buddhica 26. Leningrad, 1930–32.
———. *The Central Conception of Buddhism*. Prize Publication Fund, vol. 7. London, 1923.
———. *The Conception of Buddhist Nirvana*. Leningrad,1927.
———. "The Doctrine of the Buddha." *Bulletin of the School of Oriental and African Studies* 6 (1930–32): 867–96.
———. "The Soul Theory of the Buddhists." *Bulletin de l'Academie des Sciences de Russie*. Petrograd, 1920.
———. "The 'Dharmas' of Buddhists and the 'Guṇas' of the Sāṃkhyas." *Indian Historical Quarterly* 10 (1934): 737–60.
Suzuki, D. T. "The Analytic and the Synthetic Approach to Buddhism." *Middle Way* 24 (1954): 102–4.
Takakusu, J., and M. Aneski. "The Abhidharma Literature of the Sarvāstivādins."-*Journal of the Pali Text Society* (1904–5): 67–146.
———. *The Essentials of Buddhist Philosophy*. Edited by W. T. Chan and C. A. Moore. Honolulu, 1947.
Tatia, N. "Paṭiccasamuppāda." *Nava-Nalanda Research Publication* 1 (1957): 177–239.
Thomas, E. J. *History of Buddhist Thought*. London, 1933.
———. "State of the Dead (Buddhist)." In Hastings, *Encyclopaedia of Religion and Ethics*, vol. 11, 829–33.
Vaidya, P. L. *Etudes sur Āryadeva et son Catuḥṣataka*. Paris, 1923.
Waddell, L. A. "Buddha's Secret from a Sixth-Century Pictorial Commentary and Tibetan Tradition." *Journal of the Royal Asiatic Society* (1894): 367–84.
———. *The Buddhism of Tibet: Or, Lamaism, with Its Mystic Cults, Symbolism, and Mythology, and Its Relation to Indian Buddhism*. 2nd ed. Cambridge, 1958.
Warder, A. K. "On the Relationships between Early Buddhism and Other Contemporary Systems." *Bulletin of the School of Oriental and African Studies* 18 (1956): 43-63.
Wijesekara, O. H. de A. "Upanishadic Terms for Sense-Functions." *University of Ceylon Review* 2 (1944): 14–24.
———. "Vitalism and Becoming: A Comparative Study." *University of Ceylon Review* 1 (1943): 49–58.
Winternitz, M. *History of Indian Literature*, vol. 2. Calcutta, 1933.
———. "Problems of Buddhism." *Visva-Bharati Quarterly* 2 (1936): 41–56.

INDEX

Q

R

S

T

ABOUT THE AUTHOR

Y. Karunadasa, PhD (London), PhD Honoris Causa (Mahamakut Buddhist University, Thailand), DLitt Honoris Causa (Kelaniya), is Professor Emeritus at the University of Kelaniya and a former director of its Postgraduate Institute of Pali and Buddhist Studies. He was a Commonwealth Academic Staff Fellow (1974–75) and Visiting Professor at SOAS University of London (1993), Distinguished Numata Chair Professor at the University of Calgary (2001), and Tung Lin Kok Yuen Visiting Professor at the University of Toronto (2008). Subsequently he served as the MaMa Charitable Foundation Visiting Professor at the University of Hong Kong. Among his published works are *Early Buddhist Teachings: The Middle Position in Theory and Practice* and *The Theravāda Abhidhamma: Inquiry into the Nature of Conditioned Reality.*

WHAT TO READ NEXT FROM WISDOM PUBLICATIONS

Early Buddhist Teachings
The Middle Position in Theory and Practice
Y. Karunadasa

Discover the birth of Buddhism and the essentials of Buddhist teachings with this comprehensive explanation of early Buddhism's key doctrines.

The Theravāda Abhidhamma
Inquiry into the Nature of Conditioned Reality
Y. Karunadasa

The renowned Sri Lankan scholar Y. Karunadasa examines Abhidhamma perspectives on the nature of phenomenal existence.

Abhidhamma Studies
Buddhist Explorations of Consciousness and Time
Nyanaponika Thera
Edited and introduced by Bhikkhu Bodhi

". . . one of the most profound and lucid interpreters of Buddhist psychology in our time."—Daniel Goleman, author of *Emotional Intelligence*

About Wisdom Publications

Wisdom Publications is the leading publisher of classic and contemporary Buddhist books and practical works on mindfulness. To learn more about us or to explore our other books, please visit our website at wisdomexperience.org or contact us at the address below.

Wisdom Publications
199 Elm Street
Somerville, MA 02144 USA

We are a 501(c)(3) organization, and donations in support of our mission are tax deductible.

Wisdom Publications is affiliated with the Foundation for the Preservation of the Mahayana Tradition (FPMT).